Microsoft® Official Academic Course

Windows Development
Fundamentals, Exam 98-362

WILEY

Credits

EDITOR	Bryan Gambrel
DIRECTOR OF SALES	Mitchell Beaton
EXECUTIVE MARKETING MANAGER	Chris Ruel
ASSISTANT MARKETING MANAGER	Debbie Martin
MICROSOFT SENIOR PRODUCT MANAGER	Merrick Van Dongen of Microsoft Learning
EDITORIAL PROGRAM ASSISTANT	Jennifer Lartz
CONTENT MANAGER	Micheline Frederick
SENIOR PRODUCTION EDITOR	Kerry Weinstein
CREATIVE DIRECTOR	Harry Nolan
COVER DESIGNER	Jim O'Shea
TECHNOLOGY AND MEDIA	Tom Kulesa/Wendy Ashenberg

Cover photo: Credit: © brytta/iStockphoto

This book was set in Garamond by Aptara, Inc. and printed and bound by Bind Rite Robbinsville. The cover was printed by Bind Rite Robbinsville.

Founded in 1807, John Wiley & Sons, Inc. has been a valued source of knowledge and understanding for more than 200 years, helping people around the world meet their needs and fulfill their aspirations. Our company is built on a foundation of principles that include responsibility to the communities we serve and where we live and work. In 2008, we launched a Corporate Citizenship Initiative, a global effort to address the environmental, social, economic, and ethical challenges we face in our business. Among the issues we are addressing are carbon impact, paper specifications and procurement, ethical conduct within our business and among our vendors, and community and charitable support. For more information, please visit our website: www.wiley.com/go/citizenship.

ISBN 978-0-470-88913-8

Printed in the United States of America

10 9 8 7 6 5 4 3 2 1

www.wiley.com/college/microsoft *or*
call the MOAC Toll-Free Number: 1+(888) 764-7001 (U.S. & Canada only)

Foreword from the Publisher

Wiley's publishing vision for the Microsoft Official Academic Course series is to provide students and instructors with the skills and knowledge they need to use Microsoft technology effectively in all aspects of their personal and professional lives. Quality instruction is required to help both educators and students get the most from Microsoft's software tools and to become more productive. Thus our mission is to make our instructional programs trusted educational companions for life.

To accomplish this mission, Wiley and Microsoft have partnered to develop the highest quality educational programs for Information Workers, IT Professionals, and Developers. Materials created by this partnership carry the brand name "Microsoft Official Academic Course," assuring instructors and students alike that the content of these textbooks is fully endorsed by Microsoft, and that they provide the highest quality information and instruction on Microsoft products. The Microsoft Official Academic Course textbooks are "Official" in still one more way—they are the officially sanctioned courseware for Microsoft IT Academy members.

The Microsoft Official Academic Course series focuses on *workforce development*. These programs are aimed at those students seeking to enter the workforce, change jobs, or embark on new careers as information workers, IT professionals, and developers. Microsoft Official Academic Course programs address their needs by emphasizing authentic workplace scenarios with an abundance of projects, exercises, cases, and assessments.

The Microsoft Official Academic Courses are mapped to Microsoft's extensive research and job-task analysis, the same research and analysis used to create the Microsoft Technology Associate (MTA) and Microsoft Certified Technology Specialist (MCTS) exams. The textbooks focus on real skills for real jobs. As students work through the projects and exercises in the textbooks, they enhance their level of knowledge and their ability to apply the latest Microsoft technology to everyday tasks. These students also gain resume-building credentials that can assist them in finding a job, keeping their current job, or furthering their education.

The concept of life-long learning is today an utmost necessity. Job roles, and even whole job categories, are changing so quickly that none of us can stay competitive and productive without continuously updating our skills and capabilities. The Microsoft Official Academic Course offerings, and their focus on Microsoft certification exam preparation, provide a means for people to acquire and effectively update their skills and knowledge. Wiley supports students in this endeavor through the development and distribution of these courses as Microsoft's official academic publisher.

Today educational publishing requires attention to providing quality print and robust electronic content. By integrating Microsoft Official Academic Course products, *WileyPLUS*, and Microsoft certifications, we are better able to deliver efficient learning solutions for students and teachers alike.

Bonnie Lieberman

General Manager and Senior Vice President

Preface

Welcome to the Microsoft Official Academic Course (MOAC) program for Windows Development Fundamentals. MOAC represents the collaboration between Microsoft Learning and John Wiley & Sons, Inc. publishing company. Microsoft and Wiley teamed up to produce a series of textbooks that deliver compelling and innovative teaching solutions to instructors and superior learning experiences for students. Infused and informed by in-depth knowledge from the creators of Microsoft products, and crafted by a publisher known worldwide for the pedagogical quality of its products, these textbooks maximize skills transfer in minimum time. Students are challenged to reach their potential by using their new technical skills as highly productive members of the workforce.

Because this knowledge base comes directly from Microsoft, creator of the Microsoft Certified IT Professional (MCITP), Microsoft Certified Technology Specialist (MCTS), and Microsoft Technology Associate (MTA) exams (www.microsoft.com/learning/certification), you are sure to receive the topical coverage that is most relevant to students' personal and professional success. Microsoft's direct participation not only assures you that MOAC textbook content is accurate and current—it also means that students will receive the best instruction possible to enable their success on certification exams and in the workplace.

▪ The Microsoft Official Academic Course Program

The *Microsoft Official Academic Course* series is a complete program for instructors and institutions to prepare and deliver great courses on Microsoft software technologies. With MOAC, we recognize that, because of the rapid pace of change in the technology and curriculum developed by Microsoft, there is an ongoing set of needs beyond classroom instruction tools for an instructor to be ready to teach the course. The MOAC program endeavors to provide solutions for all these needs in a systematic manner in order to ensure a successful and rewarding course experience for both instructor and student—technical and curriculum training for instructor readiness with new software releases; the software itself for student use at home for building hands-on skills, assessment, and validation of skill development; and a great set of tools for delivering instruction in the classroom and lab. All are important to the smooth delivery of an interesting course on Microsoft software, and all are provided with the MOAC program. We think about the model below as a gauge for ensuring that we completely support you in your goal of teaching a great course. As you evaluate your instructional materials options, you may wish to use the model for comparison purposes with other available products.

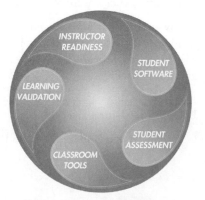

Illustrated Book Tour

■ Pedagogical Features

The MOAC textbook for Windows Development Fundamentals is designed to cover all the learning objectives for that MTA exam 98-362, which is referred to as its "exam objective." The Microsoft Technology Associate (MTA) exam objectives are highlighted throughout the textbook. Many pedagogical features have been developed specifically for the *Microsoft Official Academic Course* program.

Presenting the extensive procedural information and technical concepts woven throughout the textbook raises challenges for the student and instructor alike. The Illustrated Book Tour that follows provides a guide to the rich features contributing to the *Microsoft Official Academic Course* program's pedagogical plan. The following is a list of key features in each lesson designed to prepare students for success as they continue in their IT education, on the certification exams, and in the workplace:

- Each lesson begins with a **Lesson Skill Matrix**. More than a standard list of learning objectives, the Lesson Skill Matrix correlates each software skill covered in the lesson to the specific exam objective.

- Concise and frequent **Step-by-Step** exercises teach students new features and provide an opportunity for hands-on practice. Numbered steps give detailed, step-by-step instructions to help students learn software skills. In this textbook, some figures contain numbered call-outs that correlate to their numbered step in the exercise.

- **Illustrations**—in particular, screen images—provide visual feedback as students work through the exercises. These images reinforce key concepts, provide visual clues about the steps, and allow students to check their progress.

- Lists of **Key Terms** at the beginning of each lesson introduce students to important technical vocabulary. When these terms are used later in the lesson, they appear in bold, italic type and are defined.

- Engaging point-of-use **Reader Aids**, located throughout the lessons, tell students why a topic is relevant (*The Bottom Line*) or provide students with helpful hints (*Take Note*). Reader Aids also provide additional relevant or background information that adds value to the lesson.

- **Certification Ready** features throughout the text signal students where a specific certification objective is covered. They provide students with a chance to check their understanding of that particular MTA objective and, if necessary, review the section of the lesson where it is covered. MOAC offers complete preparation for MTA certification.

- **End-of-Lesson Questions** in the Knowledge Assessment section provide a variety of multiple-choice, true-false, matching, and fill-in-the-blank questions.

- **End-of-Lesson Exercises**, such as the Competency Assessment case scenarios and the Proficiency Assessment case scenarios, are projects that test students' ability to apply what they've learned in the lesson.

■ Lesson Features

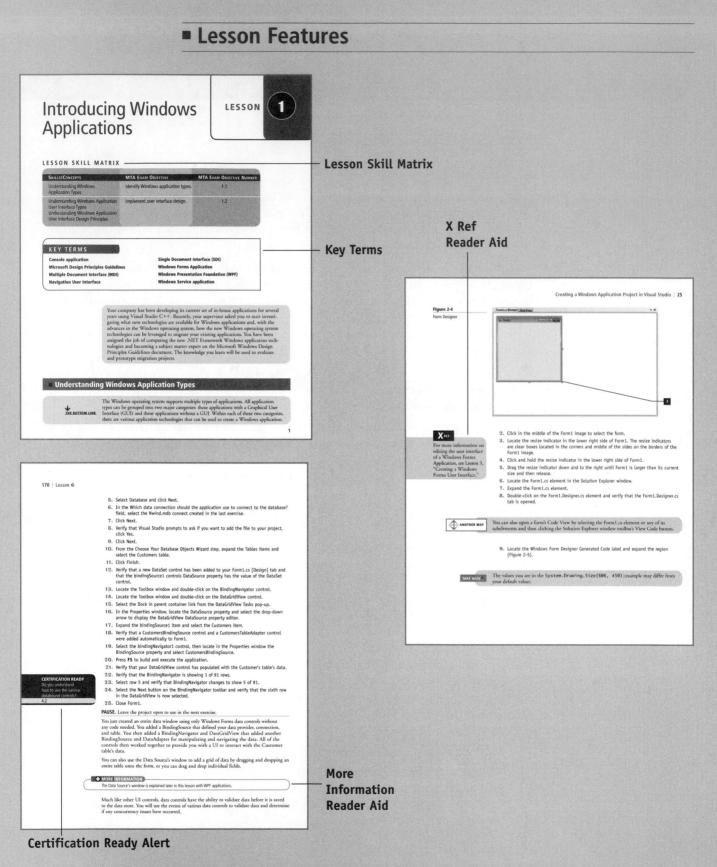

Lesson Skill Matrix

Key Terms

X Ref
Reader Aid

More
Information
Reader Aid

Certification Ready Alert

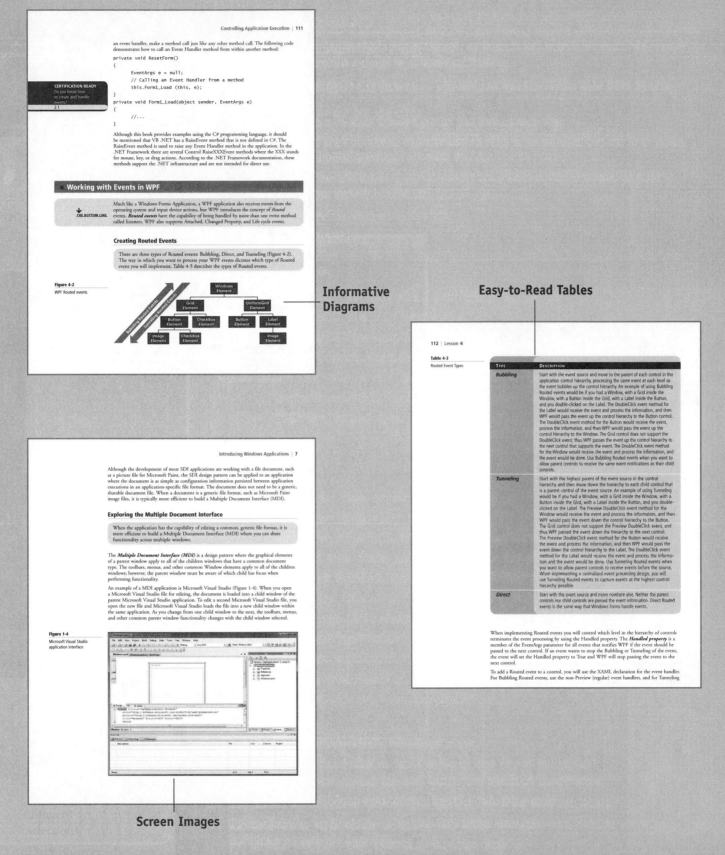

Informative Diagrams

Easy-to-Read Tables

Screen Images

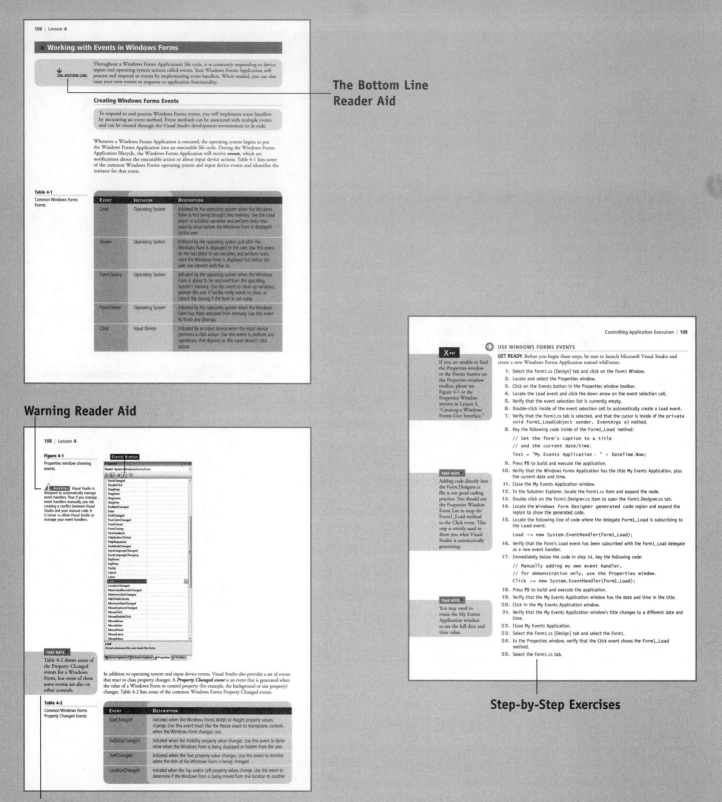

**The Bottom Line
Reader Aid**

Warning Reader Aid

**Take Note
Reader Aid**

Step-by-Step Exercises

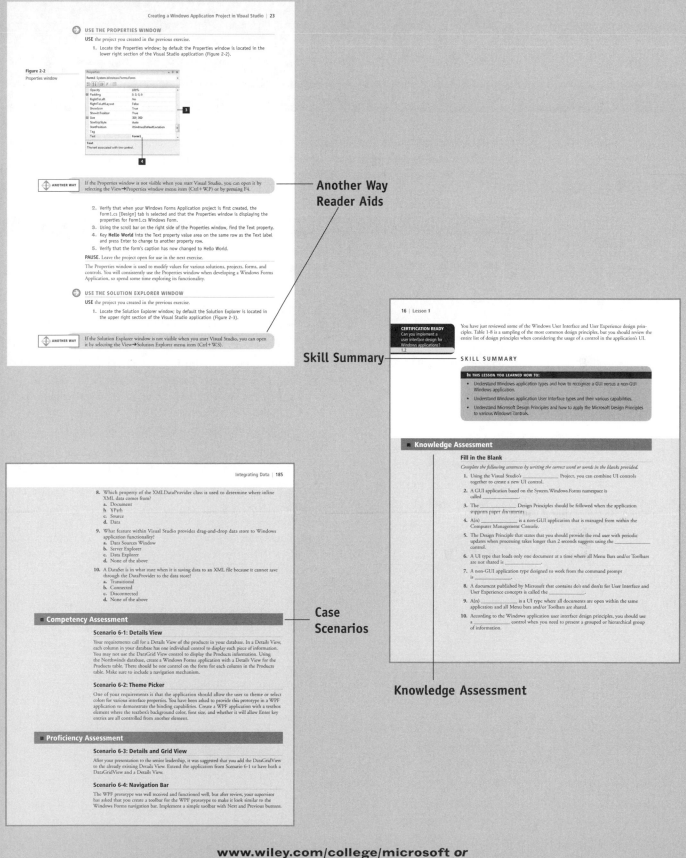

Another Way Reader Aids

Skill Summary

Case Scenarios

Knowledge Assessment

Conventions and Features Used in This Book

This book uses particular fonts, symbols, and heading conventions to highlight important information and to call attention to special steps. For more information about the features in each lesson, refer to the Illustrated Book Tour section.

CONVENTION	MEANING
↓ THE BOTTOM LINE	This feature provides a brief summary of the material to be covered in the section that follows.
CLOSE	Words in all capital letters indicate instructions for opening, saving, or closing files or programs. They also point out items you should check or actions you should take.
CERTIFICATION READY	This feature signals a point in the text where a specific certification objective is covered. It provides you with a chance to check your understanding of that particular MTA objective and, if necessary, review the section of the lesson where the objective is covered.
TAKE NOTE*	Reader aids appear in shaded boxes found in your text. *Take Note* provides helpful hints related to particular tasks or topics.
DOWNLOAD	Download provides information on where to download useful software.
X REF	These notes provide pointers to information discussed elsewhere in the textbook or describe interesting features that are not directly addressed in the current topic or exercise.
Alt + Tab	A plus sign (+) between two key names means that you must press both keys at the same time. Keys that you are instructed to press in an exercise will appear in the font shown here.
Example	Key terms appear in bold, italic font.

Instructor Support Program

The *Microsoft Official Academic Course* programs are accompanied by a rich array of resources that incorporate the extensive textbook visuals to form a pedagogically cohesive package. These resources provide all the materials instructors need to deploy and deliver their courses. Resources available online for download include:

- The **MSDN Academic Alliance** is designed to provide the easiest and most inexpensive developer tools, products, and technologies available to faculty and students in labs, classrooms, and on student PCs. A free three-year membership is available to qualified MOAC adopters.

  Note: Microsoft Windows Server 2008, Microsoft Windows 7, and Microsoft Visual Studio can be downloaded from MSDN AA for use by students in this course.

- The **Instructor's Guide** contains solutions to all the textbook exercises and Syllabi for various term lengths. The Instructor's Guide also includes chapter summaries and lecture notes. The Instructor's Guide is available from the Book Companion site (http://www.wiley.com/college/microsoft).

- The **Test Bank** contains hundreds of questions in multiple-choice, true-false, short answer, and essay formats, and is available to download from the Instructor's Book Companion site (www.wiley.com/college/microsoft). A complete answer key is also provided.

- A complete set of **PowerPoint presentations and images** is available on the Instructor's Book Companion site (http://www.wiley.com/college/microsoft) to enhance classroom presentations. Approximately 50 PowerPoint slides are provided for each lesson. Tailored to the text's topical coverage and Skills Matrix, these presentations are designed to convey key concepts addressed in the text. All images from the text are on the Instructor's Book Companion site (http://www.wiley.com/college/microsoft). You can incorporate them into your PowerPoint presentations or use them to create your own overhead transparencies and handouts. By using these visuals in class discussions, you can help focus students' attention on key elements of technologies covered and help them understand how to use these technologies effectively in the workplace.

- When it comes to improving the classroom experience, there is no better source of ideas and inspiration than your fellow colleagues. The **Wiley Faculty Network** connects teachers with technology, facilitates the exchange of best practices, and helps enhance instructional efficiency and effectiveness. Faculty Network activities include technology training and tutorials, virtual seminars, peer-to-peer exchanges of experiences and ideas, personal consulting, and sharing of resources. For details, visit www.WhereFacultyConnect.com.

MSDN ACADEMIC ALLIANCE—FREE 3-YEAR MEMBERSHIP AVAILABLE TO QUALIFIED ADOPTERS!

The Microsoft Developer Network Academic Alliance (MSDN AA) is designed to provide the easiest and most inexpensive way for universities to make the latest Microsoft developer tools, products, and technologies available in labs, in classrooms, and on student PCs. MSDN AA is an annual membership program for departments teaching Science, Technology, Engineering, and Mathematics (STEM) courses. The membership provides a complete solution to keep academic labs, faculty, and students on the leading edge of technology.

Software available in the MSDN AA program is provided at no charge to adopting departments through the Wiley and Microsoft publishing partnership.

As a bonus to this free offer, faculty will be introduced to Microsoft's Faculty Connection and Academic Resource Center. It takes time and preparation to keep students engaged while giving them a fundamental understanding of theory, and the Microsoft Faculty Connection is designed to help STEM professors with this preparation by providing articles, curriculum, and tools that professors can use to engage and inspire today's technology students.

Contact your Wiley representative for details.

For more information about the MSDN Academic Alliance program, go to:

http://msdn.microsoft.com/academic/

Note: Microsoft Windows Server 2008, Microsoft Windows 7, and Microsoft Visual Studio can be downloaded from MSDN AA for use by students in this course.

▪ Important Web Addresses and Phone Numbers

To locate the Wiley Higher Education Representative in your area, go to http://www. wiley.com/college and click on the "*Who's My Rep?*" link at the top of the page, or call the MOAC toll-free number: 1 + (888) 764-7001 (U.S. & Canada only).

To learn more about becoming a Microsoft Certified Technology Specialist and about exam availability, visit www.microsoft.com/learning/mcp/mcp.

▪ Additional Resources

Book Companion Web Site (www.wiley.com/college/microsoft)

The students' book companion site for the MOAC series includes any resources, exercise files, and Web links that will be used in conjunction with this course.

Wiley Desktop Editions

Wiley MOAC Desktop Editions are innovative, electronic versions of printed textbooks. Students buy the desktop version for up to 50% off the U.S. price of the printed text, and they get the added value of permanence and portability. Wiley Desktop Editions also provide students with numerous additional benefits that are not available with other e-text solutions.

Wiley Desktop Editions are NOT subscriptions; students download the Wiley Desktop Edition to their computer desktops. Students own the content they buy to keep for as long as they want. Once a Wiley Desktop Edition is downloaded to the computer desktop, students have instant access to all of the content without being online. Students can print the sections they prefer to read in hard copy. Students also have access to fully integrated resources within their Wiley Desktop Edition. From highlighting their e-text to taking and sharing notes, students can easily personalize their Wiley Desktop Edition as they are reading or following along in class.

▪ About the Microsoft Technology Associate (MTA) Certification

Preparing Tomorrow's Technology Workforce

Technology plays a role in virtually every business around the world. Possessing the fundamental knowledge of how technology works and understanding its impact on today's academic and workplace environment is increasingly important—particularly for students interested in exploring professions involving technology. That's why Microsoft created the Microsoft Technology Associate (MTA) certification—a new entry-level credential that validates fundamental technology knowledge among students seeking to build a career in technology.

The Microsoft Technology Associate (MTA) certification is the ideal and preferred path to Microsoft's world-renowned technology certification programs, such as Microsoft Certified Technology Specialist (MCTS) and Microsoft Certified IT Professional (MCITP). MTA is positioned to become the premier credential for individuals seeking to explore and pursue a career in technology, or augment related pursuits such as business or any other field where technology is pervasive.

MTA Candidate Profile

The MTA certification program is designed specifically for secondary and post-secondary students interested in exploring academic and career options in a technology field. It offers students a certification in basic IT and development. As the new recommended entry point for Microsoft technology certifications, MTA is designed especially for students new to IT and software development. It is available exclusively in educational settings and easily integrates into the curricula of existing computer classes.

MTA Empowers Educators and Motivates Students

MTA provides a new standard for measuring and validating fundamental technology knowledge right in the classroom while keeping your budget and teaching resources intact. MTA helps institutions stand out as innovative providers of high-demand industry credentials and is easily deployed with a simple, convenient, and affordable suite of entry-level technology certification exams. MTA enables students to explore career paths in technology without requiring a big investment of time and resources, while providing a career foundation and the confidence to succeed in advanced studies and future vocational endeavors.

In addition to giving students an entry-level Microsoft certification, MTA is designed to be a stepping stone to other, more advanced Microsoft technology certifications, like the Microsoft Certified Technology Specialist (MCTS) certification.

Delivering MTA Exams: The MTA Campus License

Implementing a new certification program in your classroom has never been so easy with the MTA Campus License. Through the one-time purchase of the 12-month, 1,000-exam MTA Campus License, there's no more need for ad hoc budget requests and recurrent purchases of exam vouchers. Now you can budget for one low cost for the entire year, and then administer MTA exams to your students and other faculty across your entire campus where and when you want.

The MTA Campus License provides a convenient and affordable suite of entry-level technology certifications designed to empower educators and motivate students as they build a foundation for their careers.

The MTA Campus License is administered by Certiport, Microsoft's exclusive MTA exam provider.

To learn more about becoming a Microsoft Technology Associate and exam availability, visit www.microsoft.com/learning/mta.

▪ Activate Your FREE MTA Practice Test!

Your purchase of this book entitles you to a free MTA practice test from GMetrix (a $30 value). Please go to www.gmetrix.com/mtatests and use the following validation code to redeem your free test: **MTA98-362-DFDBD8795F72**

The **GMetrix Skills Management System** provides everything you need to practice for the Microsoft Technology Associate (MTA) Certification.

Overview of Test features:

- Practice tests map to the Microsoft Technology Associate (MTA) exam objectives
- GMetrix MTA practice tests simulate the actual MTA testing environment
- 50+ questions per test covering all objectives
- Progress at own pace, save test to resume later, return to skipped questions
- Detailed, printable score report highlighting areas requiring further review

To get the most from your MTA preparation, take advantage of your free GMetrix MTA Practice Test today!

For technical support issues on installation or code activation, please email support@gmetrix.com.

Acknowledgments

■ MOAC MTA Technology Fundamentals Reviewers

We'd like to thank the many reviewers who pored over the manuscript and provided invaluable feedback in the service of quality instructional materials:

Yuke Wang, University of Texas at Dallas

Palaniappan Vairavan, Bellevue College

Harold "Buz" Lamson, ITT Technical Institute

Colin Archibald, Valencia Community College

Catherine Bradfield, DeVry University Online

Robert Nelson, Blinn College

Kalpana Viswanathan, Bellevue College

Bob Becker, Vatterott College

Carol Torkko, Bellevue College

Bharat Kandel, Missouri Tech

Linda Cohen, Forsyth Technical Community College

Candice Lambert, Metro Technology Centers

Susan Mahon, Collin College

Mark Aruda, Hillsborough Community College

Claude Russo, Brevard Community College

David Koppy, Baker College

Sharon Moran, Hillsborough Community College

Keith Hoell, Briarcliffe College and Queens College—CUNY

Mark Hufnagel, Lee County School District

Rachelle Hall, Glendale Community College

Scott Elliott, Christie Digital Systems, Inc.

Gralan Gilliam, Kaplan

Steve Strom, Butler Community College

John Crowley, Bucks County Community College

Margaret Leary, Northern Virginia Community College

Sue Miner, Lehigh Carbon Community College

Gary Rollinson, Cabrillo College

Al Kelly, University of Advancing Technology

Katherine James, Seneca College

Brief Contents

Contents

Introducing Windows Applications

LESSON SKILL MATRIX

Skills/Concepts	MTA Exam Objective	MTA Exam Objective Number
Understanding Windows Application Types	Identify Windows application types.	1.1
Understanding Windows Application User Interface Types Understanding Windows Application User Interface Design Principles	Implement user interface design.	1.2

KEY TERMS

Console application

Microsoft Design Principles Guidelines

Multiple Document Interface (MDI)

Navigation User Interface

Single Document Interface (SDI)

Windows Forms Application

Windows Presentation Foundation (WPF)

Windows Service application

Your company has been developing its current set of in-house applications for several years using Visual Studio C++. Recently, your supervisor asked you to start investigating what new technologies are available for Windows applications and, with the advances in the Windows operating system, how the new Windows operating system technologies can be leveraged to migrate your existing applications. You have been assigned the job of comparing the new .NET Framework Windows application technologies and becoming a subject matter expert on the Microsoft Windows Design Principles Guidelines document. The knowledge you learn will be used to evaluate and prototype migration projects.

Understanding Windows Application Types

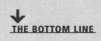

THE BOTTOM LINE

The Windows operating system supports multiple types of applications. All application types can be grouped into two major categories: those applications with a Graphical User Interface (GUI) and those applications without a GUI. Within each of these two categories, there are various application technologies that can be used to create a Windows application.

Introducing Windows GUI Applications

> To create Windows GUI applications Visual Studio provides two technologies: the Windows Forms .NET Framework and the Windows Presentation Foundation (WPF).

With the introduction of the .NET Framework, Visual Studio has enabled developers to create GUI-based Windows application by using the .NET Framework's System.Windows and System.Windows.Forms namespaces. These two namespaces combined provide all of the graphical elements required to give a rich graphical user interface and interactions. *Windows Forms* (WinForms) *applications* support all of the standard Windows application User Interface (UI) elements. Figure 1-1 represents a typical Windows Forms Application.

Figure 1-1

Windows Forms calculator

With the introduction of .NET Framework 3.0, Visual Studio enabled developers to create GUI-based Windows applications by using the *Windows Presentation Foundation (WPF).* WPF is a unified programming model for combining UI, media, and document elements into one Windows application. Figure 1-2 represents a typical WPF application.

Figure 1-2

WPF calculator

A Windows Forms and WPF application can look very similar and, based solely on the executing application, it can be nearly impossible to tell which application is based on what technology. WPF was not created to replace the Windows Forms development process so when creating an application you should not consider the two technologies to be competitors. Because each technology has its advantages, you should compare the application objectives against both technologies to identify which technology is better suited. Table 1-1 provides a brief list of Windows Forms and WPF technologies to consider when developing your Windows application.

Table 1-1

Windows Forms and WPF Technologies

TECHNOLOGY	WINDOWS FORMS	WPF
User Interface Controls	Windows Forms supports a wide range of prebuilt UI controls. There are over 70 default Windows Forms controls provided by Visual Studio in the Toolbox and by using the Custom User Control Project you can combine UI controls to create new UI controls.	WPF supports a basic set of UI controls with about 40 UI controls provided by default in the Visual Studio Toolbox. The power of the WPF UI is the ability to combine UI controls right on the Window or Page to create new controls without needing to create a new project. You can combine UI controls into other UI controls by nesting each UI control's Extensible Application Markup Language (XAML) inside of each other.
User Interface Development	Windows Forms provides a Windows Forms designer with code that implements the business logic for UI components. The UI designer and code behind are grouped into the same file and the glue code between the two is managed by the Visual Studio environment.	WPF provides a XAML editor and a separate code editor. The UI of a WPF application can be completely separated from the code that implements the business logic. In some cases, a graphics designer will use the Expression Blend application to create the UI while a developer creates the code. When both of them are done, the UI and the business logic are combined based on common XAML defined tags.
Event Handling	Windows Forms Applications can handle all of the standard Windows operating system events. Events are handled at the control level and validation and application execution is controlled by the events that are triggered.	WPF applications can handle all of the standard Windows operating system events and, in addition, WPF integrated Routed Events technology. WPF events can be routed up or down a control tree allowing various controls to validate and process application execution.
Data Integration	Windows Forms Applications have several UI controls that support direct integration with database data. The Visual Studio development environment has several built-in support tools designed to work with Windows Forms and data from databases. A Windows Forms Application that interfaces with a database can be created without one line of code.	WPF applications look at data in a different way. WPF introduced the technology of binding where properties of a control can be bound to another property, an object, or a database. The Visual Studio development environment has support for WPF and database integrations, but the real power of WPF and data is the binding capability to not only bind to database data, but to bind to anything that can have a value.

Not all applications developed for Windows need to have an interface that requires the use of a Windows Forms or WPF application. Visual Studio can also create applications that run as a Windows Service or as a Console on the command line.

Introducing Windows Non-GUI Applications

> To create Windows non-GUI applications, Visual Studio provides two technologies: the Windows Service and the Console application.

Although a Windows Service application and a Console application both do not have UIs they serve very different purposes. A ***Windows Service application*** is designed to execute and interact with the Computer Management Console. The Windows Service application is intended to be executed for monitoring, maintaining, or evaluating functionality. A Windows Service application is by definition a "service" and should function as one.

An example of a Windows Service application is the Internet Information Service (IIS). IIS does not have a user interface outside of the virtual directory and configuration management applications that are separate from the IIS application itself. IIS runs in the background of the operating system waiting for web page requests; it processes the requests and then returns the results. Table 1-2 provides a brief list of Windows Services capabilities.

Table 1-2

Windows Services Capabilities

FEATURE	DESCRIPTION
Always Executing	A Windows Service application is always running. Once you install a Windows Service application into the operating system, the application begins to execute and your Windows Service application functionality is available.
Start, Stop, Pause, Continue	A Windows Service application is always executing, thus it provides the capability to control the service's execution through the start, stop, pause, and continue functionality.
Shutdown Notification	When the operating system is about to shut down, your Windows Service application needs to stop executing and possibly clean up any service processing. A Windows Service application has the capability to be notified when the operating system is shutting down to allow for processing.

The Console application project type has been a part of Visual Studio for many years. When operating systems transitioned from Disk-based Operating System (DOS) to Windows, the concept of a command-line prompt and command-line applications did not disappear. Windows still supports the ability to open a command-line window and enter command-line commands to execute functionality within the Windows environment. A ***Console application*** is a command-line application that has no UI and is executed from the command-line prompt. A Console application is not within the scope of this book, although a Console application is another choice when considering what type of Windows application to create.

Introducing Windows Win32 Applications

> To create Windows Win32 applications, you can use either a GUI or non-GUI Visual Studio project.

A Windows Win32 application is created using the Windows Application Programming Interface (API). Although you can create an application strictly using the Win32 APIs, it is more common to use Win32 APIs within another application. The Win32 APIs provide functionality into most of the operating systems' features. Table 1-3 provides a list of some of the Windows Win32 API libraries.

Table 1-3

Windows Win32 API Libraries

LIBRARY	DESCRIPTION
Advanced Services	The Advanced Services library implements Windows interfaces not implemented in the Basic Services library but that still apply to Windows fundamental features. The Advanced Services include interfaces into the Windows Registry and User Account Management. The APIs for the Advanced Services are available from the advapi32.dll for Windows 32-bit operating systems.
Basic Services	The Basic Services library implements interfaces into the Windows operating system's fundamental resources like the file system and application threads. The APIs for the Basic Services are available from the kernel32.dll for Windows 32-bit operating systems.
User Interface	The User Interface library implements interfaces to create and manage the GUI part of Windows. The User Interface library includes interfaces for buttons, mouse, and keyboard input. The APIs for the User Interface library are available from the user32.dll for Windows 32-bit operating systems.

CERTIFICATION READY
Can you identify the various Windows application types?
1.1

For a full list of Windows Win32 API libraries and APIs, you can use the Microsoft Solutions Developer Network (MSDN) Windows API topic http://msdn.microsoft.com/en-us/library/aa383750.aspx.

■ Understanding Windows Application User Interface Types

↓
THE BOTTOM LINE

A Windows Forms or WPF application provides several options for presenting graphic information. Deciding if the application needs to have a Single document, Multiple document, or Navigation interface will affect your end user's satisfaction with the application's ability to meet his or her objective.

Exploring the Single Document User Interface

The most basic of all UI designs is the Single Document Interface (SDI).

The *Single Document Interface (SDI)* is one of the first UI designs introduced when the Windows operating system was created. SDI is a design pattern in which the graphical elements of the window apply only to the current Window where they reside. The toolbars, menus, and other common Window elements control only the functionality for the window in which they are embedded. Each window that appears will have its own set of toolbars and menus to control its functionality.

An example of a SDI application is Microsoft Paint (Figure 1-3). You can open only one picture at a time for editing within the Microsoft Paint application. To edit a second picture,

Figure 1-3

Microsoft Paint application
interface

you must close the first picture. If you open two Microsoft Paint applications, the toolbars
and menus affect only the picture loaded into the respective Microsoft Paint applications. You
cannot change the color of one picture from the other Microsoft Paint application. Table 1-4
provides a brief list of SDI application capabilities.

Table 1-4

SDI Capabilities

FEATURE	DESCRIPTION
Multiple Icons on the Windows Taskbar	As each application is executed and processes each opened document, each executing application's icon is placed on the Windows Taskbar. This provides quick and individual access to each document. Some users like having the individual icons, while others find that having all of the icons on the Windows Taskbar is too cluttered.
Isolated Functionality	Each Menu Bar and toolbar is isolated to the current window; thus end users interacting with the Menu Bar and/or toolbar will always be aware of which document the action is applicable.
Simplify Interface	Some end users find interacting with one window to be a simplified interface. The interface presents information for only one document and the end user does not need to take other documents into consideration when working with the UI.

Although the development of most SDI applications are working with a file document, such as a picture file for Microsoft Paint, the SDI design pattern can be applied to an application where the document is as simple as configuration information persisted between application executions in an application-specific file format. The document does not need to be a generic, sharable document file. When a document is a generic file format, such as Microsoft Paint image files, it is typically more efficient to build a Multiple Document Interface (MDI).

Exploring the Multiple Document Interface

> When the application has the capability of editing a common, generic file format, it is more efficient to build a Multiple Document Interface (MDI) where you can share functionality across multiple windows.

The *Multiple Document Interface (MDI)* is a design pattern where the graphical elements of a parent window apply to all of the children windows that have a common document type. The toolbars, menus, and other common Window elements apply to all of the children windows; however, the parent window must be aware of which child has focus when performing functionality.

An example of a MDI application is Microsoft Visual Studio (Figure 1-4). When you open a Microsoft Visual Studio file for editing, the document is loaded into a child window of the parent Microsoft Visual Studio application. To edit a second Microsoft Visual Studio file, you open the new file and Microsoft Visual Studio loads the file into a new child window within the same application. As you change from one child window to the next, the toolbars, menus, and other common parent window functionality changes with the child window selected.

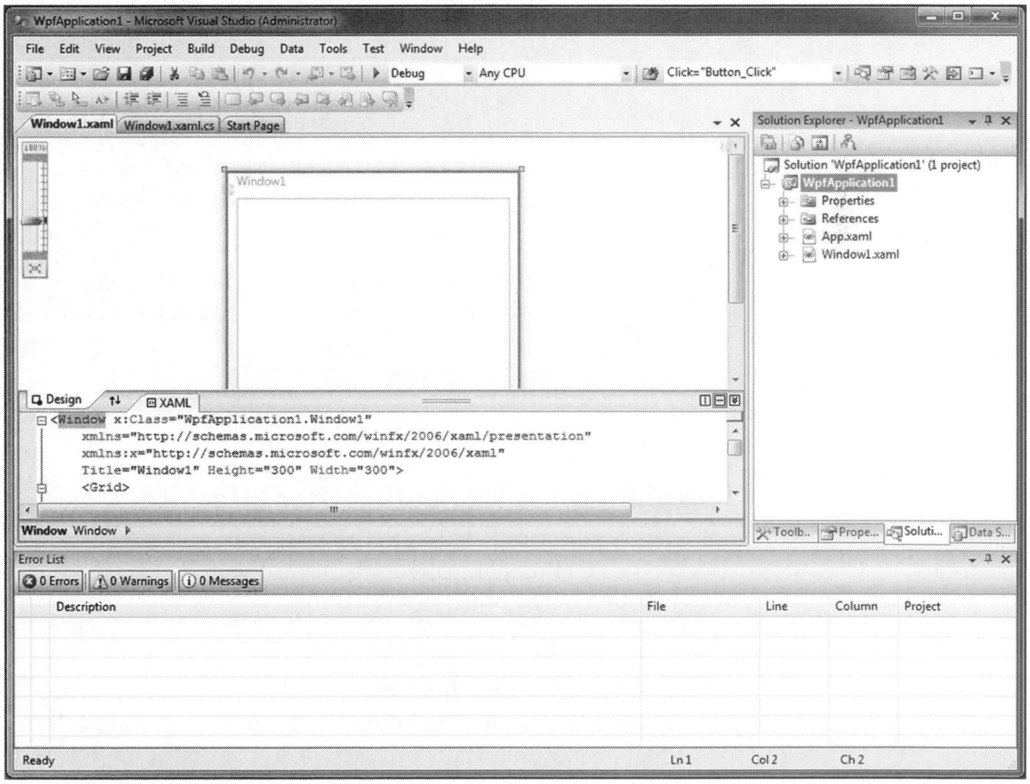

Figure 1-4

Microsoft Visual Studio
application interface

The advantage to using a MDI design pattern versus a SDI design pattern for generic documents is the ability to implement the same functionality once and then apply that capability across multiple documents (Table 1-5). You can achieve similar functionality by using the SDI design pattern and Windows inheritance, but with SDI the windows will be organized within the operating system window, versus with MDI, the Windows will be organized within the parent window. Some users will want to have separate windows, while other users will want to have all windows within one application. Understanding when to use one design pattern versus the other depends on the application objectives.

Table 1-5

MDI Capabilities

FEATURE	DESCRIPTION
Single Icons on the Windows Taskbar	As each document is opened and processed, a singular application icon is responsible for providing access to the entire list of open documents. By having a singular icon on the Taskbar, the end user does not need to identify which Taskbar Icon to select to gain access to the right document. The one application maintains the list of open documents and provides the UI mechanism for gaining focus and switching between open documents. Some users find that having the application manage the open documents and Windows, Pages, or Forms makes the application more complicated and too cluttered.
Flexible Document Switching	When using SDI, all of the documents and their applications are presented to the user on the Taskbar, but when using MDI, you have the ability to present the documents whichever way you feel best suits the user experience. You can list the documents in a List Box on the side of the Windows in a Task Pane, or add an icon to the Toolbar for direct and quick access.
Shared Functionality	When the end user is presented with a Menu Bar or Toolbar, the functionality is shared across all of the open Windows, Pages, and/or Forms. The end user must always be aware of what document is currently selected; otherwise the incorrect functionality could be applied to the wrong document. Alternatively, the end user does not need to manage multiple Menu Bars and/or Toolbars when changing between documents. The same Menu Bar and/or Toolbar applies to multiple documents. MDI provides consistency and familiarity for the overall end user experience when working with multiple documents.
Advanced Interface	Some end users find interacting with more than one document to be an advanced interface. The interface presents multiple documents and document functionality all at one time, forcing the end user to take into consideration all documents at one time rather than individually.

Exploring the Navigation User Interface

The new UI design pattern introduced with the .NET Framework 3.0 and WPF is the Navigation User Interface (UI).

The *Navigation User Interface* is used like a wizard or process flow. The Navigation UI design pattern has built-in buttons and capabilities to allow for moving forward and backward through application Pages of functionality. It can be applied to both the SDI and MDI design patterns. You can have a single document with multiple pages of information or you can have multiple documents with multiple pages of information.

An example of a Navigation UI application with an MDI design pattern is Microsoft Internet Explorer (see Figure 1-5). Earlier versions of Microsoft Internet Explorer would allow you to browse only one set of web pages at a time. The current version of Microsoft Internet Explorer provides tabs for browsing multiple documents transitioning the Microsoft Internet Explorer application from the SDI to the MDI design pattern. Table 1-6 provides a brief list of Navigation UI application capabilities.

Figure 1-5

Microsoft Internet Explorer
application interface

Table 1-6

Navigation UI Capabilities

FEATURE	DESCRIPTION
Similar to SDI	The Navigation UI is similar to SDI in that it typically loads only one document of information at a time. The Menu Bars and/or Toolbars apply only to the document of information being presented to the end user in the current application.
Supports MDI	Although the Navigation UI is similar to SDI, the Navigation UI supports some features from MDI, such as Pages. A Page is one Window of information. A Page can be used to load one document, such as a web page, then as you transition to the next web document a new Page is created to provide the next and previous functionality. Multiple web documents are being loaded, but not in a new Window.
Built-In Navigation	A unique capability of the Navigation UI is its built-in capability to provide navigation between Pages. The end user moves from one Page to the next Page as they work in the Navigation UI application. If the user wants to revert to a previous page, the Navigation UI has the ability to reload a previous page, without having to perform all of the Page initializations. The navigation capabilities of the Navigation UI are not reserved only for Internet browsers and wizard applications. The user can also use the Navigation UI for configuration applications where the user would need to transition between options, but wants to provide the ability to jump to previous configurations.

When designing a Windows application, Microsoft has provided a Design Principles guideline to help developers implement UIs that increase the end user's satisfaction level.

■ Understanding Windows Application User Interface Design Principles

↓ THE BOTTOM LINE

When designing the Windows operating system, Microsoft developed a set of User Experience design principles that increase the end user's satisfaction—Controls, Commands, Text, Messages, Interaction, Windows, Visuals, Experiences, and Windows Environment.

Introducing Design Principles

Each of the Windows UI components was designed and implemented to serve a specific purpose in the Windows operating system environment. Using each component as it was designed requires an understanding of the Do's and Don'ts of UI design.

Microsoft has compiled a complete list of design principles to consider when creating a Windows application in the *Microsoft Design Principles Guidelines* document. As each new Windows operating system is released, Microsoft updates this list of design principles to help developers understand the reasoning behind the various UI elements. You can view the list of design principles for Windows 7 and Windows Vista at http://msdn.microsoft.com/en-us/library/aa511258(v=MSDN.10).aspx or you can download a PDF formatted file from the previous web page. Table 1-7 summarizes some of the design principles for Windows 7 and Windows Vista from the Microsoft Design Principles Guidelines document.

Table 1-7

Microsoft Design Principles Guidelines

DESIGN PRINCIPLE	GUIDELINE
Small things matter, good and bad	Focuses on the little details of the application. Make sure to fix the small bugs and pay attention to the small details. Does the application solve the little problems as well as the big ones? As you are capturing the requirements and objectives for the application, pay attention to the little features that you can implement to make the user's experience better.
Be great at "look" and "do"	Focuses on the steps and obviousness of the operations that the user needs to perform. When a user looks at the application Window, Page, or Form in front of him, is it obvious what he should do? The applications should look like what the user wants to do.
Solve distractions, not discoverability	Focuses on the user experience when presented with a task. Do not allow multiple parts of the application to compete for the user's attention. The user's attention should be focused on one area where he can complete the task at hand. The user should not need to discover the task to complete. Poor discoverability should not be resolved by putting an icon on the Desktop, in the Notifications area, or having a tour.
Value the life cycle of the experience	Focuses on the application's global perspective. Don't focus on the application as an execution-only product. Consider the installation, the first time run, the regular usage, management and maintenance, and finally uninstall or upgrade. Viewing the application from all aspects of the application life cycle will enable you to provide a total user experience.
Time matters, so build for people on the go	Focuses on the proficiency of the user at using the application, and the performance of the application itself. Ensuring that users can perform operations quickly means taking into account connectivity, performance, and returning fast from processing operations.

Table 1-8 summarizes some of the design principles do's and don'ts for Windows 7 and Windows Vista.

Table 1-8

Microsoft Design Principles Do's and Don'ts

USER EXPERIENCE AREA	DO'S/DON'TS
Window	Design the application windows for a screen resolution of 800x600. When new windows are opened, position them in the center of their owner or if the window is contextual, position it near the object that opened it.
Layout	Avoid truncating text when within a control. Resize controls as their containers resize. Make a control taller, wider, or multi-line if needed. The positioning of the controls should feel balanced. Don't put too many controls on one side of a window or group controls in a tight configuration. Consider having controls fill the entire width of a window or be organized in columns and rows.
Text	Use ordinary conversational terms and focus on the functionality not the technology. Always remove redundant text from windows, controls, messages, and commands. The text should capitalize only needed names and should be blue only if the text represents a link to the Internet or additional functionality.
Keyboard	When a window opens, the first control to receive focus should be the control that the users will use the most. Any control that requires user interaction should have a tab stop and tab stops that move from left to right and top to bottom. When presenting the user with buttons, they should be ordered OK/Yes, No, Cancel, and then Apply when each of them is needed.
Wizards	Use Wizards only when other interaction methods such as dialog boxes, task panes, or single panes, will not work. Use the Next button only to advance through the Wizard without taking an action and use the Back button only to correct mistakes. When a user needs to go back through the steps, preserve the previous user selections.
Error Messages	Do not show an error message when the user does not have an action that can change the outcome. When an action can be taken, suggest the steps a user can take to correct the error. Don't assign blame or use words such as 'error' or 'failure'; use 'problem' instead.
Icons	All icons should be Aero compatible and comply with the Aero icon guidelines (see http://msdn .microsoft.com/en-us/library/aa511280.aspx). When presenting standard message boxes, use the appropriate message icon such as the Question icon when asking the user for information, the Exclamation icon when warning the user of an action, and so forth.
Help	The application should always provide a help system. Do not put help links on every window but allow the control or windows built-in help functionality to launch relevant help topics.

The Microsoft Design Principles Guidelines document also explains various user controls and specific design principles for when and how to use each control.

Applying Specific Design Principles

Each of the User Interface elements within a Windows application can apply the design principles defined within the Microsoft Design Principles Guidelines document.

See Figure 1-6 for an example. Table 1-9 summarizes some of the specific User Interface element design principles for Windows 7 and Windows Vista from the Microsoft Design Principles Guidelines document.

Figure 1-6

Microsoft specific design principles example

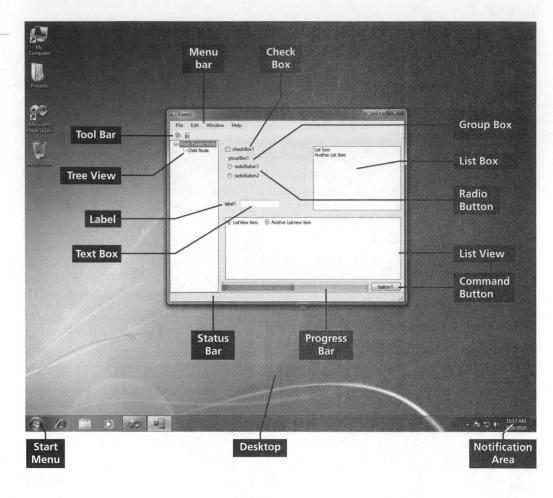

Table 1-9

Microsoft Specific Design Principles

DESIGN AREA	DESIGN ELEMENT	GUIDELINES
Controls	Check Boxes	Use a Check Box when there is a clear choice between opposites. It would be incorrect to have a Check Box with the text "Pizza" because it would not be clear if checking the box means I want pizza or not. Changing the text to "Include pizza in the order" now makes the decision much clearer. Checking the Check Box means that pizza is in the order, and not checking the Check Box means the pizza is not in the order.
	Command Button	Use a Command Button when there is an immediate action to be performed. Typically a Command Button will be the OK/Yes/No/Cancel/Apply functionality for a window or dialog. The default size of a Command Button should be used when possible.
	Group Boxes	Use a Group Box when there are controls that have a strong relationship with each other. Overpopulating a window with Group Boxes can clutter the interface and consume unnecessary amounts of window space. Never nest Group Boxes or place controls in the Group Box label area.

Table 1-9 *(continued)*

DESIGN AREA	DESIGN ELEMENT	GUIDELINES
	List Boxes	Use a List Box when there is a list of data that does not represent program options; does not need to sort, organize, or group; and does not need to drag and drop list items. List Box items should always be sorted in a logical order with options that represent None or All placed at the top of the list.
	List Views	Use a List View when a more flexible List Box is needed. The List View supports sorting, grouping, column reordering, and drag and drop.
	Progress Bars	Use a Progress Bar when the user needs to be presented with a known or deterministic end or to show the application is still working for an indeterministic end. To ensure proper feedback for the user, have the Progress Bar increment about every second. Operations that take longer than two seconds need more feedback. Whenever possible, use a percentage indicator to help the user know the exact amount of the operation that has completed.
	Status Bars	Use a Status Bar when there are notifications that need to be presented without disrupting the flow of execution. Be aware that Status Bar notifications can often be overlooked; thus, if the notification is important, consider a different design concept. The Status Bar should show the current window's status, progress, or contextual information, such as where the user's mouse is located on a drawing canvas.
	Text Boxes	Use a Text Box when the value to be entered is completely unconstrained. If the value needs to be incremented, use a Spinner; if the value needs to be entered in a specific order, use a Masked Edit Box. The Text Box is very flexible and has many design pattern applications such as a single-line data entry, multi-line textual input, or assisted data entry where the Text Box displays the value selected from another action.
	Tree Views	Use a Tree View when a grouped or hierarchical group of information needs to be presented. The Tree View is also a flexible control with several design principle applications. Always sort the Tree View nodes in a logic order. When the user expands or collapses nodes, a nodes state should be maintained between sessions.
Commands	Menus	There are several different types of Menus to consider, a Menu Bar, Toolbar Menu, a Tab Menu, a Context Menu, or a Task Pane Menu. In general, use any or several of these different kinds of Menus when you have a Primary Window or Windows with categories of functionality. Each type of Menu has its own design usages but all Menus should be well organized and follow standard Menu conventions when possible.
	Toolbars	Use a Toolbar when there are a select number of operations that the end user will need to use often. The Toolbar can be a replacement for Menu bars, but ensure that the Toolbar controls are self-explanatory, can be used directly, and that their frequency and usage are needed by the end user. There are several different design patterns and design styles a Toolbar can represent such as large icons, small icons, and property or split buttons.
	Ribbons	The Ribbon is a new control that replaces the Menu bar and Toolbar. Use the Ribbon whenever possible because it prompts discoverability and functional visibility.

(continued)

Table 1-9 *(continued)*

DESIGN AREA	DESIGN ELEMENT	GUIDELINES
Visuals	Fonts	Text is one of the most frequently used features in Windows. Users will look at text more than anything else within the applications. Windows uses a standard font called Segoe (pronounced See-go) to represent all text to the users. Ensure that the font size is 9 point or larger, and that there is a contrast between the font's color and the background color.
	Color	From background colors, to text colors, and even for buttons and labels, you have complete control over the colors users will see. The .NET Framework and especially WPF applications have the ability to theme, or colorize most aspects of the UI. When using colors in the applications, be consistent. If notification messages are red, make all of them red. If command buttons are purple, make all of them purple. Make sure that colors have meaning, convey an emphasis, or are used to differentiate an action.
	Animations and Transitions	Use an Animation or a Transition when drawing the user's attention to an action that is about to happen or is happening. Both Animation and Transitions have movement that is happening over a period of time, thus capturing users' attention and focusing them on the task. When using Animation or Transitions, make sure that the application has character and personality. Character and Personality define the type of Animation or Transition that is most appropriate. For example, if the task is for fun, then the Animation or Transition should be fun or funny; if the task is serious, then the Animation or Transition should be serious.
	Sound	Use Sound to communicate nonverbally with the end user. Sound can be used with or without a UI element. When considering Sound for the application, ensure that the Sound has a clear benefit. Does the sound spark an emotion or visual picture that is consistent with the action? Ensure that the sound is never distracting or annoying. Use an annoying sound only if the action needs to be addressed immediately, but do so sparingly.
Experiences	Setup	Although you might not consider the setup process a part of the application, it is necessary for end users to utilize this application. The Setup and installation process is a necessary evil for end users to utilize the application. Typically the first interactions end users have with the application is the installation process. Keep the installation and setup process short and quick. Remember, end users want to use the application, not the setup and installation application. Ensure that the setup application has only questions and steps that directly impact the installation process.
	First Experience	Helps an end user transition from the first time he uses the application to using it again and again. Some of the First Experience can be accomplished in the Setup application, such as gathering product codes or licensing information. The application should start with the most common set of configuration information. If there are areas that require configuration by the end user to operate, the First Experience should present the end user with only the needed customizations and then continue to the main application operations. Keep the First Experience as short and quick as possible. Again, the end user wants to use the application, not continually reconfigure it.

(continued)

Table 1-9 (*continued*)

DESIGN AREA	DESIGN ELEMENT	GUIDELINES
	Printing	Refers to the direct output of application information to paper format. Not all applications need to have Printing functionality but if the application edits, views, or works with documents, images, or data, the user will most likely need some degree of printing. Whenever possible, the application should support a What You See Is What You Get (WYSIWYG) preview feature that enables the end user to see what will be printed and how many pages of paper will be used. Remember, printing has a resource (paper, toner) cost; thus provide the end user with as much information as possible about the printing process before actually printing.
Windows Environment	Desktop	Not a part of the application, but how the application uses this shared work area can enhance the end user's experience. If the application is going to be used frequently, have the Setup application install a shortcut to the Desktop. Do not install the application to the Desktop, only a shortcut. The shortcut's label should never be truncated, so choose a label with less than 20 characters.
	Start Menu	As the initial entry point for end users into all applications in the operating system, ensure that the application does not hinder the end user from using any other applications. If the application is going to be used frequently, use the Stat Menu Pinned area to ensure that the application is always one-click away. Otherwise, the application should be organized under the Programs menu within its own folder. Put shortcuts to the program, help files, readme files, utilities, un-installation, and/or Web sites into the application's folder. Additional shortcuts should be avoided. Be sure not to create an excessive number of shortcuts.
	Notification Area	Use the Notification Area for temporary system or program level messages. The Notification Area is an excellent place to allow applications without the current focus to notify the end user of a message, but keep in mind that the user is currently performing another task, and interrupting the flow of that task might be undesirable. Also, use the Notification Area to provide Jump lists or quick access to the commonly used application commands.
	Help	Use Help as a secondary UI—not to fix a bad UI. Create Help that assists users in completing tasks and that helps those who want information the UI can't provide. At times the label of a control cannot fully explain what the setting means. Help allows further elaboration of a field's meaning and/or the impact of selecting one or more various options.
	User Account Control (UAC)	UAC was introduced with Windows Vista and has been discussed in various development forums because of its control over the privileges needed for application installation and execution within the Windows Vista and Windows 7 operating systems. Whenever possible, try to design the application to execute at the default UAC level. The UAC level can be elevated, but ensure that when the application is complete, the UAC level is returned to its original setting.

CERTIFICATION READY
Can you implement a
user interface design for
Windows applications?
1.2

You have just reviewed some of the Windows User Interface and User Experience design principles. Table 1-8 is a sampling of the most common design principles, but you should review the entire list of design principles when considering the usage of a control in the application's UI.

SKILL SUMMARY

IN THIS LESSON YOU LEARNED HOW TO:

- Understand Windows application types and how to recognize a GUI versus a non-GUI Windows application.

- Understand Windows application User Interface types and their various capabilities.

- Understand Microsoft Design Principles and how to apply the Microsoft Design Principles to various Windows controls.

■ Knowledge Assessment

Fill in the Blank

Complete the following sentences by writing the correct word or words in the blanks provided.

1. Using the Visual Studio's _____ Project, you can combine UI controls together to create a new UI control.

2. A GUI application based on the System.Windows.Forms namespace is called _____.

3. The _____ Design Principles should be followed when the application supports paper documents.

4. A(n) _____ is a non-GUI application that is managed from within the Computer Management Console.

5. The Design Principle that states that you should provide the end user with periodic updates when processing takes longer than 2 seconds suggests using the _____ control.

6. A UI type that loads only one document at a time where all Menu Bars and/or Toolbars are not shared is _____.

7. A non-GUI application type designed to work from the command prompt is _____.

8. A document published by Microsoft that contains do's and don'ts for User Interface and User Experience concepts is called the _____.

9. A(n) _____ is a UI type where all documents are open within the same application and all Menu bars and/or Toolbars are shared.

10. According to the Windows application user interface design principles, you should use a _____ control when you need to present a grouped or hierarchical group of information.

Multiple Choice

Circle the letter that corresponds to the best answer.

1. Which of the following is NOT a Design Principle based on the Microsoft Design Principles Guidelines document?
   a. Be great at "look" and "do."
   b. Value the life cycle of the experience.
   c. Simple things matter, good and bad.
   d. None of the above.

2. Which of the following labels would be best suited for use on a Check Box control?
   a. Chocolate
   b. Chocolate Ice Cream
   c. Chocolate Ice Cream Sundae
   d. Add Chocolate Ice Cream Sundae to Order

3. The Solve distractions, not discoverability Design Principle applies to all but which of the following guidelines?
   a. Application features should not compete with one another.
   b. The end user's focus should not be split between tasks.
   c. Consider how the setup and installation affect your overall application experience.
   d. You should not put an icon in the Notification Area to help end user's complete a task.

4. An application should be designed to work at what screen resolution?
   a. 800 x 600
   b. 640 x 480
   c. 1024 x 768
   d. 1280 x 960

5. The Setup process should conform to which of the following design principles?
   a. Take as much time as needed, make sure to get the installation correct.
   b. The Setup should run every time the application runs.
   c. If needed, ask the user several times the same question in different ways to make sure he/she understands.
   d. None of the above.

6. Which controls should receive keyboard focus when a Window first opens?
   a. The first control
   b. The control used the most
   c. The last control
   d. None of the above

7. Which of the following guideline(s) violations apply to a Group Box?
   a. Add as many as you want, the more the better.
   b. Grouping is great; grouping controls inside of groupings just shows good design.
   c. The Grouping Label is not graphical enough; additional controls over the label makes the application more impressive.
   d. All of the above.

8. Which of the following is a correct design principle for the Start Menu?
   a. Always put the application in the pinned area.
   b. Placing the application in the programs menu enables faster access.
   c. Placing a shortcut to the control panel is okay if the application interacts with the control panel frequently.
   d. None of the above.

9. Which command should be placed on a Toolbar?
   a. All Commands, they are all important.
   b. The most commonly used Commands.
   c. None; let the end user decide.
   d. None of the above.

10. Which of the following is NOT a Font design guideline?
   a. Font size should be 9 point or higher.
   b. Font color should be high contrast.
   c. Never change the font from the standard Segoe font.
   d. All of the above.

■ Competency Assessment

Scenario 1-1: Supervisor's Meeting

You have just completed your investigation of the various Windows application types when your supervisor calls you into his/her office. Your supervisor has a meeting in several minutes with the IT director and would like you to help prep for the meeting. Using a pen and paper or a text file, list the various Windows application options and some bullet points for each type and when each type should be used.

Scenario 1-2: User Interface Review

A coworker has brought you an interface mock-up picture to review. Using Figure 1-7 and a pen and paper or a text file, make a list of all the User Interface Do's and Don'ts you observe.

Figure 1-7

Scenario 1-2 User Interface Mock-Up

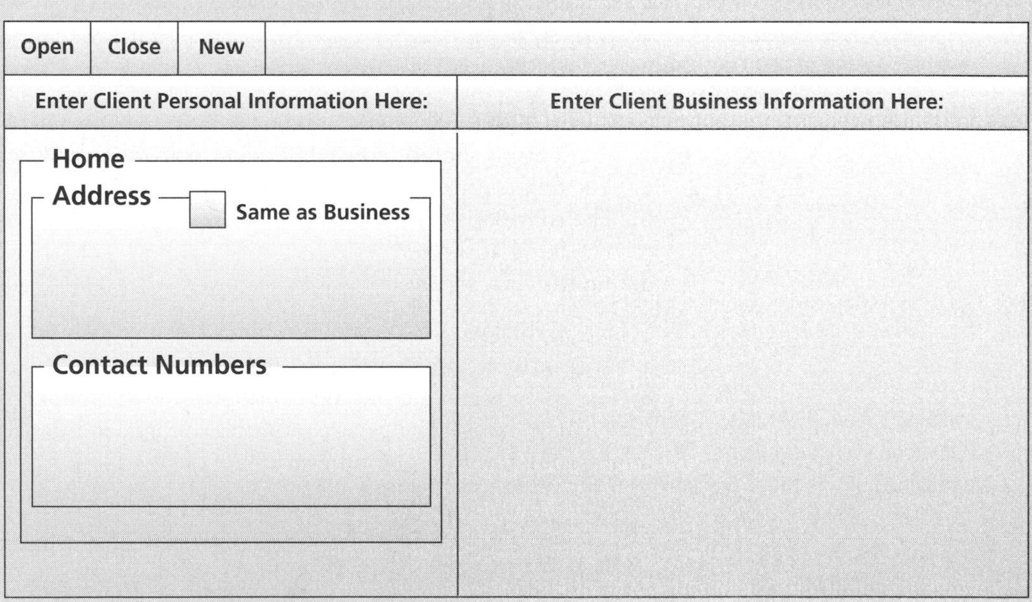

■ Proficiency Assessment

Scenario 1-3: Working with Documents

One of your coworkers is analyzing one of your existing applications to gather business requirements. One of the business requirements is the ability to manage a group of data in a document. Your coworker has come to you to understand the various Windows applications designs. Using pen and paper or a drawing application and a text file, draw each of the Windows application designs and a few bullet points to explain the differences.

Scenario 1-4: Client Information Mock-Up

Your supervisor has come to you with the assignment to create a user interface mock-up for one of your existing applications that gathers client information. Using a pen and paper or a drawing application and a text file, draw a user interface that follows the Microsoft User Interface Design Principles. The user interface mock-up should include the Main Window (with any menu bars, toolbars and/or status bars) and any other Windows you will need to edit all of the client's information.

2 LESSON

Creating a Windows Application Project in Visual Studio

LESSON SKILL MATRIX

SKILLS/CONCEPTS	MTA EXAM OBJECTIVE	MTA EXAM OBJECTIVE NUMBER
Getting Started with a Windows Forms Application Getting Started with a Windows Service Application	Create Windows-based applications by using Visual Studio.	1.3
Getting Started with a Windows Presentation Foundation Application	Supplemental	

KEY TERMS

form

New Project dialog

Page

Properties window

Solution Explorer Window

Window

Your organization is starting a new project and your supervisor has asked you to document the creation process for a Windows Forms Application, a Windows Presentation Framework (WPF) Application, and a Windows Service Application. Your report will include a comparison of these three creation processes and the differences between each project type. Your report will be used by organizational decision makers to understand which type of project(s) will be used to solve an organizational need.

■ Getting Started with a Windows Forms Application

↓ **THE BOTTOM LINE**   To begin a Windows Forms Application, you create a Windows Forms Application project. Once created, you can explore the basic structure and parts.

Creating a Windows Forms Application

Visual Studio provides several methods for creating a new Windows Forms Application project type.

To initiate the creation of a Windows Forms Application, you can use any one of the following methods:

- The Start Page
- The File→New→Project menu
- The New Project toolbar button

All three of these methods will open the same *New Project dialog* where you will select your project type and create a Windows Forms Application.

 CREATE A WINDOWS FORMS APPLICATION

GET READY. Before you begin these steps, be sure to launch Visual Studio.

1. Verify that the Start Page is displayed by default when opening Visual Studio; this is the most obvious way to start the Windows Forms Application project creation process.
2. On the Start Page, click the Projects . . . link next to the Create label inside of the Recent Projects grouping.
3. The New Project dialog (Figure 2-1) will appear.

 **ANOTHER WAY**

You can also open the New Project dialog by Selecting the File→New→Project menu item (Ctrl-Shift-N) or by clicking the New Project toolbar button positioned, by default, as the first (far left) button on the Standard toolbar.

Figure 2-1

New Project dialog

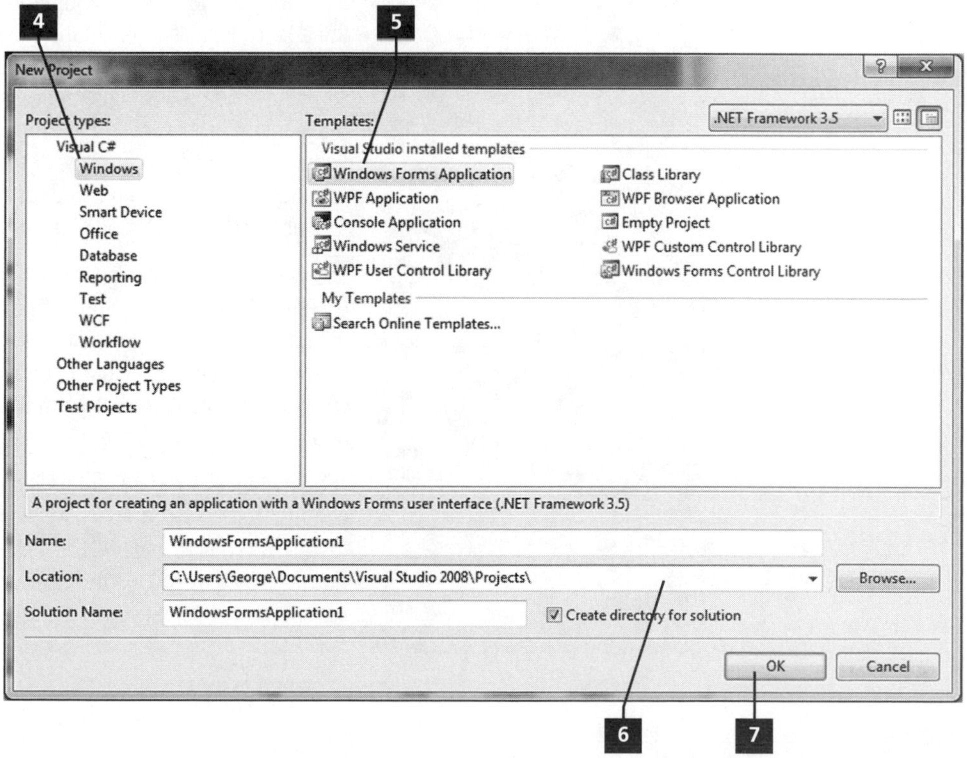

TAKE NOTE✱

Depending on which language (C# or VB.NET) you selected as your default when first running Visual Studio, your default New Project dialog project types may look different from Figure 2-1.

![New Project dialog with callouts 4, 5 (top), 6, 7 (bottom). Project types: Visual C# (Windows, Web, Smart Device, Office, Database, Reporting, Test, WCF, Workflow), Other Languages, Other Project Types, Test Projects. Templates: Windows Forms Application, WPF Application, Console Application, Windows Service, WPF User Control Library, Class Library, WPF Browser Application, Empty Project, WPF Custom Control Library, Windows Forms Control Library, Search Online Templates. Name: WindowsFormsApplication1. Location: C:\Users\George\Documents\Visual Studio 2008\Projects\. Solution Name: WindowsFormsApplication1. Create directory for solution checked. OK / Cancel buttons.]

TAKE NOTE✲

By default, Visual Studio will associate your new project with the version of the .NET Framework indicated by the .NET Framework selection button located in the upper right corner of New Project dialog. You can use the .NET Framework selection button to change the version of the .NET Framework your application will use.

4. Click the Windows item in the Project types: selection.

5. Click the Windows Forms Application item in the Templates: selection.

6. Enter a different Name, Location, or Solution Name if desired.

7. Click the OK button and your Windows Forms Application project is created.

PAUSE. Leave the project open for use in the next exercise.

Exploring the Windows Forms Application

Now that you have a Windows Forms Application project created, you can explore its contents.

Although this section does not cover an exhaustive list of all Windows Forms Application project features, Table 2-1 lists the most common features of the Windows Forms Application project type.

Table 2-1

Windows Forms Application Common Project Features

CERTIFICATION READY
Can you create Windows-based applications by using Visual Studio?
1.3

FEATURE	DESCRIPTION
Properties Window	The *Properties window* displays the property keys and property values for various parts of the Windows Forms Application project. Use the Properties window to change solution settings, project settings, form settings, and control settings. The Properties window is most commonly used as an alternative to changing property values in source code. You can control most of the applications' behavior by setting property values.
Solution Explorer Window	The *Solution Explorer window* contains a hierarchical view of all the files, folders, and Solution specific information within the application. Use the Solution Explorer window to manage files and folders, Project information, and Solution information. Selecting Solution elements in the Solution Explorer will display the Solution Properties in the Properties window. Use the Solution Properties to manage assembly information, application resources, and application settings. Use the Solution References to manage the application's dependency on other assemblies.
Windows Form Designer	The Windows Form Designer is a What You See Is What You Get (WYSIWYG) editor for creating and managing Windows Forms. A *form* is the building block for a Windows Forms Application and represents the top container for all other Windows Forms controls. Use the Windows Form Designer to lay out the forms and controls to create the user interface (UI).
Program.cs	The Program.cs file is a Solution file that contains the starting point for the Windows Forms Application. Use the Program.cs file to indicate which Windows Form will start the application or any functionality that you want to execute before the first Windows Form is loaded, for example, processing command-line parameters.

→ USE THE PROPERTIES WINDOW

USE the project you created in the previous exercise.

1. Locate the Properties window; by default the Properties window is located in the lower right section of the Visual Studio application (Figure 2-2).

Figure 2-2

Properties window

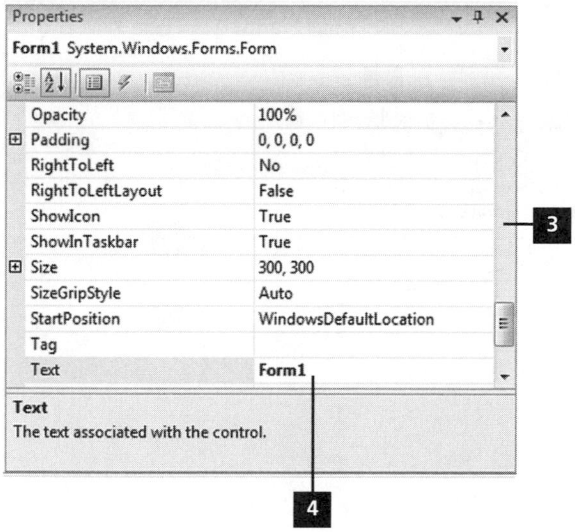

ANOTHER WAY If the Properties window is not visible when you start Visual Studio, you can open it by selecting the View→Properties window menu item (Ctrl+W,P) or by pressing F4.

---

2. Verify that when your Windows Forms Application project is first created, the Form1.cs [Design] tab is selected and that the Properties window is displaying the properties for Form1.cs Windows Form.
3. Using the scroll bar on the right side of the Properties window, find the Text property.
4. Key **Hello World** into the Text property value area on the same row as the Text label and press Enter to change to another property row.
5. Verify that the form's caption has now changed to Hello World.

PAUSE. Leave the project open for use in the next exercise.

The Properties window is used to modify values for various solutions, projects, forms, and controls. You will consistently use the Properties window when developing a Windows Forms Application, so spend some time exploring its functionality.

→ USE THE SOLUTION EXPLORER WINDOW

USE the project you created in the previous exercise.

1. Locate the Solution Explorer window; by default the Solution Explorer is located in the upper right section of the Visual Studio application (Figure 2-3).

ANOTHER WAY If the Solution Explorer window is not visible when you start Visual Studio, you can open it by selecting the View→Solution Explorer menu item (Ctrl+W,S).

2. When a Windows Forms Application project is first created, the Solution Explorer window contains a tree structure of elements. Locate the Solution element in the tree.

3. Verify that the Solution element contains both the name of the solution and the number of projects contained inside the solution. A solution can contain any number of projects and the project types do not have to match. A typical example is a solution that contains a Windows Forms Application project and the Test project to validate the Windows Forms Application.

Figure 2-3

Solution Explorer

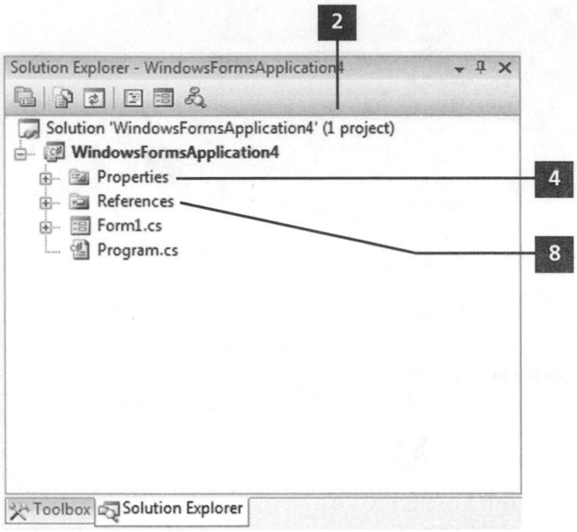

4. Verify that by default you have only one project.

5. Expand the Solution Explorer's Properties element.

6. Open the AssemblyInfo.cs element by double-clicking. The AssemblyInfo.cs file is opened into the AssemblyInfo.cs tab.

7. Locate the AssemblyVersion attribute. Changing the AssemblyVersion attribute value changes the version number of the application.

8. Expand the Solution Explorer's References element.

9. Locate the System.Windows.Forms element.

PAUSE. Leave the project open for use in the next exercise.

TAKE NOTE*

The System.Windows. Forms element is the one reference required to have a Windows Forms Application.

The Solution Explorer organizes your solution and project elements. In a Windows Forms Application, you have a Properties element that contains information about the project including the version number defined in the AssemblyInfo.cs file. The References element contains a list of assemblies used by your Windows Forms Application and includes the required System.Windows.Forms reference.

USE THE WINDOWS FORM DESIGNER

USE the project you created in the previous exercise.

1. Select the Form1.cs [Design] tab (Figure 2-4).

TAKE NOTE*

The Designer View can be identified by its WYSIWYG (What You See Is What You Get) functionality. Adding and Editing controls on the Windows Form are updated immediately and what you see in the Designer will be the same as your application.

Figure 2-4

Form Designer

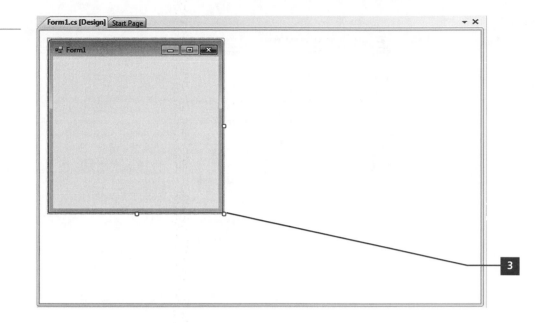

 REF

For more information on editing the user interface of a Windows Forms Application, see Lesson 3, "Creating a Windows Forms User Interface."

2. Click in the middle of the Form1 image to select the form.

3. Locate the resize indicator in the lower right side of Form1. The resize indicators are clear boxes located in the corners and middle of the sides on the borders of the Form1 image.

4. Click and hold the resize indicator in the lower right side of Form1.

5. Drag the resize indicator down and to the right until Form1 is larger than its current size and then release.

6. Locate the Form1.cs element in the Solution Explorer window.

7. Expand the Form1.cs element.

8. Double-click on the Form1.Designer.cs element and verify that the Form1.Designer.cs tab is opened.

 ANOTHER WAY

You can also open a form's Code View by selecting the Form1.cs element or any of its subelements and then clicking the Solution Explorer window toolbar's View Code button.

9. Locate the Windows Form Designer Generated Code label and expand the region (Figure 2-5).

TAKE NOTE✱

The values you see in the `System.Drawing.Size(606, 450);` example may differ from your default values.

Figure 2-5

Form Code View

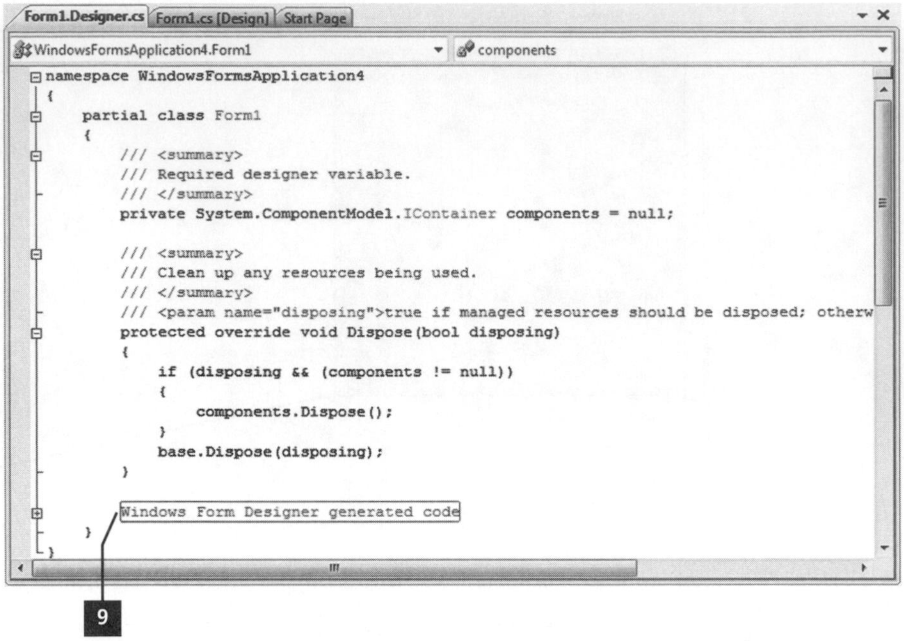

```
Form1.Designer.cs  Form1.cs [Design]  Start Page                      ▾ ✕
WindowsFormsApplication4.Form1              ▾   components              ▾
namespace WindowsFormsApplication4
{
    partial class Form1
    {
        /// <summary>
        /// Required designer variable.
        /// </summary>
        private System.ComponentModel.IContainer components = null;

        /// <summary>
        /// Clean up any resources being used.
        /// </summary>
        /// <param name="disposing">true if managed resources should be disposed; otherw
        protected override void Dispose(bool disposing)
        {
            if (disposing && (components != null))
            {
                components.Dispose();
            }
            base.Dispose(disposing);
        }

        Windows Form Designer generated code

    }
}
```

 9

10. Locate inside of the InitializeComponent method the code line:

    ```
    this.ClientSize = new System.Drawing.Size(606, 450);
    ```

11. Repeat steps 1 through 10 and verify that the Size parameters change.

PAUSE. Leave the project open for use in the next exercise.

The Windows Form Designer is the easiest way to change your Windows Forms Application look and feel. As you change layout elements in the design editor, Visual Studio is updating the generated code to match.

⊕ UNDERSTAND THE PROGRAM.CS FILE

USE the project you created in the previous exercise.

1. Locate the Program.cs element in the Solution Explorer window.
2. Double-click on the Program.cs element and verify that the Program.cs tab is open.
3. By Default the Program.cs element contains only the Main method. The Main method is by default the starting point for the Windows Forms Application.
4. Locate inside of the Main method the code:

    ```
    Application.Run(new Form1());
    ```

TAKE NOTE *

The `Application.Run` method starts your Windows Forms Application with the Form1 window. Changing the Form1 parameter to a different form name will start your application with a different form.

STOP. Save or discard the solution. It will not be used again for another exercise.

As you have just seen, the Windows Forms Application creation process only requires a few steps. The New Project dialog provides all of the interactions required to create a default Windows Forms Application.

The real work begins when you start to modify the default Windows Forms Application project elements:

- Use the Properties window to change various project elements' attribute values.
- Use the Solution Explorer window to navigate and find the parts of your Windows Forms Application.
- The Solution Explorer's Properties element contains application settings information.
- The Solution Explorer's Reference element contains a reference to the assemblies required to operate your application.
- Use the Form Designer to edit the user interface of your application.
- Use the Form Code View to edit the user interface or functionality of your application.
- Use the Program Code to edit application-level functionality and set the first form used by your application.

Getting Started with a Windows Presentation Foundation Application

↓ **THE BOTTOM LINE**

To begin a Windows Presentation Foundation (WPF) application, create a Windows Presentation Foundation Application project. Next, explore the basic structure and parts of the Windows Presentation Foundation Application project.

Creating a Windows Presentation Foundation Application Project

Visual Studio provides one WPF Application project type, but the same project type can be used to create either a WPF Navigation application or a WPF application.

In addition to standard windows applications, the Windows Presentation Foundation (WPF) Application project type introduced built-in functionality for creating navigation or wizard-like applications. All WPF Application projects are capable of using the navigation functionality, but the navigation functionality works better when a WPF Application is designed to function as a step-by-step process.

To create a WPF Navigation application, first create the default WPF Application project. Then with a few changes you can convert your WPF Application to a WPF Navigation Application.

→ **CREATE A WINDOWS PRESENTATION FOUNDATION APPLICATION**

GET READY. Before you begin these steps, be sure to launch Visual Studio.

1. On the Start Page, Click the Projects . . . link next to the Create label inside of the Recent Projects grouping.
2. The New Project dialog will appear (Figure 2-6).

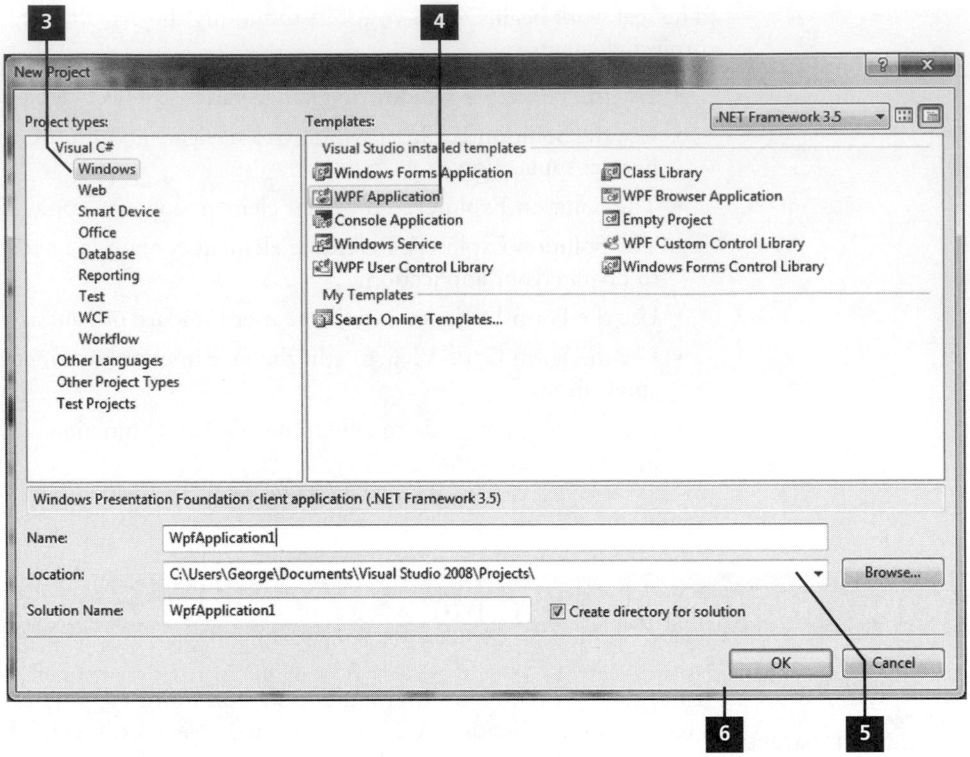

Figure 2-6

New Project dialog

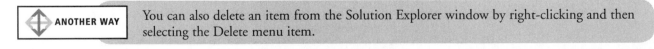

3. Click the Windows item in the Project types: selection.

4. Click the WPF Application item in the Templates: selection.

5. Enter a different Name, Location or Solution Name if desired.

6. Click the OK button and your WPF Application project is created.

PAUSE. Leave the project open for use in the next exercise.

XREF

For more information on various ways to open the New Project dialog, see the Windows Forms Application exercise in this lesson.

⊖ BUILD AND EXECUTE THE WINDOWS PRESENTATION FOUNDATION NAVIGATION APPLICATION

USE the project you created in the previous exercise.

1. Select the Window1.xaml.cs item in the Solution Explorer window.

2. Press **Delete** to remove the Windows1.xaml.cs item from the solution. A confirmation dialog will appear; click OK to complete the deletion process.

◆ ANOTHER WAY

You can also delete an item from the Solution Explorer window by right-clicking and then selecting the Delete menu item.

3. Add a new Page item to the Solution.

a. Locate the WPF Project element in the Solution Explorer window. By default the WPF Project element is named WPFApplication1, but if you changed the application name in the New Project dialog, the WPF Project element will be the name you entered into the New Project dialog Name field.

b. Right-click on the WPF Project element and a pop-up menu appears.

c. Click the Add→New Item . . . and the Add New Item dialog appears.

d. From the Categories: section, click the WPF element.

e. From the Templates: section, click the Page (WPF) element.

f. Click Add.

ANOTHER WAY You can also add a new page by using the Add→Page menu item from the same pop-up menu.

4. Locate the App.xaml item in the Solution Explorer window.

5. Double-click the App.xaml item and verify that the App.xaml tab is open.

6. On the XAML tab, locate the line of code:

StartupUri="Window1.xaml">

7. Change the Windows1.xaml code to Page1.xaml. Changing the code to Page1.xaml will instruct the application to open the Page1.xaml object when first executing the application.

8. Build and Execute the WPF Application by pressing F5 (Figure 2-7).

Figure 2-7

WPF Navigation Application

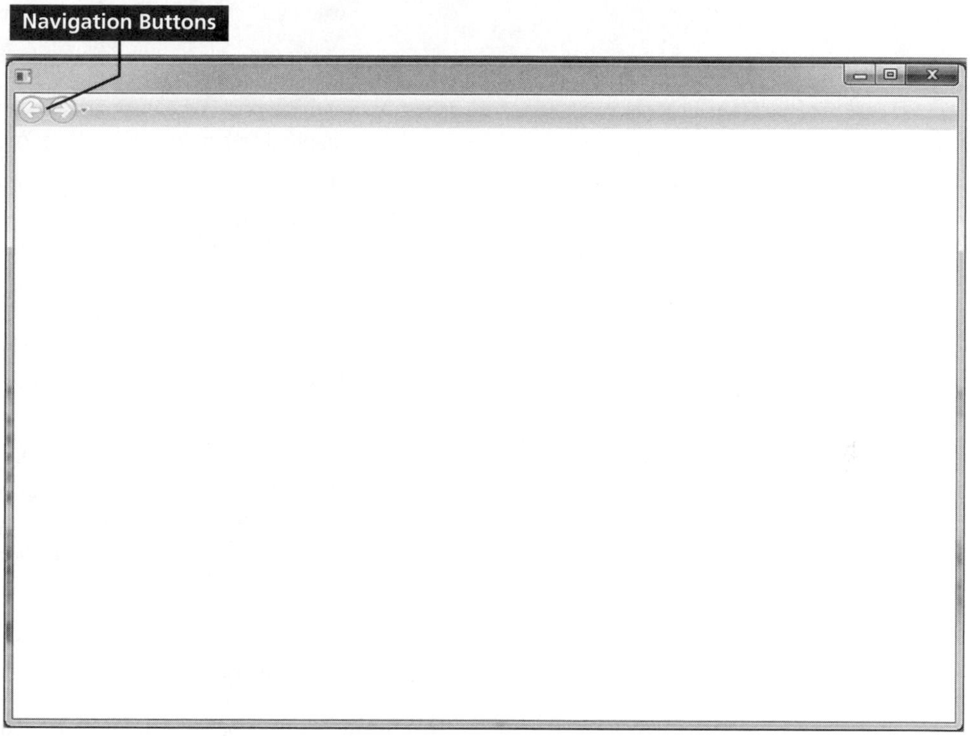

TAKE NOTE*

You can tell the difference between a WPF application and a WPF Navigation Application by the Previous and Next navigation buttons located in the upper left corner of the window.

STOP. Save or discard the solution. It will not be used again for another exercise.

You just created a WPF Application and then changed the WPF application to a WPF Navigation Application. When deciding on which type of WPF application to create, you will only want to create a WPF Navigation Application if your application requires next and previous functionality. Using the WPF Navigation Application for a non-Wizard-style application will add a level of overhead not required.

Exploring a Windows Presentation Foundation Application Project

Now that you have a WPF Application project created, you can explore its contents.

Although this section does not cover an exhaustive list of all WPF Application project features, it does discuss the most common ones. You will notice that a WPF Application shares some functionality with a Windows Forms Application, including:

- The Properties window
- The Solution Explorer window
- The Solution Properties

Table 2-2 lists some of the WPF Application elements that differ from a Windows Forms Application.

Table 2-2

WPF Application Common Project Features

FEATURE	DESCRIPTION
Solution References	You looked at the Solution Explorer and the Solution References when you created a Windows Forms Application, but for a WPF Application the Solution References have changed. In a WPF Application, the Solution References contain the PresentationCore and PresentationFramework elements. These two elements are required to have a WPF application.
Window Views	The Window Views consists of two different editors. Use the Windows Designer View to edit the Extensible Application Markup Language (XAML) or maneuver the controls in a WYSIWYG editor to configure the user interface (UI). A WPF application's UI consists of a **Window** that is the parent container of all other controls in the application. Inside a WPF Navigation Application, use a **Page** to segment a WPF Navigation Application into steps. Use the Windows Code View to edit the source code behind the Window.
App Views	The App Views consist of two different editors. Like the Window Views Designer View, the App Views has the same two editors, but the WYSIWYG editor is disabled and you will only edit XAML. Use the App Code View to edit the source code behind the App.

⊙ **USE THE WINDOW DESIGNER AND CODE VIEW**

GET READY. Before you begin these steps, be sure to launch Visual Studio and create a new WPF application.

1. Verify that the Window1.xaml tab is selected.

TAKE NOTE ✱

The Designer View for a WPF Application is different from the Designer View for a Windows Forms Application. The WPF Designer View has two tabs, one for the WYSIWYG Design and the other for Extensible Application Markup Language (XAML).

TAKE NOTE*

A WPF Application has a default Grid container inside the window; make sure you select the window and not the Grid container.

2. Verify that the Window1.xaml tab opens with the Design tab already selected. The XAML tab is visible, but the focus of the Window Designer is inside of the Design tab (Figure 2-8).

3. Click on the text Window1 at the top of the image of Window1 to select Window1.

Figure 2-8

Window Designer

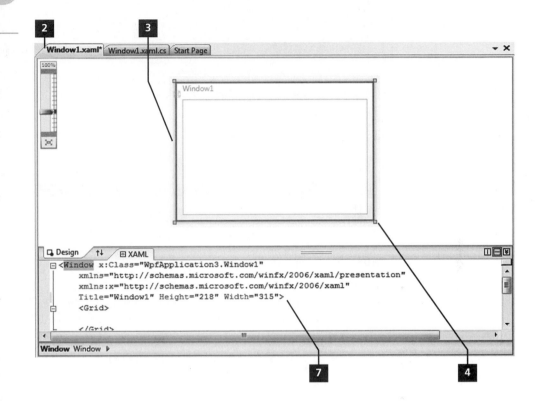

4. Locate the resize indicator in the lower right side of the window. The resize indicators are background colored boxes located in the corners of the window.

5. Click and hold the resize indicator in the lower right side of the window.

6. Drag the resize indicator down and to the right until the window is larger than its current size and then release.

7. Locate in the XAML Tab the code line:

    `Title="Window1" Height="318" Width="312"`

8. Repeat steps 4 through 6 and observe how the above line of code changes.

9. Locate the Window1.xaml element in the Solution Explorer window.

10. Expand the Window1.xaml element.

11. Double-click on the Window1.xaml.cs element and verify that the Window1.xaml.cs tab opens.

X REF

For more information on editing the user interface of a WPF Application, see Lesson 3.

ANOTHER WAY

You can also open a window's Code View by selecting the Window1.cs element or any of its subelements and then clicking the Solution Explorer window toolbar's View Code button.

12. Verify that the Window1.xaml.cs Code View does not have any code other than the Window1 class declaration and constructor (Figure 2-9).

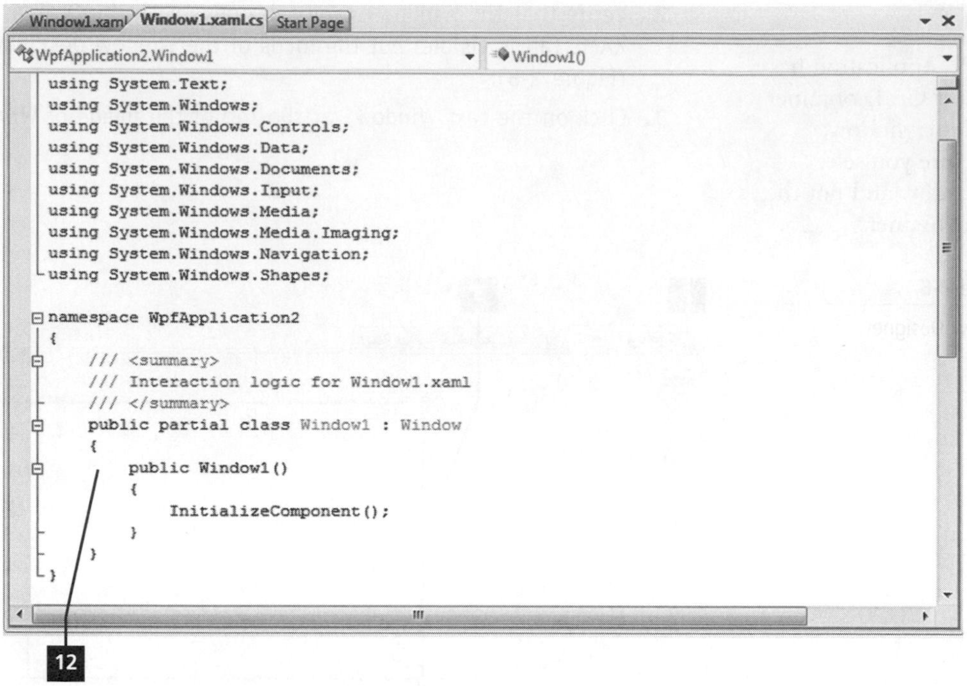

Figure 2-9

Window Code View

```
Window1.xaml  Window1.xaml.cs  Start Page                                    ▾ ×
WpfApplication2.Window1                        ▾   Window1()                  ▾
    using System.Text;
    using System.Windows;
    using System.Windows.Controls;
    using System.Windows.Data;
    using System.Windows.Documents;
    using System.Windows.Input;
    using System.Windows.Media;
    using System.Windows.Media.Imaging;
    using System.Windows.Navigation;
    using System.Windows.Shapes;

  namespace WpfApplication2
  {
      /// <summary>
      /// Interaction logic for Window1.xaml
      /// </summary>
      public partial class Window1 : Window
      {
          public Window1()
          {
              InitializeComponent();
          }
      }
  }
```

12

PAUSE. Leave the project open for use in the next exercise.

You will use the Window Designer and Code Views to edit the window containers within your application. The Window Designer is composed of both a WYSIWYG and XAML editor that work in conjunction with each other to change the UI.

➔ USE THE APP DESIGNER AND CODE VIEWS

USE the project you created in the previous exercise.

1. Locate the App.xaml element in the Solution Explorer window.
2. Double-click the App.xaml element and verify that the App.xaml tab is open.
3. Verify that in the App.xaml Design tab a message has been displayed stating that the visual designer was left blank intentionally.
4. Verify that in the App.xaml XAML tab, just below the App.xaml Design tab, the xaml code for the App.xaml file is displayed.
5. Locate the App.xaml element in the Solution Explorer window.
6. Expand the App.xaml element.
7. Locate the App.xaml.cs element in the Solution Explorer window.
8. Double-click on the App.xaml.cs element and verify that the App.xaml.cs tab is open.
9. Verify that by default the App.xaml.cs element contains only the application class definition.

TAKE NOTE✱

In a WPF Application, the Application Class does not contain a reference to the window that starts the application like a Windows Forms Application. To set the start-up window for a WPF application, change the StartupUri attribute in the App.xaml file.

STOP. Save or discard the solution. It will not be used again for another exercise.

As you have just seen, the WPF Application creation process only requires a few steps. The New Project dialog provides all of the interactions required to create a default WPF Application.

To convert your WPF Application to a WPF Navigation Application there are a few steps and some code changes, but the conversion process is also straightforward.

The real work begins when you begin to modify the default WPF Application project elements:

- Use the common elements between a Windows Forms Application and a WPF Application to change various project elements' attribute values.
- The Solution Explorer's Reference element contains a reference to the assemblies required to operate your application.
- Use the Window Designer to edit the user interface of your application.
- Use the Window Code View to edit the functionality of your application.
- Use the App Code to edit application level functionality.

■ Getting Started with a Windows Service Application

THE BOTTOM LINE

To begin a Windows Service Application, create a Windows Service Application project. Once created, you can explore the basic structure and parts of the Windows Service Application project.

Creating a Windows Service Application Project

Visual Studio provides one Windows Service Application project type.

Much like the Windows Forms Application project and the WPF Application project, the Windows Service Application project is created using the New Project dialog.

 CREATE A WINDOWS SERVICE APPLICATION

GET READY. Before you begin these steps, be sure to launch Visual Studio.

X REF

For more information on various ways to open the New Project dialog, see the Windows Forms Application exercise in this lesson.

1. On the Start Page, click the Projects . . . link next to the Create label inside of the Recent Projects grouping.
2. The New Project dialog will appear (Figure 2-10).

Figure 2-10

New Project dialog

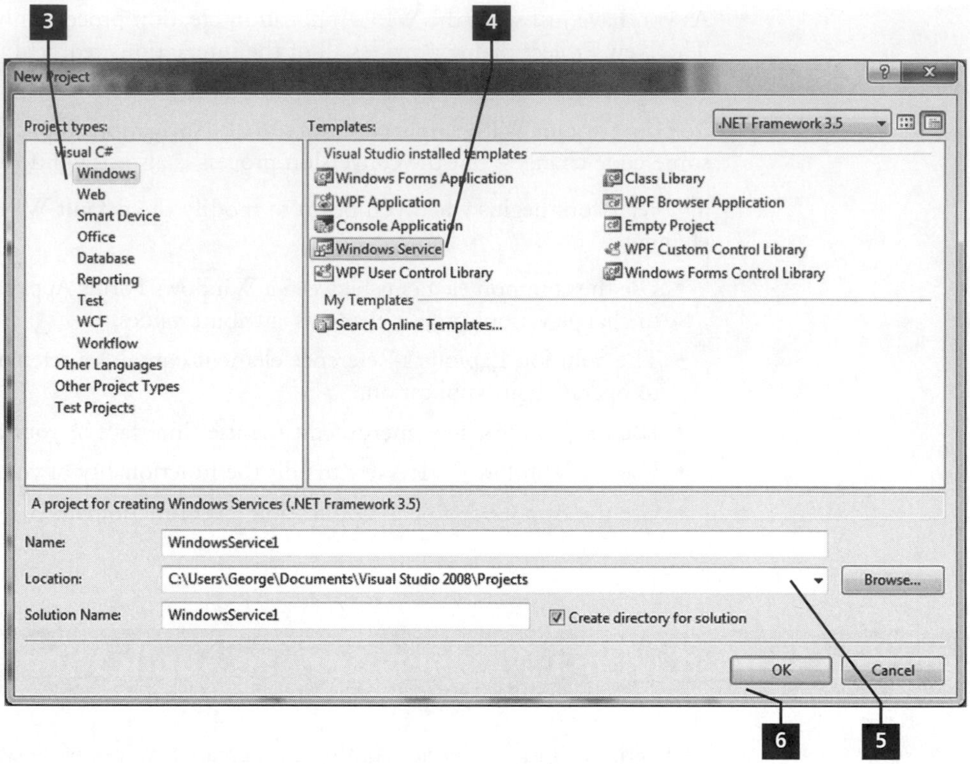

3. Click the Windows item in the Project types: selection.

4. Click the Windows Service item in the Templates: selection.

5. Enter a different Name, Location, or Solution Name if desired.

6. Click the OK button and your Windows Service Application project is created.

CERTIFICATION READY
Can you create Windows-based applications by using Visual Studio?
1.3

PAUSE. Leave the project open for use in the next exercise.

Exploring a Windows Service Application Project

Now that you have a Windows Service Application project created, you can explore its contents.

Although this section does not cover an exhaustive list of all Windows Service Application project features, it presents the most common ones. You will notice that a Windows Service Application shares some functionality with a Windows Forms Application and a WPF Application, including:

- The Properties window
- The Solution Explorer window
- The Solution Properties

Table 2-3 lists some of the Windows Service Application elements that are different from a Windows Forms Application and a WPF application.

Table 2-3

Windows Service Application
Common Project Features

FEATURE	DESCRIPTION
Solution References	Much like the Windows Forms Application and WPF Application, the Windows Service Application solution references have also changed. In a Windows Service Application, the solution references contain the System.ServiceProcess element. This element is required for a Windows Service Application.
Service Views	The Service Views consists of two different editors. The Service Designer View is available, but a Windows Service application does not have a UI and controls should not be added to the Service Designer View. The Windows Service Application contains a *Service* that is the non-UI container for all of the Windows Service Application functionality. Make the most of your changes in the Windows Service Code View where you will edit the source code behind the Service.
Program.cs	Like the Windows Forms Application, the Windows Service Application has a Program.cs element. Use the Program.cs file to indicate which Service will start the application or any functionality that you want to execute before the first Service is loaded, for example, processing command-line parameters.

USE THE SERVICE DESIGNER AND CODE VIEWS

USE the project you created in the previous exercise.

1. Verify that the Service1.cs [Design] tab is selected (Figure 2-11).

Figure 2-11

Service Designer

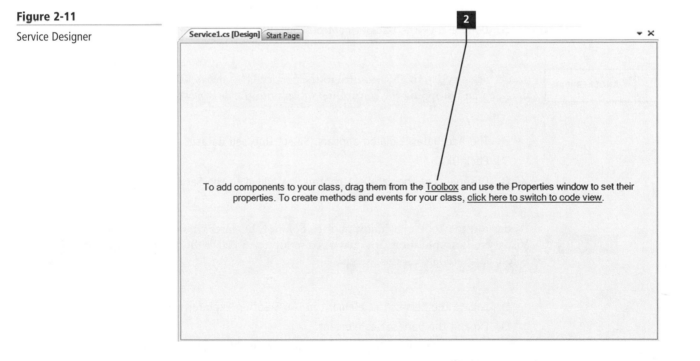

To add components to your class, drag them from the Toolbox and use the Properties window to set their properties. To create methods and events for your class, click here to switch to code view.

The Designer View for a Windows Service Application is different from the Designer View for a Windows Forms Application and WPF application. The Service Designer does not have a WYSIWYG interface. You can still add controls to the Service Designer, but watch which controls you add because a Windows Service Application is designed to operate without user interactions. If you want your Windows Service to have a UI for configuration purposes, add a Windows Form element.

2. Click the Toolbox link (Figure 2-12).

Figure 2-12

Control Toolbox

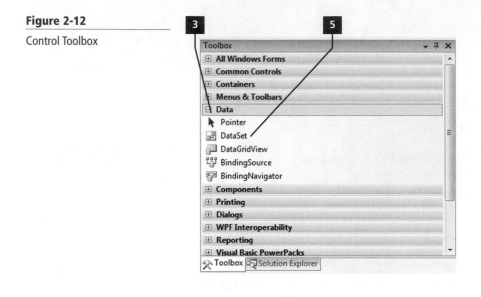

3. Locate the Data group heading in the Toolbox window.

4. Expand the Data grouping to expose the data controls.

5. Double-click the DataSet control icon.

ANOTHER WAY You can also add a Toolbox control to the Service Designer or any other designer by dragging and dropping the control-item icon onto the designer area.

6. The Add Dataset dialog appears. Select Untyped dataset.

7. Click OK.

8. Observe that the dataSet1 control was added to the Service Designer.

TAKE NOTE* By default, the Toolbox window and the Solution Explorer window share space in the Visual Studio application. You may need to locate and click the Solution Explorer tab before continuing with this exercise.

9. Locate the Service1.cs element in the Solution Explorer window.

10. Expand the Service1.cs element.

11. Open the Service1.Designer.cs element by double-clicking on the Service1.Designer.cs element.

12. Locate the Component Designer generated code label and expand the region (Figure 2-13).

Figure 2-13

Service Code View

TAKE NOTE*

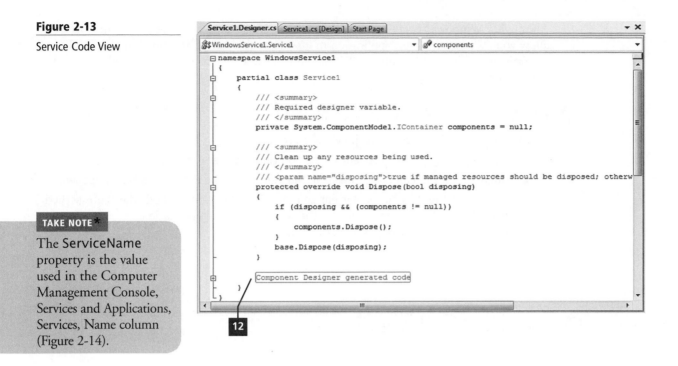

The ServiceName property is the value used in the Computer Management Console, Services and Applications, Services, Name column (Figure 2-14).

13. Locate inside of the InitializeComponent method the code line:

```
this.ServiceName = "Service1";
```

PAUSE. Leave the project open for use in the next exercise.

Figure 2-14

Computer Management Console

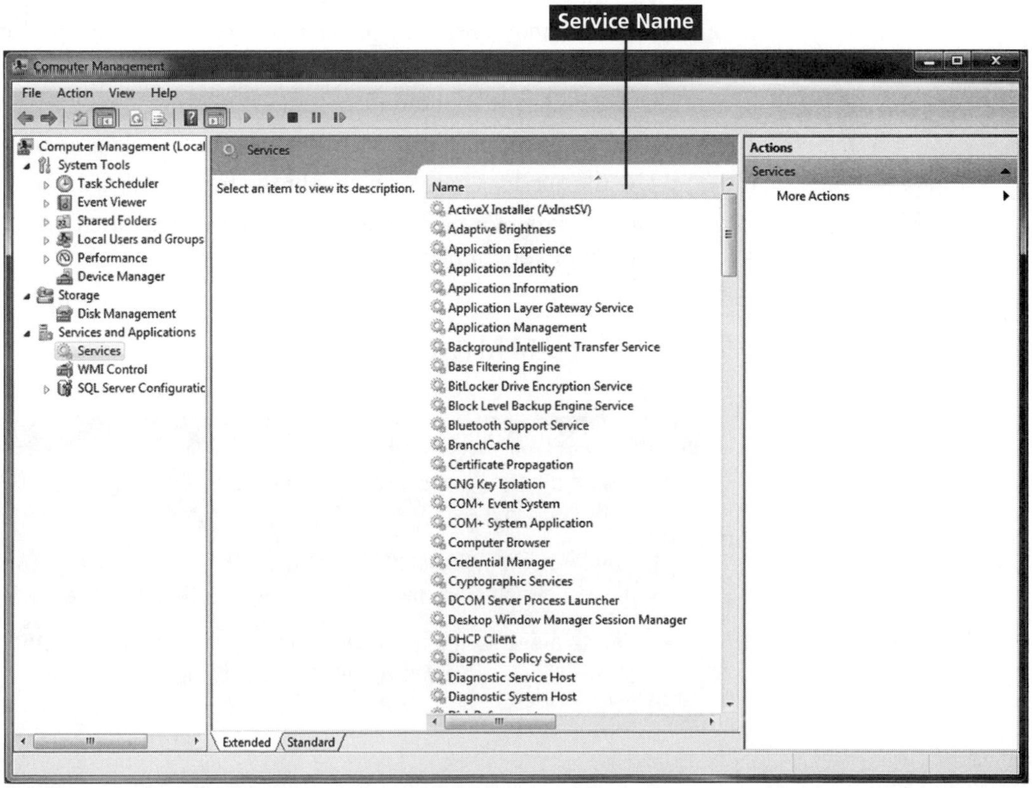

Although a Windows Service application does not have a UI, you can add data controls to allow your Windows Service application to interact with database information. Adding UI controls should be avoided, but is allowed and will cause reference errors that will need to be corrected before you can execute.

→ UNDERSTAND THE PROGRAM.CS FILE

USE the project you created in the previous exercise.

1. Locate the Program.cs element in the Solution Explorer window.
2. Double-click the Program.cs element and verify that the Program.cs tab is opened.
3. Verify that the Program.cs element contains only the Main method. The Main method is by default the starting point for the Windows Service application.
4. Locate inside of the Main method the code:

```
new Service1()
```

TAKE NOTE * The `new Serivce()` line of code is wrapped inside an array assignment. Multiple services can be started at the same time.

STOP. Save or discard the solution. It will not be used again for another exercise.

As you have just seen, the Windows Service Application creation process requires only a few steps. The New Project dialog provides all of the interactions required to create a default Windows Service Application.

The real work begins when you start to modify the default Windows Service Application project elements:

- Use the common elements between a Windows Forms Application, a WPF Application, and a Windows Service Application to change various project elements' attribute values.
- The Solution Explorer's Reference element contains a reference to the assemblies required to operate your application.
- Use the Service Designer to edit the controls of your application.
- Use the Service Code View to edit the functionality of your application.
- Use the Program Code to edit application-level functionality and set the list of services to start with your application.

SKILL SUMMARY

IN THIS LESSON YOU LEARNED HOW TO:

- Create a new Windows Forms Application. You then explored the most common elements of the Windows Forms Application you created.

- Create a new WPF Application and a WPF Navigation Application. You then explored the most common elements of the WPF Application you created.

- Create a new Windows Service Application. You then explored the most common elements of the Windows Service Application you created.

Knowledge Assessment

Fill in the Blank

Complete the following sentences by writing the correct word or words in the blanks provided.

1. The Visual Studio dialog used to create a new project is _____.

2. You can use the _____ button to change the version of the .NET Framework your Application will use.

3. The _____ window contains all of the projects and project elements for a solution.

4. The reference required for a Windows Forms Application is _____.

5. To change the values of various attributes of a solution, project, form, and/or control use the _____.

6. The project type that contains the functionality of a Windows Service Application is _____.

7. The _____ file is a Solution file which contains the starting point for your Windows Forms Application.

8. The reference required for a Windows Service Application is _____.

9. The Designer View's _____ functionality ensures that the when you add or edit controls, Windows Forms are updated immediately and what you see in the designer will be the same as your application.

10. The project type that contains the functionality of a Windows Forms Application is _____.

Multiple Choice

Circle the letter that corresponds to the best answer.

1. Which of the following is NOT a way to access the New Project Dialog?
   a. The Start Page
   b. The File→New→Project menu item
   c. The New Project button on the Solution Explorer window toolbar
   d. The New Project button on the Visual Studio Standard toolbar

2. Which of the following application types do NOT have a Designer?
   a. Windows Forms
   b. Windows Service
   c. WPF
   d. None of the above

3. Which of the following methods can you use to create a new Windows Forms Application?
   a. The Start Page
   b. The File→New menu
   c. The New Project toolbar button
   d. All of the above

4. What project element and method defines which Services are started in a Windows Service Application?
   a. Program, Main
   b. App, Main
   c. Program, Start
   d. App, Start

5. You need to change the settings of controls on your Windows form. Which of the following Visual Studio windows should you use?
   a. Properties window
   b. Solution Explorer window
   c. Windows Form Designer window
   d. Server Explorer window

6. You need to change the layout of the controls on your Windows form. Which of the following Visual Studio windows should you use?
   a. Properties window
   b. Solution Explorer window
   c. Windows Form Designer window
   d. Server Explorer window

7. Which method starts the Windows Forms Application and displays the specified form on the screen?
   a. Application.Run
   b. Form.Show
   c. Main
   d. Drawing.Size

8. What is the name of the project element used to change the version number of an application?
   a. Settings.settings
   b. Assembly.info
   c. App.cs
   d. None of the above

9. Which of the following project types canNOT have controls placed on its Designer?
   a. Windows Service
   b. Windows Form
   c. WPF
   d. None of the above

10. Which of the following project types does NOT have a WYSIWYG Designer?
    a. Windows Forms
    b. Windows Service
    c. WPF
    d. None of the above

■ Competency Assessment

Scenario 2-1: Executive Summary

You have completed your report for the decision makers in your organization, but due to the amount of information needed for the comparison, the decision makers have requested that you create an executive summary. Using a pen and paper, create three columns labeled Windows Forms, WPF, and Windows Services; then in bullet format, list the differences between each column's application type.

Scenario 2-2: Project Creation Demonstration

One of the decision makers would like to see firsthand the project creation process. Using a pen and paper, list the steps you will follow to demonstrate how to create a Windows Forms Application, a WPF Application, and a Windows Service Application.

Proficiency Assessment

Scenario 2-3: Windows Forms Designer Demonstration

One of the decision makers would like to see how the WYSWYG functionality of the Windows Forms works to create the layout of controls on a Windows form. Create a new Windows Forms Application for a demonstration. Using pen and paper, list the steps you will follow to demonstrate how to arrange controls on the Windows Forms Designer.

Scenario 2-4: Synchronized Version Numbers

You have been given a project where you will be creating a Windows Forms Application and a Windows Service Application. A requirement of your solution is that you keep the version numbers between the two Applications synchronized. Create a Windows Forms Application and a Windows Service Application, and then set both applications to have a version number of 1.0.0.1.

3 LESSON

Creating a Windows Forms User Interface

LESSON SKILL MATRIX

Skills/Concepts	MTA Exam Objective	MTA Exam Objective Number
Working with Windows Forms Working with Windows Forms Controls	Create Windows Forms Applications by using Visual Studio.	2.1
Creating Windows Forms Inheritance	Understand Windows Forms inheritance.	2.2
Creating Custom Windows Forms Controls	Understand how to create new controls and extend existing controls.	2.3

KEY TERMS

Inheritance

Multiple Document Interface (MDI)

Override method

Single Document Interface (SDI)

Virtual method

Windows Forms Design View

Windows Forms Control Library

Your organization has decided that part of its overall solution should be developed as a Windows Forms Application. You have been given the Use Case requirements and have been assigned the task of designing and creating a prototype user interface. To create your interface, you will need multiple forms that look the same, but represent different entities. You will need to divide the forms into sections, provide a navigation system, and add a variety of controls to present and gather information. You will need the application to be customizable for colors and fonts. Your supervisor has asked that the prototype contain some basic error and help functionality in addition to the defined processing indicators. Your prototype will be the base for the design phase.

■ Working with Windows Forms

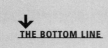
↓
THE BOTTOM LINE

Now that you can create a Windows Forms project and a default Windows Form, you will modify the default Windows Form's behavior by setting property values or by using the Windows Forms Design View editor. Once you can create and modify one Windows Form, you will add and modify additional Windows Forms to create a Multiple Document Interface (MDI).

Setting Windows Forms Properties

As one of the few activities that does not require coding, you can modify the appearance of Windows Forms by using the Properties window.

The Properties window contains a list of properties and their values (Figure 3-1). By changing a property's value, you are able to modify a Windows Form's appearance. To show the Properties window, select View→Properties Window (Ctrl-W,P) or F4.

Figure 3-1

Properties window

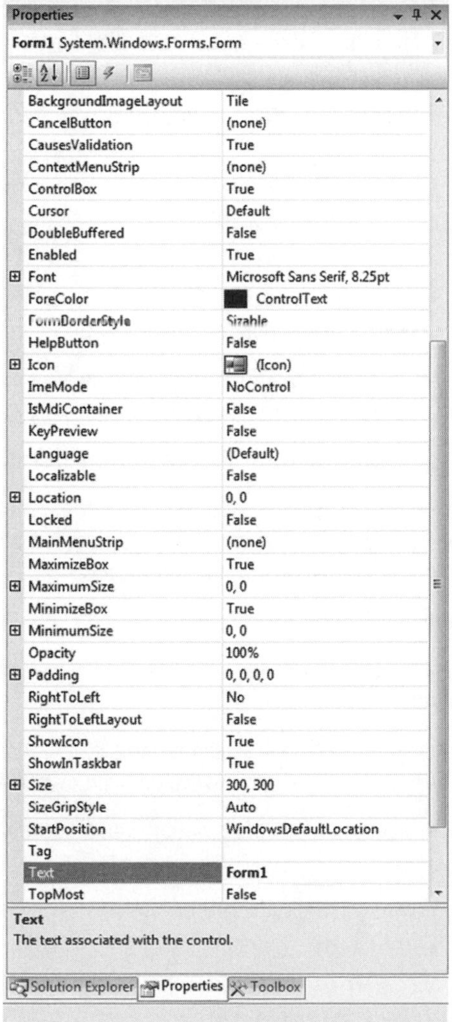

Properties	▾ ⫢ ✕
Form1 System.Windows.Forms.Form	▾
BackgroundImageLayout	Tile
CancelButton	(none)
CausesValidation	True
ContextMenuStrip	(none)
ControlBox	True
Cursor	Default
DoubleBuffered	False
Enabled	True
⊞ Font	Microsoft Sans Serif, 8.25pt
ForeColor	■ ControlText
FormBorderStyle	Sizable
HelpButton	False
⊞ Icon	(Icon)
ImeMode	NoControl
IsMdiContainer	False
KeyPreview	False
Language	(Default)
Localizable	False
⊞ Location	0, 0
Locked	False
MainMenuStrip	(none)
MaximizeBox	True
⊞ MaximumSize	0, 0
MinimizeBox	True
⊞ MinimumSize	0, 0
Opacity	100%
⊞ Padding	0, 0, 0, 0
RightToLeft	No
RightToLeftLayout	False
ShowIcon	True
ShowInTaskbar	True
⊞ Size	300, 300
SizeGripStyle	Auto
StartPosition	WindowsDefaultLocation
Tag	
Text	Form1
TopMost	False

Text
The text associated with the control.

Solution Explorer | Properties | Toolbox

Table 3-1 lists some of the properties for Windows Forms. This table is not an exhaustive list, but represents some of the more common properties.

Table 3-1

Common Windows Forms Properties

PROPERTY	DESCRIPTION
ControlBox	Determines if the form's Icon, Minimize, Maximize, and Close buttons will appear in the Windows form titlebar. When the ControlBox property has a value of True, the form's Icon, Minimize, Maximize, and Close buttons are all visible. When the ControlBox property has a value of False, the form's Icon, Minimize, Maximize, and Close buttons are all hidden. To control each button individually, use the following properties: • ShowIcon • MinimizeBox • MaximizeBox
FormBorderStyle	Determines the type of Windows Forms border. FormBorderStyle has the following options: • None—No border, this value also removes the Windows Forms titlebar and any ability to graphically resize or move the window. • FixedSingle—Nonsizable border with the Windows Forms titlebar. • Fixed3D—Nonsizable border with the Windows Forms titlebar, but the titlebar, side and bottom borders are all raised to create a 3D effect. • FixedDialog—Nonsizable border with the Windows Forms titlebar, but the icon is missing from the titlebar. • Sizable—Sizable border with the Windows Forms titlebar. • FixedToolWindow—Nonsizable border with a reduced height Windows Forms titlebar, but only the Close button is visible. • SizableToolWindow—Sizable border with a reduced height Windows Forms titlebar, but only the Close button is visible. The FormBorderStyle does not affect the Minimize and Maximize button features but it can affect whether buttons are visible.
Icon	Sets the icon image used in the Windows Forms titlebar.
Location	Determines where on the screen the upper leftmost point (X,Y) of the Windows Form is positioned. The Location property can be overridden by the StartPosition or WindowState properties.
ShowIcon	Determines if the icon will be displayed in the Windows Forms titlebar.
ShowInTaskbar	Determines if the Windows Forms Application will appear in the Windows taskbar.
StartPosition	Determines the default screen position of the Windows Forms Application when it first appears after being executed. StartPosition has the following options: • Manual—Uses the Location.X and Location.Y properties. • CenterScreen—In the middle of the user's screen. • WindowsDefaultLocation—Allows Windows to determine the position. • WindowsDefaultBounds—Position is determined by the operating system. • CenterParent—In the middle of the Windows Form that created the new Windows Form.

Table 3-1 (*continued*)

PROPERTY	DESCRIPTION
Size	Sets the width and height of the Windows Form. The Size property can be overridden by the WindowState property.
Text	Sets the caption of the application in the Windows Forms titlebar.
TopMost	Determines if the Windows Form is always on top of all other Windows applications.
WindowState	Sets the default state of the Windows Form when it first appears after being executed. WindowState has the following options: • Normal—The size set by the Size.Width and Height properties. • Maximized—Full size of the screen. • Minimized—Not visible on the screen, only in the taskbar.

WORK WITH THE WINDOWS FORMS PROPERTIES WINDOW

GET READY. Before you begin these steps, be sure to launch Microsoft Visual Studio and create a new Windows Forms Application project called wfaFormProperties.

1. Select the Form1.cs [Design] tab and then select Form1 by clicking anywhere on Form1.
2. In the Properties window, locate the (Name) property and select the Form1 value.
3. Press **Delete.**
4. Key **frmFormProperties** and press **Enter.**
5. Locate the Text property and key **Hello World.**
6. Locate the Size property and expand the plus sign to show the Width and Height properties.
7. In the Width property, key **600.**
8. Locate the FormBorderStyle property and choose the FixedDialog option.
9. Locate the TopMost property and choose the True option.
10. Press **F5** to build and run your application.
11. Verify the following:
    • The Windows Forms Application icon is not visible.
    • You cannot resize the Windows Forms Application by its edges.
12. Click on the Maximize button.
13. Verify that you can maximize the Windows Form.
14. Click on the Close button in the Windows Forms titlebar to exit the application and return to the Visual Studio development environment.
15. In the Properties window, locate the MaximizeBox property and select the False option.
16. Press **F5** to build and run your application.
17. Verify that you cannot resize the Windows Forms Application by its edges, nor can you use the Maximize button.

PAUSE. Leave the project open to use in the next exercise.

You have just created a Windows Forms Application by changing some of the Windows Forms properties. In the exercise, you created a Windows Forms Application and changed some form properties to create a fixed dialog form. Here are a few other ways a Windows form's properties can be changed to enhance the user interface:

- Splash Screen—FormBorderStyle property value set to None.
- Data Entry Screen—FormBorderStyle property value set to Fixed Dialog, ControlBox property value set to False.
- Main Application Screen—FormBorderStyle property value set to Sizable.

In addition to setting properties, a Windows Form can be modified using the Design View editor. You will work more with the Design View editor later in this lesson when you work with controls.

A Windows Forms Application with just one Windows Form is uncommon. Most Windows Forms Applications require many Windows Forms. In the next sections, you will add more Windows Forms to your project and find how to create a Multiple Document Interface (MDI) Windows Forms Application.

Adding Multiple Windows Forms

By using the Add New Item dialog you can add multiple Windows Forms to your application. You can organize multiple Windows Forms into a Single Document Interface (SDI) or a Multiple Document Interface (MDI).

During the development of your Windows Forms Application, you may find the need to have more than one Windows Form. You can add as many Windows Forms as needed by using the Add New Item dialog. When you have more than one Windows Form, you will need to decide which Windows Form is displayed first. You will also need to organize the relationship between your Windows Forms. In a *Single Document Interface (SDI)* application, your Windows Forms operate independent of each other. In a *Multiple Document Interface (MDI)* application, your Windows Forms are encompassed into a parent Windows Form where their functionality is coordinated.

⊕ USE THE ADD NEW ITEM DIALOG

USE the project you created in the previous exercise. Ensure that the Solution Explorer is visible in the Visual Studio environment. If the Solution Explorer is not visible, select View→Solution Explorer (Ctrl-W,S).

1. Select Project→Add New Item. The Add New Item dialog appears (Figure 3-2).

 ANOTHER WAY You can also open the Add New Item dialog by selecting your Project in the Solution Explorer, right-clicking to show the pop-up menu and then selecting Add→New Item.

2. Select Windows Forms from the Categories list.
3. Select Windows Forms from the Templates list.

TAKE NOTE * The Name control in the Add New Item dialog box does not need to be changed, but as a good coding practice changing the name to a value more descriptive is suggested.

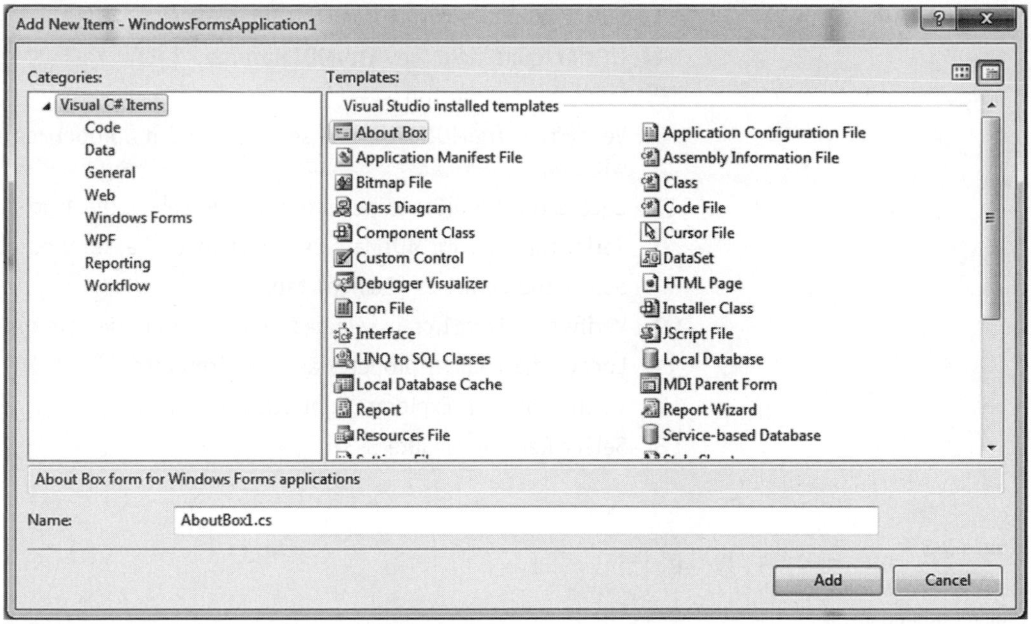

Figure 3-2

Add New Item dialog

Add New Item - WindowsFormsApplication1

Categories:

▲ Visual C# Items
    Code
    Data
    General
    Web
    Windows Forms
    WPF
    Reporting
    Workflow

Templates:

Visual Studio installed templates

About Box	Application Configuration File
Application Manifest File	Assembly Information File
Bitmap File	Class
Class Diagram	Code File
Component Class	Cursor File
Custom Control	DataSet
Debugger Visualizer	HTML Page
Icon File	Installer Class
Interface	JScript File
LINQ to SQL Classes	Local Database
Local Database Cache	MDI Parent Form
Report	Report Wizard
Resources File	Service-based Database

About Box form for Windows Forms applications

Name: AboutBox1.cs

Add   Cancel

4. Select the contents of the Name field.

5. Key **frmDataEntry.cs**

6. Click the Add button.

7. Verify that a new Windows Form was added to the solution.

8. In the Solution Explorer, double-click Program.cs. This will open the Program.cs file in a code editor.

9. Locate the following code:

```
Application.Run(new frmFormProperties());
```

10. Replace the `frmFormProperties` form reference with the `frmDataEntry` form reference.

11. Press **F5** to build and run the application.

12. Verify that the frmDataEntry form appeared first.

STOP. Save or discard the solution. It will not be used again for another exercise.

In the last exercise, you created an additional Windows Form, added it to your existing project, and changed the first Windows Form to appear when the application starts. An application where each form is independent of one another is typically considered a Single Document Interface (SDI) application.

You will now use the Add New Item dialog to add multiple Windows Forms to a MDI application. You will notice that in a MDI application, the Windows Forms are related to one another and work together to provide the application's functionality.

CREATE A MULTIPLE DOCUMENT INTERFACE WINDOWS FORMS APPLICATION

GET READY. Before you begin these steps, be sure to launch Microsoft Visual Studio and create a new Windows Forms Application project.

1. Select Project→Add New Item. The Add New Item dialog appears.

2. Select Windows Forms from the Categories list.

3. Select Windows Forms from the Template list.

4. In the Name field, key **frmMDIMain.cs**

5. Click the Add button.

6. Verify that frmMDIMain.cs is selected, and its properties are visible in the Properties window.

7. Locate the IsMdiContainer property and select the True option.

8. Verify that the frmMDIMain.cs has changed background colors.

9. Select the Form1.cs [Design] tab.

10. Verify that Form1.cs is selected, and its properties are visible in the Properties window.

11. Locate the (Name) property and key **frmChild**

12. In the Solution Explorer, right-click on Form1.

13. Select Rename (Figure 3-3).

Figure 3-3

Windows Forms Solution
Explorer pop-up menu

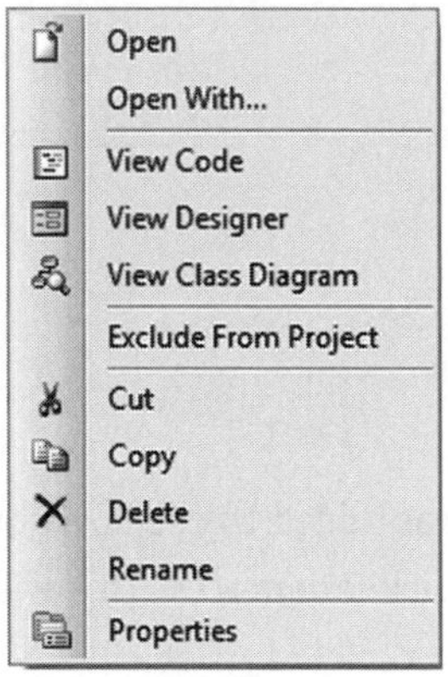

	Open
	Open With...
	View Code
	View Designer
	View Class Diagram
	Exclude From Project
	Cut
	Copy
	Delete
	Rename
	Properties

14. Key **frmChild.cs**

15. In the Solution Explorer, double-click Program.cs.

16. Locate the following code:

```
Application.Run(new Form1());
```

17. Replace the Form1 form reference with the frmMDIMain form reference.

18. Press **F5** to build and run the application.

19. Verify that frmMDIMain is the only Windows Form to appear.

20. Close frmMDIMain.

21. Select the frmMDIMain.cs [Design] tab.

22. In the Properties window, select the Events button (Figure 3-4).

Figure 3-4

Properties Window toolbar

Properties	▾ ⏻ ✕
Form1 System.Windows.Forms.Form	▾

22

23. Locate the Load event and double-click in the set method cell.

24. Key the following code into the frmMDIMain_Load method:

```
// Create a new form derived
// from the frmChild form.
frmChild frmX = new frmChild();
// Make the new form's parent the MdiParent form.
frmX.MdiParent = this;
// Show the derived frmChild form.
frmX.Show();
```

25. Press **F5** to build and run the application.

26. Verify that frmMDIMain now contains a frmChild Windows Form.

27. Close frmMDIMain, which also closes frmChild.

Visual Studio also provides a MDI Parent Form template in the Add New Item dialog. The MDI Parent Form template builds a standard set of menus and toolbars to support MDI functionality.

PAUSE. Leave the project open to use in the next exercise.

You have now created a new Windows Form that you have changed to behave as a Multiple Document Interface (MDI) Windows Form. A MDI Windows Forms Application can contain many Windows Forms. When working with MDI applications, it is common to have a base Windows Form that then gets inherited multiple times. *Inheritance* is the process of creating one Windows Form from another Windows Form.

■ Creating Windows Forms Inheritance

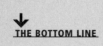

Much like other object-oriented environments, Visual Studio enables you to create Windows Forms inheritance. You can instantiate new Windows Forms from other Windows Forms. You can inherit new Windows Forms from other Windows Forms and then extend your inherited Windows Forms to add additional functionality.

Instantiating and Inheriting Windows Forms

Instantiating a Windows Form from another Windows Form is performed at run time in code. Inheriting a Windows Form from another Windows Form is performed at design time by using the Add New Item dialog.

You used Windows Forms instantiation in the last exercise when you entered the code:

```
frmChild frmX = new frmChild();
```

In this code sample, you created a new Windows Form, frmX, as an instantiation of Windows Form frmChild. It was created with all of the same properties and events as the base, frmChild, Windows Forms class. By changing the properties and events of the instantiated Windows Form, you can customize the instantiated Windows Form's functionality.

→ INSTANTIATE WINDOWS FORMS IN CODE

USE the project you created in the previous exercise.

1. Select the frmMIDMain.cs tab.
2. Locate the frmMDIMain_Load method.
3. Replace the current code with the following code:

```
// Create a new instantiated form
// base on the frmChild form.
frmChild frmOne = new frmChild();
// Make the instantiated form's parent
// the MdiParent form.
frmOne.MdiParent = this;
// Change the instantiated form's caption.
frmOne.Text = "Instantiated frmOne";
// Show the instantiated form.
frmOne.Show();
// Create another instantiated form
// based on the frmChild form.
frmChild frmTwo = new frmChild();
// Make the second instantiated form's
// parent the MdiParent form.
frmTwo.MdiParent = this;
// Change the second instantiated form's caption.
frmTwo.Text = "Instantiated frmTwo";
// Show the second instantiated form.
frmTwo.Show();
```

> **TAKE NOTE** *
>
> You may need to increase the size of the MDI Windows Form and move the position of the topmost inherited Windows Form to see both forms.

4. Press **F5** to build and run the application.
5. Verify that the MDI Window appears and that you have two child windows with different captions.
6. Close frmMDIMain, which closes frmOne and frmTwo.
7. Select the frmChild.cs [Design] tab.
8. In the Properties window, select the Text property.
9. Key **Base Form**
10. Select the frmMDIMain.cs tab.
11. Locate and delete the following code lines:

```
// Change the instantiated form's caption.
frmOne.Text = "Instantiated frmOne";
```

12. Press **F5** to build and run the application.
13. Verify the following:
    • One form has the caption Base Form. This is the frmOne Windows Form.
    • One form has the caption Instantiated frmTwo.
14. Close frmMDIMain, which closes frmOne and frmTwo.

PAUSE. Leave the project open to use in the next exercise.

You have just created two instantiated Windows Forms. An instantiated Windows Form can use the properties and events provided by the base Windows Forms class as shown in `frmOne`, or override them as show in `frmTwo`. Both of these exercises use run-time code to create an instantiated Windows Form in real time. Inherited Windows Forms are created at design time using the Add New Item dialog and the Windows Forms Inheritance template.

⊘ USE ADD NEW ITEM DIALOG FOR INHERITANCE

USE the project you created in the previous exercise.

1. Select Project→Add New Item. The Add New Item dialog appears.
2. Select Windows Forms from the Categories list.
3. Select Inherited Form from the Template list.
4. Select the Name field and key **frmInherited.cs**
5. Click the Add button and the Inheritance Picker dialog appears (Figure 3-5).

Figure 3-5

Inheritance Picker dialog

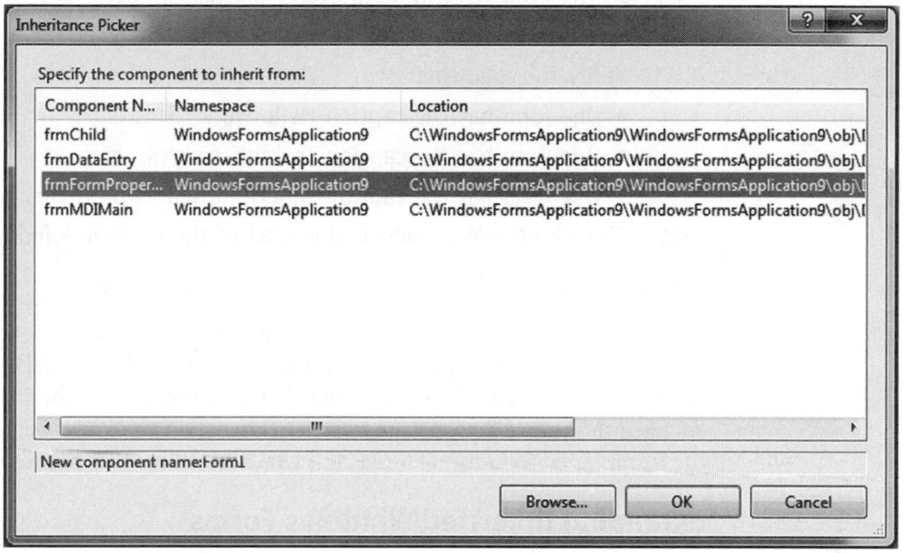

6. Select frmChild from the Specify the component to inherit from list.
7. Click OK.
8. Select the frmMDIMain.cs tab.
9. Locate the `frmMDIMain_Load` method and add the following code at the end of the method:

```
// Create a new instantiated form based
// on the frmInherited form.
frmInherited frmX = new frmInherited();
// Make the instantiated form a child to
// the MdiParent form.
frmX.MdiParent = this;
// Show the instantiated form.
frmX.Show();
```

10. Press **F5** to build and run the application.

11. Verify the following:
    - Two forms have the caption Base Form. One form is the frmOne and the other form is the frmInherited form.
    - One form has the caption Instantiated frmTwo.
12. Close frmMDIMain, which closes all of the children Windows Forms.
13. Select the frmChild.cs [Design] tab.
14. In the Properties window, select the Text property and key **Hello World.**
15. Press **F5** to build and run the application.
16. Verify the following:
    - Two forms have the caption Hello World. One form is the frmOne and the other form is the frmInherited form.
    - One form has the caption Instantiated frmTwo.
17. Close frmMDIMain, which closes all of the children Windows Forms.
18. Select the frmInherited.cs [Design] tab.
19. In the Properties window, select the Text property and key **Inherited Hello World.**
20. Press **F5** to build and run the application.
21. Verify the following:
    - One form has the caption Hello World. This is the frmOne form.
    - One form has the caption Instantiated frmTwo.
    - One form has the caption Inherited Hello World. This is the frmInheritied form.
22. Close frmMDIMain, which closes all of the children Windows Forms.

PAUSE. Leave the solution open to use in the next exercise.

You have just created a design-time inherited Windows Form. A design-time inherited Windows Form uses the same properties and events as the base Windows Forms class. When a property or event on the base Windows Forms class is changed, the inherited design-time class is also changed. Not until a property or event is changed in the instantiated Windows Forms class does the instantiated Windows Forms class override the base Windows Forms class behavior.

Extending Inherited Windows Forms

The power of an inherited Windows Forms class is in its ability to add to the inherited Windows Class to provide customized functionality while maintaining a generic Windows Forms class.

In previous exercises, you have altered instantiated Windows Forms properties to change the instantiated Windows Forms behavior. Inherited Windows Forms can also be extended to process information differently. By using Virtual methods in the base Windows Forms class, inherited Windows Forms can Override the methods and extend the base class's functionality. A *Virtual method* tells the Windows Forms class that this method will use the base class defined functionality, unless a derived class has an Override method. An *Override method* is a method declaration that replaces the Virtual method in the base class with new functionality.

USE VIRTUAL AND OVERRIDE METHODS

USE the project you created in the previous exercise.

1. Select frmChild.cs [Design] tab.
2. In the Properties window, click the Events button.
3. Locate the Load event and double-click in the set method cell.

TAKE NOTE✱

The frmChild_Load event is fired after the properties values are applied; thus the Text property values applied at run time and design time are overwritten with the value in the ChangeTitlebarText method.

X REF

To understand the Windows Forms Event life cycle, please see Lesson 4 "Controlling Application Execution."

4. Key the following code inside of the frmChild_Load method:

```
// Call the ChangeTitlebarText Method.
ChangeTitlebarText();
```

5. Just below the frmChild_Load method, key the following code:

```
// Change TitlebarText Method
// This method is a virtual method that
// can be overridden in an inherited class.
public virtual void ChangeTitlebarText()
{
  // Change the form's caption.
  this.Text = "Base Windows Form";
}
```

6. Press **F5** to build and run the application.

7. Verify that all three instantiated Windows Forms now have the caption Base Windows Form.

8. Close frmMDIMain.

9. In the Solution Explorer locate the frmInherited.cs element, right-click to display the Solution Explorer pop-up menu and select View Code.

10. Select the frmInherited.cs tab.

11. Just below the frmInherited constructor, key the following code:

```
// The ChangeTitlebarText Method
// This is the override to the base class method.
// This method has different functionality.
public override void ChangeTitlebarText()
{
  // Change the form's caption
  this.Text = "Inherited Windows Form";
}
```

12. Press **F5** to build and run the application.

13. Verify the following:
    • Two forms have the caption Base Windows. These are the frmOne and frmTwo forms.
    • One form has the caption Inherited Windows Form. This is the frmInheritied form.

14. Close frmMDIMain.

CERTIFICATION READY
Do you understand Windows Forms inheritance?
2.2

STOP. Save or discard the solution. It will not be used again for another exercise.

You just created a Virtual method in the base class and then overrode the Virtual method using an Override declaration. When you create a base Windows Forms class, you can add generic functionality that is used by most inherited Windows Forms. When you need special processing, you will override the base Virtual method and implement the special functionality.

Designing and implementing the Windows Form is only the beginning for creating a Windows Forms Application. The Windows Form is the base container where all other controls are placed.

■ Working with Windows Forms Controls

↓
THE BOTTOM LINE
When designing a Windows Forms Application, there are various Windows Forms controls that can be used to create a functional user interface. The challenge is to select and organize the right Windows Forms controls to perform your application's desired result.

While implementing a Windows Forms Application, you will need to work with several types of controls, including:

- Container controls
- Menu and Toolbar controls
- Basic Input controls
- Advanced Input controls
- Component controls
- Dialog controls

Controls can be combined in multiple ways to create the desired user interface.

Working with Container Controls

Dividing up a Windows Form's Graphical User Interface (GUI) into manageable areas can be accomplished using container controls. Container controls group other controls together and provide a more organized user interaction.

Table 3-2 lists several common Windows Forms container controls and their functionality.

Table 3-2

Common Windows Forms
Container Controls

CONTAINER CONTROL	DESCRIPTION
Panel	One of the most generic container controls, with no inherent functionality other than to contain other controls. The Panel container control is used when you want to place multiple controls in a specific region, like all docked on the left side of the application window.
SplitContainer	The default SplitContainer container control has inherent functionality that creates two panels separated by a divider. The divider can be moved horizontally or vertically to cause the two panels automatically to be resized and fill the entire SplitContainer area. A common example of the SplitContainer container control is Windows Explorer.
TabControl	The default TabControl container control has inherent functionality that creates two tabs that act like file folder tabs. Within each tab is a TabPage container control. You can add as many tabs as you would like and the TabControl container control will provide tab navigation and a TabPage for each new tab added.
GroupBox	The default GroupBox container control has inherent functionality that creates a lined box with a label to describe what is being grouped. The GroupBox container control is typically used to group the Option Input Control.

USE CONTAINER CONTROLS

GET READY. Before you begin these steps, be sure to launch Microsoft Visual Studio and create a new Windows Forms Application project named wfaContainerControls.

1. Verify that the Toolbox window is visible in the Visual Studio environment. If the Toolbox window is not visible, select View→Toolbox (Ctrl-W, X)

2. Select the Form1.cs [Design] tab.

3. In the Properties window, locate the (Name) property and key **frmWindowsContainer**

4. In the Solution Explorer, rename Form1 to frmWindowsContainer.

5. In the Toolbox window, locate the containers group (Figure 3-6) and click the plus sign to expand the grouping.

Figure 3-6

Containers toolbox

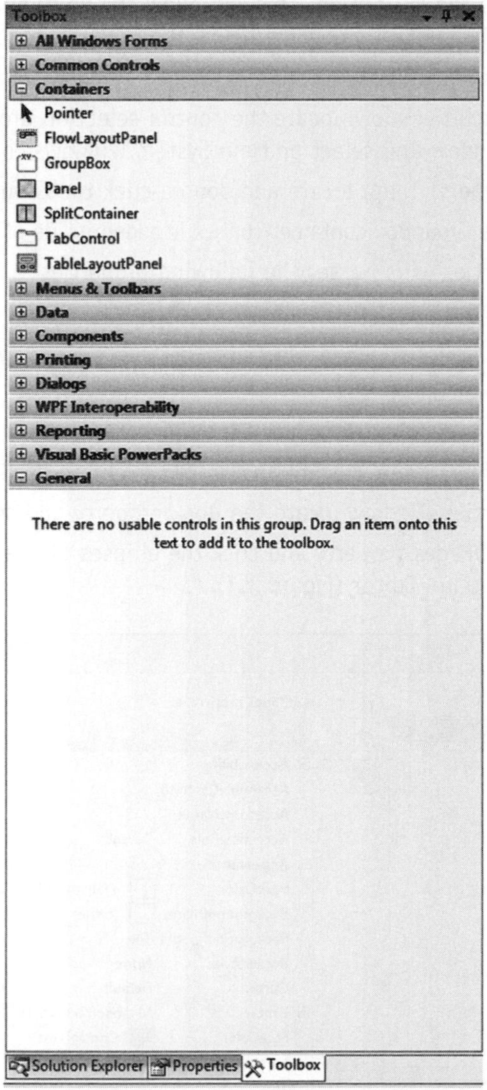

6. In the containers group, locate and double-click the Panel container control to add a Panel container control to the frmWindowsContainer Windows Form.

ANOTHER WAY You can also add controls by dragging and dropping Toolbox icons from the Toolbox area onto a Form's designer.

7. In the Properties window, set the following properties:
   - Name: pnlMain
   - Dock: Top (Select the Top Button)

8. In the Properties window, locate the control selection drop-down at the top of the Properties window and select frmWindows Container System.Windows.Forms.Form.

TAKE NOTE *

When using the double-click method to add controls to the Form Designer, you need to ensure that the right container control is selected before double-clicking. Otherwise you will have container controls contained inside of other container controls when that is not desired.

9. In the containers group, locate and double-click the SplitContainer container control. Verify that the SplitContainer container control is added with its Dock property already set to the Fill option. This will allow the SplitContainer to fill the remaining area of frmWindowsContainer just below the pnlMain container control.

10. In the Properties window, locate the (Name) property and key **spcMain**

11. In the Properties window, locate the control selection drop-down at the top of the Properties window and select pnlMain System.Windows.Forms.Panel.

12. In the containers group, locate and double-click the GroupBox container control.

13. Verify that the GroupBox container control is added inside of the pnlMain container control.

14. In the Properties window, set the following properties:
   - Name: grbMain
   - Dock: Fill
   - Text: My First Group Box

15. Select the Panel2 container control inside of the spcMain container control.

16. In the containers group, locate and double-click the TabControl container control.

17. In the Properties window, locate the Dock property and select the Fill option.

18. Select the TabPages property and click the ellipses at the end of the row to show the TabPage Collection Editor (Figure 3-7).

Figure 3-7

TabPage Collection Editor

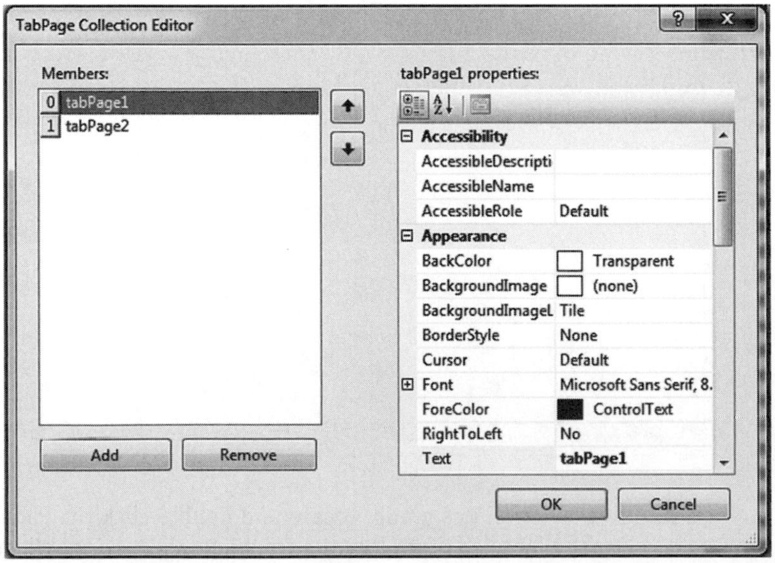

19. Select the Text property from the tabPage1 properties list and key **My Tab 1**

20. Click OK.

21. Press **F5** to build and run the application.

22. Close frmWindowsContainers.

STOP. Save or discard the solution. It will not be used again for another exercise.

You have just created a Windows Forms Application using several container controls. Each container control added to the user interface divided up the Windows Forms area. You added container controls to container controls and set container control properties to change default behavior.

Other types of specialized container controls are the Menu and Toolbar controls. Unlike the container controls you just used, the Menu and Toolbar controls cannot contain just any control, they can only contain Menu and Button controls.

Working with Menu and Toolbar Controls

It is very common in a Windows Forms Application to add navigation functionality in the form of menus and toolbars. Menu and Toolbar controls are a special category of container controls that only hold Menu and Button controls.

Table 3-3 lists all of the standard Menu and Toolbar controls in the Visual Studio Toolbox window.

Table 3-3

Windows Forms Menu and Toolbar Controls

MENU AND TOOLBAR CONTROL	DESCRIPTION
MenuStrip	Creates a system of menus and sub-menus for the user to navigate the functionality of an application. A MenuStrip control can have multiple top-level and sub-level ToolStripMenuItems. The ToolStripMenuItem can be a MenuItem, a Check Mark, a Separator, a ComboBox, or a TextBox where each ToolStripMenuItem control type provides the user with a different type of interaction. All of the ToolStripMenuItem control types support the option to add an image that is placed to the left of ToolStripMenuItem control.
ContextMenuStrip	Has all of the same features as the MenuStrip control, with the exception that the ContextMenuStrip control does not automatically appear when the application runs. To make the ContextMenuStrip control visible, you must use the **Show** method.
ToolStrip	Creates a toolbar of ToolStripButton controls to access application functionality. A ToolStripButton can be a Button, a Label, a SplitButton, a DropDownButton, a Separator, a ComboBox, a TextBox, or a ProgressBar. All of the ToolStripButton control types support the option to have no image, just an image, just text, or an image and text.
ToolStripContainer	Holds multiple ToolStrip controls. You can place multiple ToolStrip controls on a Form without the ToolStripContainer, but all of the ToolStrip controls will expand to fill the entire height or width of its container. To allow multiple ToolStrip controls to share a toolbar area, you must use a ToolStripContainer.
StatusStrip	Creates a Status toolbar that can contain multiple ToolStripStatusLabel controls. The StatusStrip control is typically placed at the bottom of the application to provide feedback to the user about application processing. A ToolStripStatusLabel control can be a HyperLink, StatusLabel, ProgressBar, DropDownButton, or a SplitButton. All ToolStripStatusLabel control types, except the ProgressBar type, can support the option to have no image, just an image, just text, or an image and text. When a ToolStripStatusLabel control is a StatusLabel type, the **Spring** property can be used to automatically resize the control's width to fill the entire StatusStrip control.

USE MENU CONTROLS

GET READY. Before you begin these steps, be sure to launch Microsoft Visual Studio and create a new Windows Forms Application project named wfaMenuControls.

1. In the Toolbox window, locate the Menus & Toolbars grouping and click the plus sign to expand the grouping (Figure 3-8).

Figure 3-8

Menus & Toolbars group

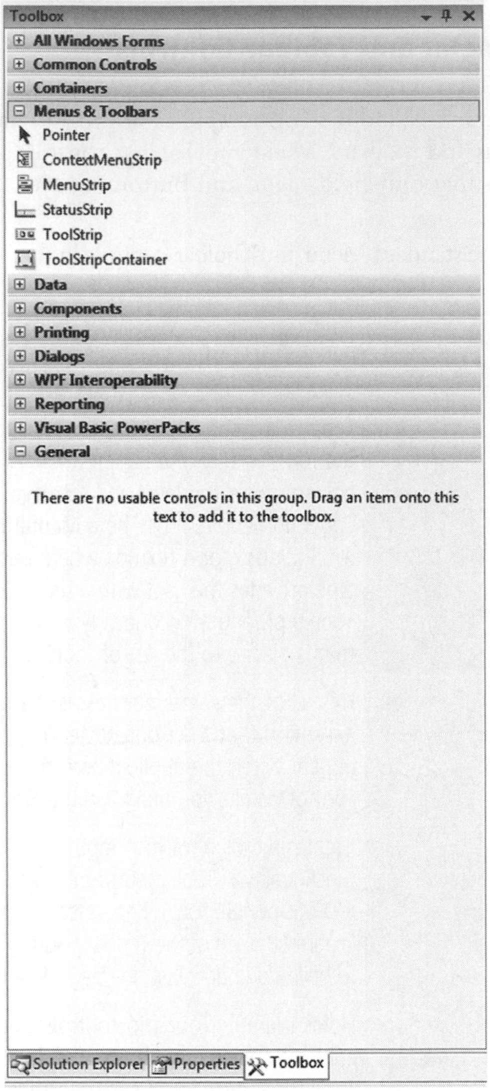

2. In the Menus & Toolbars group, locate and double-click the MenuStrip control.

3. Locate on the MenuStrip control the first ToolStripMenuItem control labeled with Type Here.

4. Key **&File** and Press **Enter**.

5. Under the File ToolStripMenuItem control, locate the first ToolStripMenuItem control labeled Type Here.

6. Key **&New**

7. Right-click on the &New ToolStripMenuItem control to display the pop-up menu (Figure 3-9).

TAKE NOTE*

The ampersand (&) is used to set the quick key access character.

Figure 3-9

Menu Item pop-up menu

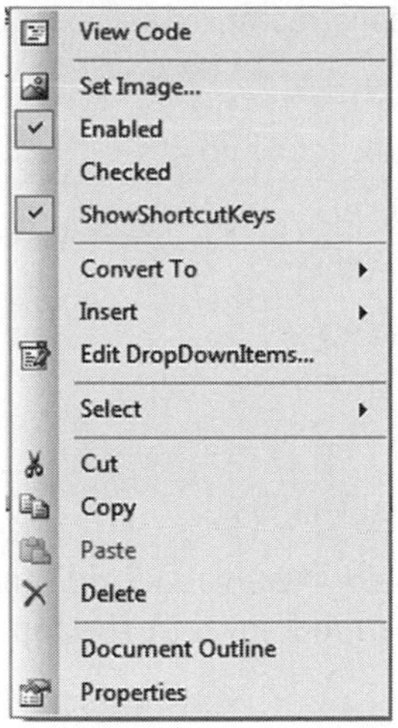

🖳	View Code
🖼	Set Image...
✓	Enabled
	Checked
✓	ShowShortcutKeys
	Convert To ▶
	Insert ▶
📝	Edit DropDownItems...
	Select ▶
✂	Cut
📋	Copy
📋	Paste
✕	Delete
	Document Outline
🔧	Properties

8. Select Checked.

9. Verify that the &New ToolStripMenuItem control now has a check mark to the left of the text.

10. Select Form1.cs [Design] tab.

11. In the Properties window, change the (Name) property to the value frmMenusMain.

12. Rename the Form1.cs Project item to frmMenusMain.cs.

13. In the Properties window, select the newToolStripMenuItem System.Windows.Forms .ToolStripMenuItem from the drop-down at the top of the properties list.

14. Click the Events button.

15. Locate the Click event and double-click in the method selection cell.

16. Insert the following code into the newToolStripMenuItem_Click method:

```
// Check to see if the New menu item is checked
if (newToolStripMenuItem.Checked)
    // The New menu item is checked, so uncheck it.
    newToolStripMenuItem.Checked = false;
else
    // The New menu item is unchecked, so check it.
    newToolStripMenuItem.Checked = true;
```

17. Press **F5** to build and execute the application.

18. Verify that when you click the New menu item, the check mark next to the menu will appear and disappear.

19. Close frmMenusMain.

20. Locate the next available ToolStripMenuItem control under the &File ToolStripMenuItem control.

21. Key **Select a color:**

22. Right-click on the Select a color: ToolStripMenuItem control to display the pop-up menu.

23. Select Convert To→ComboBox.

24. Verify that the Select a color: ToolStripMenuItem control is now a ComboBox control.

25. Select the frmMenusMain.cs tab.

26. At the end of the frmMenusMain constructor, add the following code:

```
// Add several colors to the
// Select a color: ComboBox control.
selectAColorToolStripMenuItem
    .ComboBox.Items.Add("Red");
selectAColorToolStripMenuItem
    .ComboBox.Items.Add("Blue");
selectAColorToolStripMenuItem
    .ComboBox.Items.Add("Yellow");
```

27. In the Properties window, select selectAColorToolStripMenuItem System.Windows .Forms.ToolStripMenuItem from the drop-down at the top of the properties list.

28. Click the Events button.

29. Locate the TextChanged event and double-click in the method selection cell.

30. Add the following code inside of the selectAColorToolStripMenuItem_ TextChanged method:

```
// Switch on the color selected in the
// Select a color: ComboBox control.
switch (selectAColorToolStripMenuItem
    .ComboBox.Text)
{
    // Color selected is red.
    case "Red":
        // Change the form's background to red.
        this.BackColor = Color.Red;
        break;

    // Color selected is blue.
    case "Blue":
        // Change the form's background to blue.
        this.BackColor = Color.Blue;
        break;

    // Color selected is yellow.
    case "Yellow":
        // Change the form's background to yellow.
        this.BackColor = Color.Yellow;
        break;

    // If the user types a color and it is not listed.
    default:
        // Change the form's background to gray.
        this.BackColor = Color.Gray;
        break;
}
```

31. Press **F5** to build and execute the application.

32. Click File→Select a color: and select Red.

33. Verify that the background color for frmMenusMain is now Red.

34. Close frmMenusMain.

35. In the Menus & Toolbars grouping, locate and double-click the ContextMenuStrip control.

36. Locate the first available ToolStripMenuItem control under the ContextMenuStrip control.

37. Key **&New**

38. In the Properties windows, select frmMenusMain System.Windows.Forms.Form from the drop-down at the top of the properties list.

39. Click the Events button.

40. Locate the MouseDown event and double-click in the method selection cell.

41. Add the following code inside of the frmMenusMain_MouseDown method:

```
// Display the pop-up menu at the position
// the mouse was clicked down.
contextMenuStrip1.Show(this,e.X, e.Y);
```

42. Press **F5** to build and execute the application.

43. Click anywhere inside of the frmMenusMain window area.

44. Verify that the ContextStripMenu control appears.

45. Close frmMenusMain.

STOP. Save or discard the solution. It will not be used again for another exercise.

You have just created MenuStrip and ContextMenuStrip controls. MenuStrip and ContextMenuStrip controls can hold any number of ToolStripMenuItem controls at multiple levels. The ToolStripMenuItem controls can be configured to show check marks or converted to different control types like the ComboBox.

Very similar to the MenuStrip and ContextMenuStrip controls, the ToolStrip and ToolStripContainer controls provide navigation functionality.

 USE TOOLBAR CONTROLS

GET READY. Before you begin these steps, be sure to launch Microsoft Visual Studio and create a new Windows Forms Application project named wfaToolbarControls.

1. In the Menus & Toolbar grouping, locate and double-click the ToolStrip control.

2. On the ToolStrip control, locate and click the Add ToolStripButton button.

3. Select the new ToolStripButton control and right-click to display the pop-up menu (Figure 3-10).

Figure 3-10

ToolStripButton pop-up menu

4. Select Convert To→DropDownButton.

5. Locate the first ToolStripMenu item under the DropDownButton control.

6. Key **Red** and Press **Enter**.

7. In the next ToolStripMenu item, key **Blue** and Press **Enter**.

8. In the next ToolStripMenu item, key **Yellow** and Press **Enter**.

9. Select the Red ToolStripMenu control.

10. In the Properties window, click the Events button.

11. Locate the Click event and double-click in the method selection cell.

12. Key the following code into the redToolStripMenuItem_Click method:

    ```
    // Change the form's background color to red.
    this.BackColor = Color.Red;
    ```

13. Select the Form1.cs [Design] tab.

14. In the Properties window, locate and select the blueToolStripMenuItem from the drop-down at the top of the properties list.

15. Locate the Click event and double-click in the method selection cell.

16. Key the following code into the blueToolStripMenuItem_Click method:

    ```
    // Change the form's background color to blue.
    this.BackColor = Color.Blue;
    ```

17. Select the Form1.cs [Design] tab.

18. In the Properties window, locate and select the yellowToolStripMenuItem from the drop-down at the top of the properties list.

19. Locate the Click event and double-click in the method selection cell.

20. Key the following code into the yellowToolStripMenuItem_Click method:

    ```
    // Change the form's background color to yellow.
    this.BackColor = Color.Yellow;
    ```

21. Press **F5** to build and execute the application.

22. Click the ToolStripButton and verify that the drop-down menu appears.

23. Click the Red menu item and verify that the form's background color changes to Red.

24. Click the Blue menu item and verify that the form's background color changes to Blue.

25. Close Form1.

26. Select the Form1.cs [Design] tab.

27. Click the Add ToolStripButton on the ToolStrip control.

28. Right-click on the new ToolStripButton to display the pop-up dialog.

29. Select Display Style→Text.

30. In the Properties window, locate the Text property and key **Press Me**

31. Click the Events button.

32. Locate the Click event and double-click in the method selection cell.

33. Add the following code to the toolStripButton2_Click method:

    ```
    // Show a message box.
    MessageBox.Show("Thanks for pressing me.");
    ```

34. Press **F5** to build and execute the application.

35. Key **Press Me**

36. Verify that the message box appears.

37. Click OK.

38. Close Form1.

39. Select the Form1 [Design] tab.

40. Click the ToolStrip Tasks menu button (Figure 3-11).

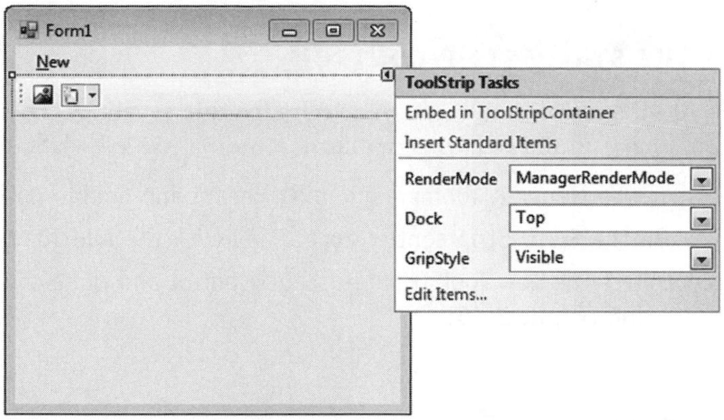

Figure 3-11

ToolStrip Tasks menu

41. Click Embed in ToolStripContainer.

42. In the ToolStripContainer Task menu, click Dock Fill in Form (Figure 3-12).

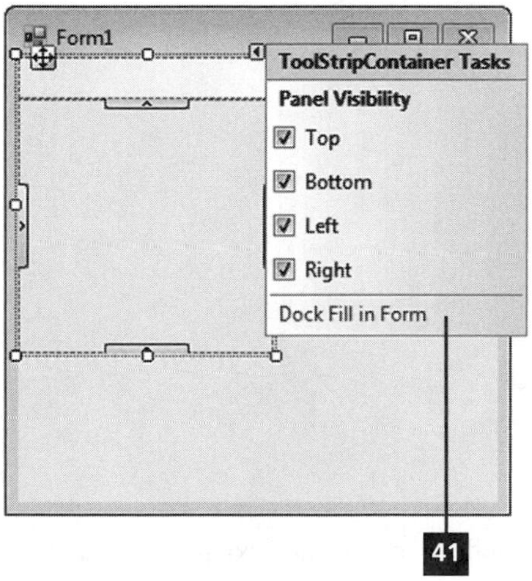

Figure 3-12

ToolStripContainer Tasks menu

43. In the Menus & Toolbars grouping, double-click on the ToolStrip control.

44. Drag and drop ToolStrip2 using the reposition indicator to the left side of the ToolStripContainer control.

45. Press **F5** to build and execute the application.

46. Using the ToolStrip grips, drag and drop ToolStrip2 from the left side of Form1 to the right side.

47. Verify that the ToolStripContainer undocks ToolStrip2 from the left side and redocks ToolStrip2 on the right side.

48. Close Form1.

STOP. Save or discard the solution. It will not be used again for another exercise.

You have just created a ToolStrip control and added ToolStripButtons. ToolStripButtons can be configured to perform various types of activities that include a drop-down menu and buttons. You can add multiple ToolStrip controls to one form and organize them using the ToolStripContainer control.

In addition to the MenuStrip and ToolStrip controls, Visual Studio also provides a StatusStrip control. The StatusStrip control is typically located at the bottom of a form and is used to provide run-time feedback.

⊙ USE THE STATUSSTRIP CONTROL

GET READY. Before you begin these steps, be sure to launch Microsoft Visual Studio and create a new Windows Forms Application project named wfaStatusStripControl.

1. In the Menus & Toolbars grouping, locate and double-click the StatusStrip control.
2. On the StatusStrip control, locate and click the Add ToolStripStatusLabel button.
3. Select the new ToolStripStatusLabel control and right-click to display the pop-up menu (Figure 3-13).

Figure 3-13

ToolStripStatusLabel pop-up menu

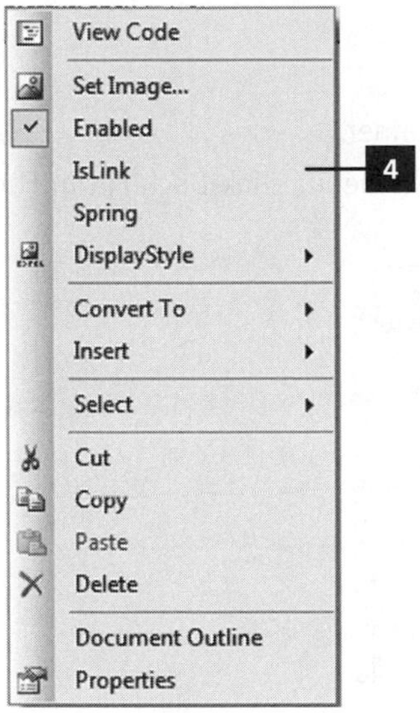

4. Click IsLink.
5. In the Properties window, locate the Text property and key **http://www.microsoft.com**
6. In Solution Explorer, select the Form1.cs element and right-click to display the Solution Explorer pop-up menu and select View Code.
7. Select the Form1.cs tab.
8. Locate the code:

   using System.Windows.Forms;

9. Immediately following this code, key the following code:

   // Add the diagnostics namespace for the
   // process functionality.
   using System.Diagnostics;

10. Select the Form1.cs [Design] tab.

11. In the Properties window, select the ToolStripStatusLabel1 System.Windows.Forms .ToolStripStatusLabel from the drop-down at the top of the properties list.

12. Click the Events button.

13. Locate the Click event and double-click in the method selection cell.

14. Add the following code into the `toolStripStatusLabel1_Click` method:

```
// Cast the sender parameter of the
// Click event to a ToolStripLabel
ToolStripLabel myHyperLinkLabel
    = (ToolStripLabel)sender;
// Starting a process will not work if
// an internet browser is not installed.
// Placing the call inside of a try catch
// will keep the application from crashing.
try
{
    // Open the default web browser with
    // the hyperlink from the tool bar.
    Process.Start(new ProcessStartInfo(
        myHyperLinkLabel.ToString()));
}
// Catch the exception if any.
catch (Exception err)
{
    // Notify the user that an error has occurred.
    MessageBox.Show("Error launching browser: "
      + err.Message);
}
```

15. Press **F5** to build and execute the application.

16. Click the http://www.microsoft.com hyperlink in the statusbar.

17. Verify that a browser opens and the Microsoft.com Web site is loaded.

18. Close Form1.

19. Select the Form1.cs [Design] tab.

20. Select ToolStripStatusLabel1 and right-click to display the pop-up menu.

21. Select Spring.

22. Verify that the ToolStripStatusLabel1 has now expanded to fill the entire ToolStrip.

23. Click the Add ToolStripStatusLabel button.

24. Verify that the ToolStripStatusLabel1 has now resized to allow the ToolStripStatusLabel2 control space on the ToolStrip.

25. Right-click the new ToolStripStatusLabel control to display the pop-up menu.

26. Select Convert To→Progressbar.

27. In the Properties window, select Form1 System.Windows.Forms.Form from the drop-down at the top of the properties list.

28. Click the Events button.

29. Locate the Click event and double-click in the method selection cell.

30. Add the following code into the Form1_Click method:

```
// Create a loop to increment the progress bar.
for (int counter = 1; counter <= 100; counter++)
{
// Increment the progress bar
this.ToolStripStatusLabel2
    .ProgressBar.Value = counter;
// Delay the loop processing
System.Threading.Thread.Sleep(50);
}
```

31. Press **F5** to build and execute the application.

32. Click in the middle of Form1.

33. Verify that the ToolStripLabel2 control's progress bar transitions.

34. Close Form1.

STOP. Save or discard the solution. It will not be used again for another exercise.

You have just created a StatusStrip control and added ToolStripLabel controls. You can add multiple ToolStripLabel controls and configure them to perform various functionalities.

Working with Input Controls

Gathering inputs from a user during the execution of your application can be a vital function. Visual Studio provides both basic and advanced input controls for creating a user interface.

Earlier in this lesson, you used the Properties window to configure control properties. In addition to using the Properties window, you will learn to use the Design View editor to move, align, resize, and configure your user interface controls.

You will also work with input controls that will be grouped into two categories:

- Basic Input Controls: Controls that have a specific functionality with several common properties and methods.
- Advanced Input Controls: Controls that have multiple functionalities with unique properties and methods.

WORKING WITH THE WINDOWS FORMS DESIGN VIEW EDITOR

As an alternative to changing property values in the Properties window, Visual Studio provides you with a What You See Is What You Get (WYSIWYG) editor. The *Windows Forms Design View* editor provides you with a real-time view of how your application's user interface will appear at run time.

Using the Windows Forms Design View editor, you can perform the following:

- Move controls
- Resize controls
- Align controls

As you drag and drop controls within the Design View editor, vertical and horizontal spacing indicators will appear to show you how much space you have between controls. When you are working with more than one control, the control alignment indicator will appear to show you how the two controls are aligning.

Visual Studio also provides a set of menus to format your controls consistently. You use the following menu items under the Format menu:

- Align
- Make Same Size
- Horizontal Spacing
- Vertical Spacing
- Center in Form

USE THE WINDOWS FORMS DESIGN VIEW EDITOR

GET READY. Before you begin these steps, be sure to launch Microsoft Visual Studio and create a new Windows Forms Application project named wfaDesignViewEditor.

1. In the Toolbox window, expand the Common Controls grouping and double-click the Label control.
2. In the Form1 [Design] tab, click and drag the label1 control to the right and down until you see the vertical and horizontal spacing indicators, then unclick (Figure 3-14).

Figure 3-14

Design View Editor spacing indicators

3. Verify that the Location property for the label1 control has a value of 12,9.
4. In the Toolbox window, locate and double-click the TextBox control.
5. In the Form1 [Design] tab, click and drag the textBox1 control to the left and up until you see the horizontal spacing indicator and the control alignment indicator (Figure 3-15).

Figure 3-15

Design View Editor control alignment indicator

6. Verify that the Location property for the textBox1 control has a value of 53,6.

7. Locate the textBox resize handle on the right side of the textBox1 control (Figure 3-16).

Figure 3-16

Design View Editor control resize handle

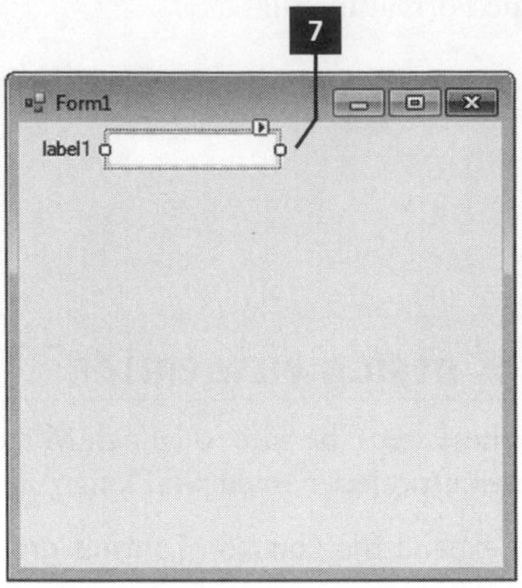

8. Click and drag the textBox1 control handle to the right to resize the textBox1 control larger.

9. Add another Label control.

10. Click on the label1 control.

11. Press **Ctrl** and click on the label2 control to select both controls at the same time.

12. Select Format→Align→Left.

13. Select only the label2 control.

14. Click and drag the label2 control down until you see the vertical and horizontal spacing indicators then unclick.

15. Add a new TextBox control.

16. Move the textBox2 control to align with the right side of textBox1 and the center of label2.

17. Click on textBox1.

18. Press **Ctrl** and click on the textBox2 control to select both controls at the same time.

19. Select Format→Make Same Size→Width.

20. Verify that both textBox1 and textBox2 have the same width.

STOP. Save or discard the solution. It will not be used again for another exercise.

You have just used the Design View editor to create a user interface. Your user interface was organized by moving, resizing, and aligning controls graphically. You used both the drag-and-drop method and the Format menu.

You now have two ways to create your user interface. You can use the Design View editor or you can use the Properties window. Now that you have the ability to design and organize your user interface, you will be adding more types of controls.

WORKING WITH BASIC INPUT CONTROLS

Visual Studio provides a set of controls that all have a common set of properties and methods. These Basic Input controls are used to build basic functionality in your application's user interface.

Most of the applications you will create will require you to gather user input. Different users come from different backgrounds and each user will interpret the User Interface functionality uniquely. Selecting the right user input control and configuring the control to perform the right functionality to gather the right input can be a challenge. For example, you add a Text control with a character mask for a personal identification number (PIN) input. Some users will be familiar with a character mask and understand why they can't see their numbers as they type. Other users will wonder why all of their typing keeps changing to this odd character. Using various input controls, you can provide most users with enough direction to enable effective input gathering.

Table 3-4 lists some of the Basic Input controls supported by Visual Studio with some of their common properties and methods. This is not an exhaustive list. For a full list of controls, see the Toolbox window's Common Controls grouping.

Table 3-4

Basic Input Controls

INPUT CONTROL	PROPERTY/METHOD	DESCRIPTION
All Input Controls		There are several properties that apply to all of the Basic Input controls. The following properties perform the same functionality for all of the controls listed in Table 3-4.
	Anchor	When an Input control is placed on a sizable Windows Form, you will want the control to move and/or resize based on how the Windows Form resizes. The Anchor property determines what sides of the Windows Form the Input Control is going to monitor and move and/or resize based on changes. For example, if an Input control has an Anchor property value of Left, Top, Right, then as the Windows Form gets taller, the Input control stays at the top of the Windows Form. As the Windows Form gets wider, the Input control also gets wider because it is anchored to the right side of the Windows Form and grows wider as the Windows Form grows wider.
	Text	The most common property across most Input controls, which determines any text that the Input control presents to the user.
	TextAlign	Determines on what side of the Input control text will be presented. The TextAlign property can have a value of Left, Right, or Center.
Label		A read-only text area you use to provide information to the user. A Label control is typically associated with each Input control and does have any additional common properties or methods.
TextBox		A read/write text area that can be used in multiple ways. When you assign a value to the PasswordChar property, the TextBox control will mask all text entries so no one can see what was typed. By default, the TextBox control is a single-line text area. When you set the Multiline property to True, the TextBox control can be resized to have multiple lines.
	Lines	An array of string values that represents each line of the text area. The Lines property provides you with access to each line of the text area individually.

(continued)

Table 3-4 *(continued)*

INPUT CONTROL	PROPERTY/METHOD	DESCRIPTION
	MaxLength	Determines how many characters the TextBox control can hold. When the text length is equal to the MaxLength property value, the TextBox control will stop accepting and showing newly entered characters. Do not underestimate the number of characters needed for user input. You should only limit the number of characters when your data storage medium also has a limited length.
	Multiline	Determines if the TextBox will allow the text area to have more than a single line of text.
	PasswordChar	Determines what character will be placed in the text area, in place of the actual text being entered. You have seen this property in action when entering your password in the Windows login screen.
	ScrollBars	When the Multiline property is True, the ScrollBars property determines how the text area scrollbars will work. The ScrollBars property can have a value of None, Horizontal, Vertical, or Both.
	WordWrap	When the Multiline property is True, the WordWrap property determines if the text area will automatically move to the next line when it reaches the end of the viewable text area.
	AppendText (string text)	Takes the text passed in and appends the text to the existing text in the TextBox control.
	Clear ( )	Removes all text from the Text property.
	ClearUndo ( )	Removes any undo operations for the TextBox control. When the ClearUndo method is called, any past changes the user has made will not be able to be undone using the Undo method.
	Cut ( )	Takes the currently selected text and places it on the Clipboard while removing it from the Text property value.
	Copy ( )	Takes the currently selected text and places it on the Clipboard.
	Paste ( )	Takes the current Clipboard contents and inserts the text into the text area at the current cursor position.
	DeselectAll ( )	Clears the selection indicator.
	SelectAll ( )	Sets the selection indicator for all of the text in the text area.
	Select (int start, int length)	Starts the selection indicator at the start parameter's value and then selects all of the text that is included in the length parameter's value.
	Undo ( )	Undoes the most recent text change.
ListBox		A set of rows where each row contains a piece of information. The ListBox controls can have single or multiple columns.
	HorizontalScrollbar	Determines if the ListBox will show a horizontal scrollbar when an Item's text extends beyond the ListBox's width.

Table 3-4 (*continued*)

INPUT CONTROL	PROPERTY/METHOD	DESCRIPTION
	IntegraHeight	Determines the behavior the ListBox control's height. When the IntegraHeight property's value is True, the ListBox control's height is automatically resized to show only whole rows. When the IntegraHeight property's value is False, the ListBox control's height can be set to a value that shows a partial row.
	ItemHeight	Determines the height of each row in the ListBox control.
	Items	A collection of Item objects. Each Item object represents one row in the ListBox control.
	Items.Count	Returns the number of rows in the ListBox control.
	MultiColumn	Determines if the ListBox control can show more than one column of text.
	FindString (string text, int startIndex)	Searches for the first ListBox item after the startIndex parameter that starts with the text parameter. The FindString method is not a case sensitive search.
	Items.Add (object item)	Used to add new rows to the ListBox control.
	Items.Clear ( )	Used to remove all rows from the ListBox control.
	Items.Remove (object item)	Used to remove a specific row from the ListBox control.
ComboBox		A TextBox and ListBox control. The ListBox can be configured to be visible all of the time or drop down when needed. The TextBox control supports direct text entry and/or can be limited to only ListBox Items.
	AutoCompleteMode	Determines if the ComboBox will try to complete your entry based on what it is able to find in the list. When the property value is Suggest, a suggestion window appears below the ComboBox when a possible match is found. When the property value is Append, the ComboBox will add the characters for the first match to the end of the text in the ComboBox as you type. When the property value is SuggestAppend, the ComboBox will do both.
	AutoCompleteSource	Determines where the ComboBox will look to find a match when performing the auto complete functionality. The AutoCompleteSource can have one of the following options: None, FileSystem, HistoryList, RecentlyUsedList, AllUrl, AllSytemResources, FileSystemDirectories, CustomResources, or ListItems. The most common source is the ListItems that represents the list associated with the ComboBox.
	DropDownHeight	Determines how far the drop-down list will appear when expanded.
	DropDownStyle	Determines the behavior between the ComboBox's TextBox and ListBox controls. When the property value is set to Simple or DropDown, the ComboBox's TextBox control will accept text entries, but when the value is DropDownList, the ComboBox's TextBox control will only display the ComboBox's ListBox control's selected value. When the property value is set to Simple, the

(*continued*)

Table 3-4 (*continued*)

INPUT CONTROL	PROPERTY/METHOD	DESCRIPTION
		drop-down arrow disappears and the ComboBox's ListBox control is always visible. This is unlike when the property value is DropDown or DropDownList where the drop-down arrow is always present and the ComboBox's ListBox control only appears when the drop-down button is pressed.
	DropDownWidth	Determines how wide the ListBox control will be when visible. The DropDownWidth does not have to be the same width as the ComboBox control. You can make the ListBox control part of the ComboBox much wider or narrower based on the size of information you want to place in each ListBox item.
	MaxDropDownItems	Determines how many rows of the ComboBox's ListBox control will be visible to the user. More rows can be in the ComboBox's ListBox control, but the user will need to use the vertical scrollbars to see the additional rows.
CheckBox		A Label control with a CheckBox control. The CheckBox control can be Checked, UnChecked, or Indeterminate.
	Checked	Determines if the CheckBox control has a check mark in the box.
	CheckState	Determines if the CheckBox control has a check mark in the box, but also determines if the CheckBox is in the indeterminate state. The indeterminate state is a checked checkbox, but the checkbox is grayed out. The indeterminate state is typically used when your CheckBox control is summarizing the state of several other CheckBox controls and the other CheckBox controls have both checked and unchecked states.
RadioButton		A Label control with a round (Radio) CheckBox control. When you place several RadioButton controls together on a container, like a GroupBox container, only one of the RadioButton controls can be checked at a time.
Button		A Label control inside of a Button control. The Button control can be configured to generate a standard Event result using the DialogResult property.
	DialogResult	Determines if the Button control generates an Event results enumeration. The DialogResult property can have a value None, OK, Cancel, Abort, Retry, Ignore, Yes, or No.
	PerformClick ( )	Generates an Event that executes the Button control's Click event. The PerformClick method can be useful if you want to perform the Button control's functionality from within code.

→ USE BASIC INPUT CONTROLS

GET READY. Before you begin these steps, be sure to launch Microsoft Visual Studio and create a new Windows Forms Application project named wfaBasicInputControls.

1. In the Toolbox window, locate the Common Controls grouping and expand the group (Figure 3-17).

Figure 3-17

Common Controls group

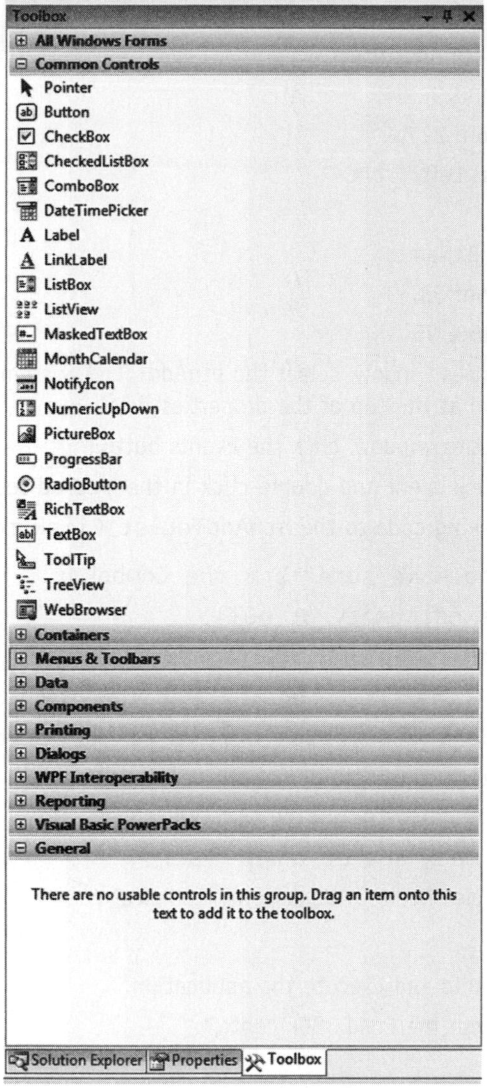

Toolbox	▾ ▯ ✕
⊞ **All Windows Forms**	
⊟ **Common Controls**	
➤ Pointer	
▣ Button	
☑ CheckBox	
▦ CheckedListBox	
▤ ComboBox	
▦ DateTimePicker	
A Label	
A LinkLabel	
▤ ListBox	
▦ ListView	
▣ MaskedTextBox	
▦ MonthCalendar	
▦ NotifyIcon	
▦ NumericUpDown	
▦ PictureBox	
▭ ProgressBar	
◉ RadioButton	
▦ RichTextBox	
▣ TextBox	
▧ ToolTip	
▦ TreeView	
▦ WebBrowser	
⊞ **Containers**	
⊞ **Menus & Toolbars**	
⊞ **Data**	
⊞ **Components**	
⊞ **Printing**	
⊞ **Dialogs**	
⊞ **WPF Interoperability**	
⊞ **Reporting**	
⊞ **Visual Basic PowerPacks**	
⊟ **General**	

There are no usable controls in this group. Drag an item onto this
text to add it to the toolbox.

Solution Explorer ｜ Properties ｜ Toolbox

2. Using either the Properties window, or the Design View editor, configure Form1 with the following controls and property values:

   a. Label

     • Name: lblName

     • Text: Name:

     • Location: 12,9

   b. ComboBox

     • Name: cboName

     • Location: 53,6

     • Size: 158, 21

     • Anchor: Top, Left, Right

     • AutoCompleteMode: Suggest

     • AutoCompleteSource: ListItems

    c. Button
- Name: btnAddToList
- Text: Add
- Location: 217,4
- Anchor: Left, Right

    d. ListBox
- Name: lstNames
- Location: 53,33
- Size: 158, 95

3. In the Properties window, select the btnAddToList System.Windows.Forms.Button from the drop-down at the top of the properties list.

4. In the Properties window, click the Events button.

5. Locate the Click event and double-click in the method selection cell.

6. Add the following code to the btnAddToList_Click method:

```
// Check to make sure that the ComboBox
// text is not empty or null.
if (!string.IsNullOrEmpty(cboName.Text))
{
    // Add the ComboBox's text to the ListBox.
    lstNames.Items.Add(cboName.Text);
    // Add the ComboBox's text to the
    // Combox's drop-down list.
    cboName.Items.Add(cboName.Text);
}
```

7. Press **F5** to build and execute the application.

8. Key a name into the ComboBox control.

9. Press Add.

10. Verify that the name was added to the ComboBox and ListBox controls.

11. Add five more names.

12. Add a name similar to one of your previous names.

13. Verify that the ComboBox control auto completes.

14. Resize the width of Form1.

15. Verify that the ComboBox control resized, the Button control stayed on the right side of the form, and the Label control did not move.

16. Close Form1.

STOP. Save or discard the solution. It will not be used again for another exercise.

You have just created an application using some basic Windows Forms controls. You used the Label, ComboBox, Button, and ListBox controls to create a user interface for working with names. Basic Input controls have overlapping properties and perform basic information gathering operations in a Windows Forms Application.

Windows Forms Applications also provide for more complex and advanced Windows Forms controls. Advanced Windows Forms controls can be used to gather more complex or multi-step inputs.

Working with Advanced Input Controls

To build a more complex user interface, Visual Studio provides additional Advanced Input controls that perform multi-step input features. Each Advanced Input control typically has very specific functionality and is designed to extend the Basic Input controls.

Table 3-5 lists some of the Advanced Input controls supported by Visual Studio with some of their common properties and methods. Visual Studio supports more than the listed controls; for a full list of controls see the Toolbox window's Common Controls grouping.

Table 3-5

Advanced Input Controls

INPUT CONTROL	PROPERTY/METHOD	DESCRIPTION
TreeView		A hieratical view of information. Information is organized into nodes with sub-levels of nodes into a tree-like structure. The user can expand, collapse, and explore various levels.
	CheckBoxes	Determines if there will be a CheckBox control next to each node.
	FullRowSelect	Determines if the selection indicator will stretch from edge to edge (full row) of the Treeview control, or be the same size as the node text.
	HotTracking	Determines if node selection follows the mouse cursor or waits for a mouse click.
	ImageList	A collection of graphics that can be associated with an individual node.
	ShowLines	Determines if there will be lines between the nodes to show branches.
	ShowPlusMinus	Determines if there will be plus signs on the left side of nodes with sub-level children nodes.
	ShowRootLines	Determines if there will be lines on nodes with no parent node.
	Nodes.Clear ( )	Removes all nodes.
	Nodes.Add (string text)	Has seven different overloads for adding a new node to the Treeview control.
	CollapseAll ( )	Closes all open nodes.
ListView		Provides the user with multiple ways to view a list of information. A user can view and select an item from the list when the list is in LargeIcon, Details, List, SmallIcon, or Tile. Set which type of list is presented by changing the View property.
	Columns	A collection of Column controls that define the column headers when the View property has a value of Details.
	Groups	Determines how the list items can be grouped into categories.
	HeaderStyle	Determines how the column headers will look when the View property has a value of Details.
	LabelWrap	Determines if long text in an item will wrap to the next line when the View property has a value of LargeIcon or Tile.

(continued)

Table 3-5 (*continued*)

INPUT CONTROL	PROPERTY/METHOD	DESCRIPTION
	LargeImageList	A collection of graphics used when the View property has a value of LargeIcon or Tile.
	MultiSelect	Determines if more than one list item can be selected at a time.
	SmallImageList	A collection of graphics used when the View property has a value of SmallIcon, Details, or List.
	Sorting	Determines how the list items are sorted.
	Items.Clear ( )	Removes all list items.
	Items.Add (string key, string text, int imageIndex)	Adds an item to the list. There are five overloads on the Add method.
	ArrangIcons ( )	Reorganizes the current view of icons into orderly rows and columns.
	FindItemWithText (string text)	Finds the first list item that begins with the provided text.
	FindNearestItem ( )	Finds the next list item that is geographically closest to the current item.
DateTimePicker		Provides the user with graphical calendar functionality. The DateTimePicker control only allows the selection of valid dates and times.
	Format	Determines how the date and/or time will be displayed. The Format property can have the value: Long (Date), Short (Date), Time, or Custom.
	MaxDate	Determines the highest date and time that can be entered into the DateTimePicker control.
	MinDate	Determines the lowest date and time that can be entered into the DateTimePicker control.
	ShowUpDown	Determines if the drop-down calendar is going to show or if the DateTimePicker control will only have up and down arrows for date value changes.
	Value	The currently entered date and time.
CheckListBox		Provides all of the same functionality as the ListBox control, but in addition, the CheckListBox control provides a CheckBox control on each row. Unlike the ListBox control, the CheckListBox control cannot support multi-selection of list items. The CheckListBox control provides the same functionality by allowing the user to check multiple CheckBox controls.
	CheckOnClick	Determines if the CheckBox control will change states when a single click is performed anywhere on the list item versus only when the CheckBox control is clicked.
	ThreeDCheckBoxes	Determines if the CheckBox controls on each list item will have raised (3D) edges.
MaskedTextBox		Provides the user with TextBox control functionality, but all of the inputted values are validated before being displayed in the control. The MaskedTextBox is used most often for Input that has a defined format like phone numbers, zip codes, area codes, and so on.

Table 3-5 (*continued*)

INPUT CONTROL	PROPERTY/METHOD	DESCRIPTION
	Cursor	Determines what type of mouse cursor is displayed when over the MaskedTextBox control.
	HideSelection	Determines if the selection indicator is hidden or visible.
	Mask	Determines the how and what will be allowed when entering text into the control. The Mask property has a built-in dialog that provides a list of predefined Mask property values.
	SkipLiterals	Determines if the literals in the Mask value are stored with the control value or left out.
	Cut ( )	Copies the selected text to the clipboard and removes the text from the MaskedEditBox control.
	Copy ( )	Copies the selected text to the clipboard.
	Paste ( )	Inserts the text currently on the clipboard into the current cursor position.
	ResetText ( )	Clears all text.
	Select (int start, int length)	Highlights with the selection indicator all text from the start parameter to the end of the length parameter.
	SelectAll ( )	Highlights all text with the selection indicator.

⊕ USE THE TREEVIEW AND LISTVIEW INPUT CONTROLS

GET READY. Before you begin these steps, be sure to launch Microsoft Visual Studio and create a new Windows Forms Application project named wfaTreeviewListview.

1. In the Toolbox window, expand the Containers grouping and double-click the SplitContainer control.
2. Select Panel1.
3. In the Toolbox window, expand the Common Controls grouping and double-click the Treeview control.
4. In the Properties window, locate the Dock property and choose the Fill option by selecting the center button.
5. Select Panel2.
6. In the Toolbox window, double-click the Listview control.
7. In the Properties window, locate the Dock property and select the Fill option.
8. In the drop-down control at the top of the Properties window, select Form1 System. Windows.Forms.Form.
9. Select the Events button.
10. Locate the Load event and double-click in the method selection cell.
11. Key the following code in the Form1_Load method:

```
// Declare a tree node for parent nodes.
TreeNode trnParent;
// Declare a tree node for child nodes.
TreeNode trnSubChildParent;
```

```
// Add a parent node.
trnParent = treeView1.Nodes.Add("Root Node 1");
// Add two child nodes.
trnParent.Nodes.Add("Child Node 1");
trnParent.Nodes.Add("Child Node 2");
// Add a child node that is also a parent
trnSubChildParent =
    trnParent.Nodes.Add("Parent Node 3");
// Add two child nodes to the child parent node.
trnSubChildParent.Nodes.Add("Child Node 4");
trnSubChildParent.Nodes.Add("Child Node 5");
// Add a child node to the original parent node.
trnParent.Nodes.Add("Child Node 6");
// Add another parent node.
trnParent = treeView1.Nodes.Add("Root Node 2");
```

12. Press **F5** to build and execute the application.

13. Click Root Node 1 to expand and see the nodes underneath.

14. Click Parent Node 3 to expand and see the nodes underneath.

15. Close Form1.

16. Select the Form1.cs [Design] tab.

17. In the Properties window, select the treeview1 System.Windows.Forms.Treeview item from the drop-down list at the top of the properties list.

18. Select the Events button.

19. Locate the AfterSelect event and double-click in the method selection cell.

20. Key the following code into the treeView1_AfterSelect method:

```
// Remove all ListView items.
this.listView1.Items.Clear();
// Switch on the text of the
// node that was selected
switch (e.Node.Text)
{
    // Root Node 1 was selected.
    case "Root Node 1":
        // Add an item to the ListView
        this.listView1.Items.Add("Listview Item 1");
        break;
    // Parent Node 3 was selected
    case "Parent Node 3":
        // Add an item to the ListView
        this.listView1.Items.Add("Listview Item 2");
        break;
    // Root Node 2 was selected
    case "Root Node 2":
```

```
                    // Add an item to the ListView
                    this.listView1.Items.Add("Listview Item 3");
                    break;
            // Any other node was selected
            default:
                    // Add an item to the ListView
                    this.listView1.Items.Add("All Other Items");
                    break;
        }
```

21. Press **F5** to build and execute the application.
22. Click Root Node 1.
23. Click Child Node 1 and verify that the Listview control now shows All Other Items.
24. Click Parent Node 1 and verify that the Listview control now shows Listview Item 2.
25. Close Form1.
26. Select the Form1.cs [Design] tab.
27. Select Listview1.
28. In the Properties window, locate the View property and select the List option.
29. Press **F5** to build and execute the application.
30. Click Root Node 1.
31. Click Child Node 1 and verify that the Listview control now shows All Other Items.
32. Click Root Node to expand and see the nodes underneath.
33. Click Parent Node 3 to expand and see the nodes underneath.
34. Close Form1.

STOP. Save or discard the solution. It will not be used again for another exercise.

You have just created a TreeView and ListView control. You added nodes to the Treeview control and list items to the ListView control. You expanded, collapsed, and explored the Treeview control's node hierarchy to see how nodes interact. You changed the ListView control's View property to ensure that all of the text for a list item was visible.

You will now look at a few other Advanced Input controls.

USE ADVANCED INPUT CONTROLS

GET READY. Before you begin these steps, be sure to launch Microsoft Visual Studio and create a new Windows Forms Application project named wfaAdvancedInputControls.

1. In the Toolbox Window, expand the Common Controls group and double-click the DateTimePicker control.
2. Set the following DateTimePicker1 control property values:
   - Location: 12,12 (Top = 12, Left = 12)
   - Size: 268,20 (Width = 268, Height = 20)
   - Format: Custom
   - CustomFormat: dd-MMM-yyyy (hh:mm:ss tt)
3. Double-click the CheckedListBox control.

4. Set the following ClickListBox1 control property values:
   - Location: 12,38 (Top = 38, Left = 12)
   - Size: 268,94 (Width=268, Height = 94)
   - MultiColumn: True

5. Double-click the MaskedTextBox control.

6. Set the following MaskedTextBox1 control property values:
   - Location: 12,138 (Top = 138, Left = 12)
   - Size: 268,20 (Width=268, Height = 20)
   - TextMaskFormat: ExcludePromptAndLiterals
   - Mask: 90/90/0000 90:90:90

7. Select the Form1 [Design] tab.

8. Select the dateTimePicker1 Input control.

9. In the Properties window, click the Events button.

10. Locate the ValueChanged event and double-click in the method selection cell.

11. Key the following code into the dateTimePicker1_ValueChanged method:

```
// Add the current date time value to the ListBox.
checkedListBox1.Items.Add(dateTimePicker1.Value);
```

12. Select the Form1 [Design] tab.

13. Select the checkListBox1 Input control.

14. Locate the ItemCheck event and double-click in the method selection cell.

15. Key the following code into the checkedListBox1_ItemCheck method:

```
// Set the MaskedTextBox text to
// the ListBox item selected.
maskedTextBox1.Text =
    checkedListBox1.SelectedItem.ToString();
```

TAKE NOTE*

Clicking on the Month name displays a list of the Months, and clicking on the Year displays a scrolling Year selection for quicker Month and Year selections.

16. Press **F5** to build and execute the application.

17. Click the drop-down arrow on the right side of the dateTimePicker1 control.

18. Select the date January 1, 2010.

19. Verify that the date January 1, 2010 was added to the checkListBox1 Input control.

20. In the checkListBox1 Input control, select the January 1, 2010 list item.

21. Click the checkbox next to the January 1, 2010 list item.

22. Verify that the value of the maskedTextBox1 Input control has changed to January 1, 2010, but the date is displayed incorrectly.

23. Click in the far leftmost position in the maskedTextBox1.

24. Enter **0**.

25. Move two characters to the right and enter another **0**.

26. Verify that the date is shifted to the right and is now displayed correctly because you have added the nonrequired number characters.

27. Close Form1.

TAKE NOTE*

The Mask property for the maskedTextBox1 used both the 9, optional numerical value, and 0, required numerical value.

PAUSE. Leave the solution open to use in the next exercise.

You have just created DateTimePicker, MaskedEditBox, and CheckListBox Advanced controls. You used the Format property to determine how the date and time were going to appear in the DateTimePicker control. You used the CheckListBox checkbox click to add the selected date time item to the MaskedEditBox control. You used the Mask property to control the value that can be assigned to the MaskedEditBox control.

Much like the Advanced Input controls, component controls encompass a variety of functionality into one control. The main difference between Advanced Input controls and component controls is the ability of component controls to add an additional property to each control in a container or create a new thread of operation.

Working with Component Controls

Most component controls extend other controls and provide centralized common functionality.

Table 3-6 lists some of the component controls supported by Visual Studio with some of their common properties and methods. Visual Studio supports more than the listed controls. For a full list of controls see the Toolbox window's component controls grouping.

Table 3-6

Component Controls

COMPONENT CONTROL	PROPERTY/METHOD	DESCRIPTION
ErrorProvider		Provides centralized functionality for notifying the user that an error has occurred in the application. Usually the ErrorProvider control is used to notify the user that an input field has an invalid value. The ErrorProvider control has very few properties, but it does add several new properties to every control within the same container control.
	BlinkRate	Determines how fast the icon associated with the error will appear and disappear.
	BlinkStyle	Determines when the icon will blink. The BlinkStyle property can have a value of BlinkIfDifferentError, BlinkAlways, or BlinkNever.
	Icon	Determines what icon appears when the error is displayed.
	GetError (Control control)	Gets the current error string associated with the control specified.
	SetError (Control control, string value)	Sets a string value on the specified control.
HelpProvider		Much like the ErrorProvider control, the HelpProvider control provides centralized functionality for creating a help system. The HelpProvider has very few properties, but it does add several new properties to every control within the same container control.
EventLog		Provides centralized functionality to monitor, add, or delete events from the current machines or from a remove machines event log. Event logs are often used to save error or status messages without notifying the user.
	EnableRaisedEvents	Determines if the EventLog control monitors the Event Logs for changes.

(continued)

Table 3-6 (continued)

COMPONENT CONTROL	PROPERTY/METHOD	DESCRIPTION
	Log	Determines which Event Log to use to monitor or add entries.
	MachineName	Determines the machine name that will be included with each event log entry.
	Source	Determines the source value that will be included with each event log entry.
	Clear ( )	Removes all entries from the event log.
	ModifyOverflowPolicy (OverflowAction action, int retentionDays)	Changes how the Event Log responds when the log has reached the maximum number of entries.
	WriteEntry ( )	Writes an entry to the Event log.
	WriteEvent ( )	Writes an event to the Event log.
BackgroundWorker		Centralizes the functionality of creating new threads of execution. The BackgroundWorker component control is typically used when the application has a process that will take a significant amount of time and you still want to allow the user to continue using the application.
	WorkerReportsProgress	Determines if the BackgroundWorker control will report its progress back to the main thread while executing.
	WorkerSupportsCancellation	Determines if the main thread can cancel the BackgroundWorker control thread.
	IsBusy	A run-time-only property. The IsBusy property is used to see if the BackgroundWorker control thread is still working (busy).
	CancelAsync ( )	Requests the cancellation of the current BackgroundWorker control's thread.
	ReportProgress ( )	Used to send messages from the BackgroundWorker control's thread to the main thread. The main thread will monitor the ProgressChanged event to receive the reports generated using this method.
	RunWorkerAsync ( )	Starts the BackgroundWorker control's thread in an asynchronous process.

 USE THE ERRORPROVIDER CONTROL

USE the project created in the last exercise.

1. Select the Form1.cs [Design] tab.
2. In the Toolbox window, locate the Components grouping and expand the group (Figure 3-18).

Figure 3-18

Components group

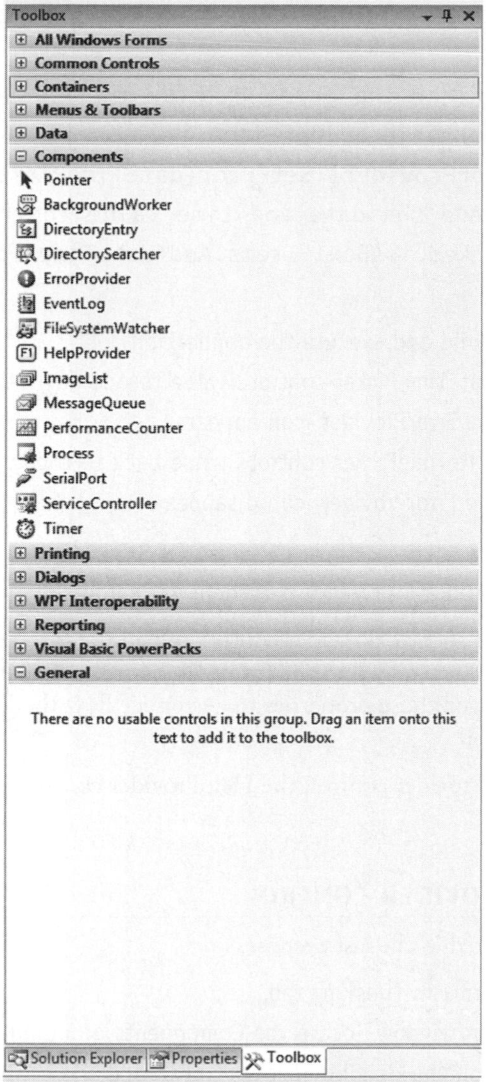

The ErrorProvider control is not added to the Form1 form area. The ErrorProvider control is added at the bottom of the form's Design View window.

3. Double-click on the ErrorProvider control to add the ErrorProvider control to Form1.

4. Select the dateTimePicker1 control.

5. In the Properties window, verify that there are three new properties:
   - Error on errorProvider1
   - IconAlignment on errorProvider1
   - IconPadding on errorProvider1

6. Select the IconPadding on errorProvider1 property and Enter **5**.

7. Select the Form1.cs tab and replace the existing code in the dateTimePicker1_ ValueChanged method with the following:

```
// Check to see if the date and time value
// is greater than the current time.
if (System.DateTime.Now.CompareTo(
    dateTimePicker1.Value) < 0)
        // Set the error provider to warn the user.
        errorProvider1.SetError(dateTimePicker1,
          "Future dates are not allowed.");
```

Once the Error text is assigned for an ErrorProvider, the icon will blink next to the control. You may need to resize your form to ensure that the ErrorProvider Icon is not covered by another control in the form. Also, by setting the ErrorProvider text to an empty string, the ErrorProvider icon is removed.

```
        else
        {
                // Clear the error to hide the
                // error provider icon.
                errorProvider1.SetError(dateTimePicker1, "");
                // Add the date and time value to the ListBox.
                checkedListBox1.Items.Add(dateTimePicker1.Value);
        }
```

8. Press **F5** to build and execute the application.
9. Change the dateTimePicker control's value to one day into the future.
10. Verify that the ErrorProvider icon appears.
11. Change the dateTimePicker control's value back to today.
12. Verify that the ErrorProvider icon disappears.
13. Close Form1.

PAUSE. Leave the solution open to use in the next exercise.

You have just created an ErrorProvider control and added it to a form. When the ErrorProvider control was added to the form, all controls on that form received several new properties. You changed those properties to customize how the ErrorProvider would work for the individual control.

Much like the ErrorProvider control, the HelpProvider control adds several new properties to each control.

USE THE HELPPROVIDER CONTROL

The HelpProvider control is not added to the Form1 form area. The HelpProvider control is added at the bottom of the form's Design View window.

USE the project created in the last exercise.

1. Select the Form1.cs [Design] tab.
2. In the Toolbox window, locate the Components grouping and expand the group.
3. Double-click on the HelpProvider control to add the control to Form1.
4. Select the dateTimePicker1 control.
5. In the Properties window, verify that there are three new properties:
   - HelpKeyword on helpProvider1
   - HelpNavigator on helpProvider1
   - HelpString on helpProvider1
6. Select the HelpString on helpProvider1 property and key **This is the pop-up help for the dateTimePicker1 control**
7. Press **F5** to build and execute the application.
8. Select the dateTimePicker1 control and press **F1**.
9. Verify that the HelpString appears.
10. Close Form1.

PAUSE. Leave the solution open to use in the next exercise.

You have just added a HelpProvider control to a Windows Form and enabled help capabilities for all controls. You set the HelpString property on the dateTimePicker1 control to enable the pop-up help to provide information when F1 is pressed. The HelpProvider control can also be used to link to an external help system by setting the HelpKeyword and HelpNavigator properties.

The EventLog Component control can also be helpful when trying to understand if your application has issues. Use the EventLog control to save entries or events to the Application Event Log, where you can then review them later.

→ USE THE EVENTLOG CONTROL

USE the project created in the last exercise.

TAKE NOTE*

The EventLog control is not added to the Form1 form area. The EventLog control is added at the bottom of the form's Design View window.

1. In the Toolbox window, locate the Components grouping and expand the group.
2. Double-click the EventLog control to add the control to Form1.
3. In the Properties window, set the following properties for the EventLog Control:
   - Log: Application
   - Source: My Windows Forms Application
4. Select the Form1.cs tab.
5. Replace the existing code in the dateTimePicker1_ValueChanged method with the following code:

```
// Check to see if the date and time value is
// greater than the current time.
if (System.DateTime.Now.CompareTo(
   dateTimePicker1.Value) < 0)
       // Set the error provider to warn the user.
       errorProvider1.SetError(dateTimePicker1,
       "Future dates are not allowed.");

else
{
       // Clear the error to hide the
       // error provider icon.
       errorProvider1.SetError(dateTimePicker1, "");
       // Add the date and time value to the ListBox.
       checkedListBox1.Items.Add(dateTimePicker1.Value);
       // Write the event to the event log.
       eventLog1.WriteEntry(
          dateTimePicker1.Value.ToString()
       + " was selected.",
       System.Diagnostics
       .EventLogEntryType.Information);
}
```

TAKE NOTE*

Depending on how Windows was installed, the My Computer icon might be called just Computer and the Computer Management window might have a different set of menu selections.

6. Press **F5** to build and execute the application.
7. Change the dateTimePicker control's value to one day in the past.
8. Close Form1.
9. Locate the My Computer icon on your Desktop or from the Start Menu.
10. Right-click the My Computer icon and Select the Manage menu item to open the Computer Management window.

TAKE NOTE *

Some of the information in the Event Properties dialog will be different as you move from one network and/or machine to another.

11. Double-click the Event Viewer icon to expand the Event Viewer node and the list of Event logs appears on the right-hand side of the window.

12. Double-click the Application list item to see all of the Application Event log entries.

13. Locate the Event Log entered by My Windows Forms Application and double-click to see the Event Properties dialog.

14. Verify that the Description has the date and time selected in the application.

15. Click OK.

16. Close the Computer Management window.

PAUSE. Leave the solution open to use in the next exercise.

You have just created an EventLog control and added it to your Windows Forms Application. You then generated an event based on an action taken on the dateTimePicker1 control. The EventLog can be used both to save entries to the Event Log and to monitor changes in the Event Log.

The BackgroundWorker control is a simplified way to add multi-threading capabilities to your Windows Forms Application. You use the BackgroundWorker control to start and stop asynchronous operations while leaving your main execution thread available to interact with the user.

USE THE BACKGROUNDWORKER CONTROL

USE the project you created in the previous exercise.

1. In the Toolbox window, locate the Components grouping and expand the group.

2. Double-click the BackgroundWorker control to add the control to Form1.

3. In the Properties window, set the following backgroundWorker1 properties:
   - WorkerReportsProgress: True
   - WorkerSupportsCancellation: True

4. Select the Form1.cs tab.

5. Replace the existing code in the dateTimePicker1_ValueChanged method with the following code:

TAKE NOTE *

The BackgroundWorker control is not added to the Form1 form area. The BackgroundWorker control is added at the bottom of the form's Design View window.

```
// Check to see if the date and time value is
// greater than the current time.
if (System.DateTime.Now.CompareTo(
    dateTimePicker1.Value) < 0)
        // Set the error provider to warn the user.
        errorProvider1.SetError(dateTimePicker1,
        "Future dates are not allowed.");

else
{
        // Clear the error to hide the
        // error provider icon.
        errorProvider1.SetError(dateTimePicker1, "");
        // Add the date and time value to the ListBox.
        checkedListBox1.Items.Add(dateTimePicker1.Value);
        // Write the event to the event log.
        eventLog1.WriteEntry(
            dateTimePicker1.Value.ToString()
        + " was selected.",
```

```
              System.Diagnostics.EventLogEntryType.Information);
              // Check to see if the background
              // thread is still working.
              if (!backgroundWorker1.IsBusy)
                      // Background thread is not working,
                      // so start it.
                      backgroundWorker1.RunWorkerAsync();
      }
```

6. Select the Form1.cs [Design] tab.

7. In the Properties window, click the Events button.

8. Locate the DoWork event and double-click in the method selection cell.

9. Key the following code into the backgroundWorker1_DoWork method:

```
// Local variable.
bool keepRunning = true;


// Check to see if the background thread
// should keep running.
while (keepRunning)
{
        // Delay the next loop of processing.
        System.Threading.Thread.Sleep(2000);
        // Show a message box and ask if the user
        // wants to continue the background thread.
        System.Windows.Forms.DialogResult response =
                MessageBox.Show("Background Worker Thread... "
                + "Do you want to continue?",
                + "Working...",
                MessageBoxButtons.OKCancel,
                MessageBoxIcon.Question);
        // Check the message box response
        if (response == DialogResult.Cancel)
        {
            // The user wants to cancel process,
            // stop the looping.
            keepRunning = false;
            // Stop the background thread.
            backgroundWorker1.CancelAsync();
        }
}
```

10. Press **F5** to build and execute the application.

11. Change the dateTimePicker control's value to one day into the past.

12. Verify that after 2 seconds the Working dialog appears. Click OK.

13. Verify that after 2 more seconds the Working dialog appears again.

14. Click Cancel.

15. Verify that the Working dialog does not appear again.

16. Close Form1.

PAUSE. Leave the solution open to use in the next exercise.

You have just created a multi-threaded application. You added the BackgroundWorker control to a Windows Form, and then set some properties to allow the background thread to report back to the main execution thread. You then started the multi-threading process by calling the RunWorkerAsync.

The last of the component controls you will use is the Dialog controls. The Dialog controls provide a set of standard folder browsing, file open and save, and color and font selection functionality.

Working with Dialog Controls

> The Dialog controls provide a centralized functionality for selecting a folder, files, color, or font. Each Dialog control presents the user with an intuitive interface for making an appropriate selection.

Table 3-7 lists all of the Dialog controls supported by Visual Studio with some of their common properties and methods. The Dialog controls can be seen in the Toolbox window's Dialog grouping.

Table 3-7

Dialog Controls

DIALOG CONTROL	PROPERTY/METHOD	DESCRIPTION
ColorDialog		Provides a prebuilt color picker and color management control.
	AllowFullOpen	Determines if the color dialog will show both the Standard color selection and the Custom color selection controls.
	AllowAnyColor	Determines if the color dialog will allow the user to select any color from the Custom color palette.
	Color	The color selected by the user.
	FullOpen	Determines if the Custom colors portion of the color dialog will be visible initially.
	ShowHelp	Determines if the Help button will be visible.
	SolidColorOnly	Determines if the color dialog will show only solid colors.
	ShowDialog ( )	Shows the color dialog form.
FontDialog		Provides a prebuilt font picker and font management control.
	AllowScriptChange	Determines if the user will be allowed to change the font style to script.
	Color	Determines the color of the font.
	Font	Determines the name of the font that is currently selected or defaulted. Use the Font property to assign the selected font to a control.

Table 3-7 (continued)

DIALOG CONTROL	PROPERTY/METHOD	DESCRIPTION
	FontMustExist	Determines if a font must be in the font list for selection.
	ShowApply	Determines if the Apply button will appear. If the ShowApply property is set to True, the user can click the Apply button to see the font applied immediately. To support the Apply button, you must implement the Apply Event.
	ShowColor	Determines if the color selection field is visible in the font dialog.
	ShowEffects	Determines if the effects field is visible in the font dialog.
	ShowHelp	Determines if the Help button will be visible on the font dialog.
	ShowDialog ( )	Shows the font dialog form.
FolderBrowserDialog		Provides a prebuilt File Folder exploration and selection control.
	RootFolder	Determines which file folder will be the root of the folder browser dialog. The root folder is the top-most folder in the folder structure.
	SelectedPath	The full path of the folder that was selected.
	ShowNewFolderButton	Determines if the New Folder button is visible on the folder browser dialog. The New Folder button allows you to add a new folder into the current file folder system without having to leave the folder browser dialog.
	ShowDialog ( )	Shows the folder browser dialog form.
OpenFileDialog		Provides a prebuilt file dialog for opening files in the file system. The OpenFileDialog control implements the standard File → Open functionality.
	AddExtension	Determines if the default extension property's value is added to a file when opened.
	CheckFileExists	Determines if the open file dialog will check to make sure that a file exists when the user clicks OK. If the file does not exist, the open file dialog will display a message to the user notifying him/her.
	CheckPathExists	Determines if the open file dialog will check to make sure that the file path exists when the user clicks OK. If the file path does not exist, the open file dialog will display a message to the user notifying him/her.
	DefaultExtension	Determines a file's initial extension. The DefaultExtension property is used in conjunction with the AddExtension property to manage file extensions.
	Filter	A list of strings that determines the filtering values for the Filter field. The Filter property value is defined as Text Documents|*.txt|All Files|*.*.
	FilterIndex	Determines which of the Filter values will be the default filter.
	InitialDirectory	Determines in what directory the open file dialog will show initially.
	MultiSelect	Determines if the open file dialog can open more than one file at a time. When more than one file is selected, the FileNames property can be used to determine the path and file for all selected files.

(continued)

Table 3-7 *(continued)*

Dialog Control	Property/Method	Description
	ReadOnlyChecked	Determines if the Read Only checkbox on the open file dialog has been checked. To show the Read Only checkbox, use the ShowReadOnly property.
	ShowReadOnly	Determines if the Read Only checkbox will be visible in the open file dialog.
	ShowHelp	Determines if the Help button will be visible in the open file dialog.
	SupportMultiDottedExtensions	Determines if the open file dialog will allow the user to select a file with multiple extensions separated by dots.
SaveFileDialog		Provides a prebuilt file dialog for saving files in the file system. The SaveFileDialog control implements the standard File→Save As functionality.
	AddExtension	Determines if the DefaultExtension's property value will be appended automatically to a file before it is saved.
	CheckFileExists	Determines if the save file dialog will check to see if a file already exists with the same file name and path. If a file already exists, the save file dialog will notify the user of a duplicate name and ask if he/she wants to overwrite it.
	CheckPathExists	Determines if the save file dialog will check to see if a path already exists. If a path already exists, the save file dialog will notify the user of a duplicate path and ask if he/she wants to overwrite.
	CreatePrompt	Determines if the save file dialog will notify the user when the file he/she wants to save does not currently exist and will need to be created.
	DefaultExtension	Determines the file's extension when the AddExtention property is set to True.
	Filename	The value selected by the user in the save file dialog.
	Filter	A list of strings that determines the filtering values for the Filter field. The Filter property values are defined as Text Documents|*.txt|All Files|*.*.
	FilterIndex	Determines which of the Filter values will be the default filter.
	InitialDirectory	Determines in what directory the save file dialog will show initially.
	OverwritePrompt	Determines if the save file dialog will notify the user when a file with same path and name already exists.
	ShowHelp	Determines if the Help button is visible.
	SupportMultiDottedExtensions	Determines if the save file dialog will allow the user to save a file with multiple extensions separated by dots.
	ValidateNames	Determines if the save file dialog will check the FileName property for any invalid characters not allowed in a file name by the operating system.

USE FORMATTING DIALOG CONTROLS

USE the project you created in the previous exercise.

1. Select the Form1.cs [Design] tab.
2. In the Toolbox window, locate and expand the Dialogs grouping (Figure 3-19).

Figure 3-19

Dialogs group

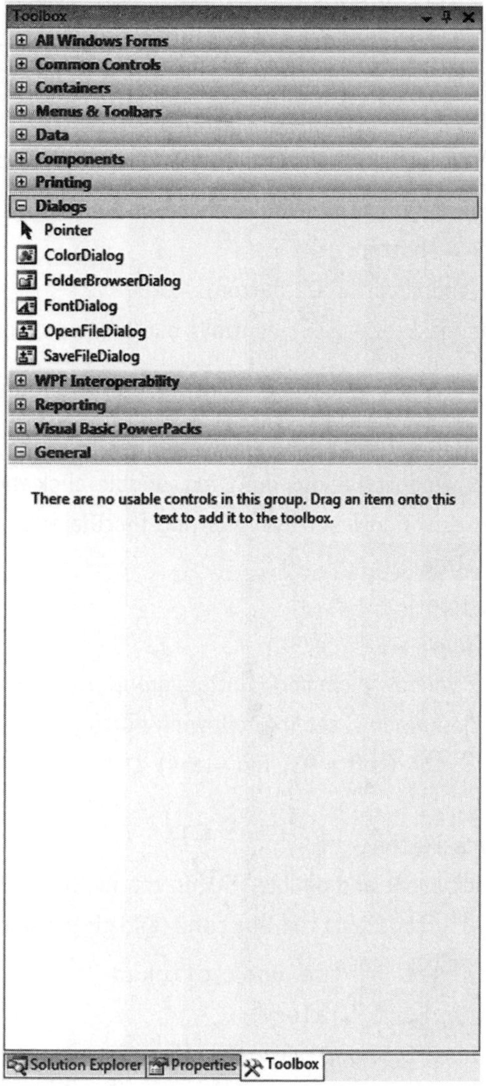

Toolbox

- ⊞ All Windows Forms
- ⊞ Common Controls
- ⊞ Containers
- ⊞ Menus & Toolbars
- ⊞ Data
- ⊞ Components
- ⊞ Printing
- ⊟ Dialogs
  - ⬆ Pointer
  - ColorDialog
  - FolderBrowserDialog
  - FontDialog
  - OpenFileDialog
  - SaveFileDialog
- ⊞ WPF Interoperability
- ⊞ Reporting
- ⊞ Visual Basic PowerPacks
- ⊟ General

There are no usable controls in this group. Drag an item onto this text to add it to the toolbox.

Solution Explorer | Properties | Toolbox

3. Double-click the ColorDialog control.
4. In the Properties window, set the following colorDialog1 properties:
   - AnyColor: True
   - FullOpen: True
   - ShowHelp: True
5. In the Toolbox window, locate and expand the Common Controls grouping.
6. Double-click the Button control.
7. In the Properties window, set the following button1 properties:
   - Location: 12, 164 (Left = 12, Top = 164)
   - Text: Color ...

TAKE NOTE *

The ColorDialog control is not added to the Form1 form area. The ColorDialog control is added at the bottom of the form's Design View window.

8. Click the Events button.

9. Locate the Click event and double-click in the method selection cell.

10. Key the following code into the button1_Click method:

```
// Check if the user pressed the
// Color Dialog's OK button.
if(colorDialog1.ShowDialog() ==
    System.Windows.Forms.DialogResult.OK)
        // The user selected a color, change the
        // MaskedTextBox's background color.
        maskedTextBox1.BackColor = colorDialog1.Color;
```

11. Press **F5** to build and execute the application.

12. Click the Color ... button.

13. Select a color and click the OK button.

14. Verify that the maskedtextBox1 control's background color changed to your selected color.

15. Close Form1.

16. Select the Form1.cs [Design] tab.

17. In the Toolbox window, Dialogs grouping, double-click the FontDialog control.

18. In the Properties window, set the following fontDialog1 properties:
    • ShowApply: True
    • ShowColor: True
    • ShowHelp: True

19. In the Toolbox window, Common Controls grouping, double-click the Button control.

20. In the Properties window, set the following button2 properties:
    • Location: 93, 164 (Left = 93, Top = 164)
    • Text: Font ...

21. Click the Events button.

22. Locate the Click event and double-click in the method selection cell.

23. Key the following code into the button2_Click method:

```
// Check to see if the user clicked
// OK in the Font Dialog.
if (fontDialog1.ShowDialog() ==
    System.Windows.Forms.DialogResult.OK)
{
        // The user selected OK, change the MaskedTextBox
        // Font and Font Color.
        maskedTextBox1.Font = fontDialog1.Font;
        maskedTextBox1.ForeColor =
    fontDialog1.Color;
}
```

24. Select the Form1.cs [Design] tab.

25. In the Properties window, select the fontDialog Control from the controls drop-down list, locate the Apply event, and double-click in the method selection cell.

TAKE NOTE *

If you click on the Help button, nothing will happen. No default help topics are provided for the ColorDialog control. Use the HelpRequest Event to show help when the ColorDialog Help button is pressed.

TAKE NOTE *

The FontDialog control is not added to the Form1 form area. The FontDialog control is added at the bottom of the form's Design View window.

26. Key the following code into the button2_Apply method:

```
// Set the sender parameter of Apply
// event to a FontDialog.
FontDialog fdX = (FontDialog)sender;
// Change the MaskedTextBox Font and Font Color.
maskedTextBox1.Font = fdX.Font;
maskedTextBox1.ForeColor = fdX.Color;
```

27. Press **F5** to build and execute the application.

28. Click the Font ... button.

29. Select a font, select Bold, select Size 16, check Strikeout, and click the Apply button.

30. Verify that all of the changes made thus far have been applied to the maskedTextBox1 control.

31. Select the color red.

32. Click the OK button.

33. Verify that the maskedtextBox1.control's font, including the background color, have been changed to your selection.

34. Close Form1.

STOP. Save or discard the solution. It will not be used again for another exercise.

You have just created a ColorDialog and FontDialog control. You added the ColorDialog and FontDialog controls to a Windows Form and used the controls to set other controls' properties. You used the ColorDialog to select a background color for the masked edit box control. You also used the FontDialog to select the font, size, effect, and color of the same masked edit box control.

More common than the ColorDialog and FontDialog controls are the FolderBrowserDialog, FileOpenDialog, and FileSaveDialog controls. The folder and file dialog controls are typically used for all user interactions when working with folders and files.

➔ USE THE FOLDER AND FILE DIALOG CONTROLS

GET READY. Before you begin these steps, be sure to launch Microsoft Visual Studio and create a new Windows Forms Application project named wfaFoldersFiles.

1. In the Toolbox window, locate the Common Controls grouping and expand the group.

2. Double-click the TextBox control.

3. In the Properties window, set the following textBox1 properties:
   - Location: 12,12 (Top = 12, Left = 12)
   - Size: 268,20 (Width = 268, Height = 20)

4. In the Toolbox window, double-click the Button control.

5. In the Properties window, set the following Button1 properties:
   - Location: 12,38 (Top = 38, Left = 12)
   - Size: 268,23 (Width = 268, Height = 23)
   - Text: Select Folder ...

6. In the Toolbox window, locate the Dialogs grouping and expand the group.

7. Double-click the FolderBrowserDialog control.

8. Select the button1 control, and then in the Properties window click the Events button.

9. Locate the Click event and double-click in the method selection cell.

10. Key the following code into the `button1_Click` Method:

```
// Check to see if the user selected OK on
// the Folder Browser Dialog.
if (folderBrowserDialog1.ShowDialog()
    == DialogResult.OK)
    // User selected a folder, assign the selected
    // path to the TextBox.
textBox1.Text = folderBrowserDialog1.SelectedPath;
```

11. Press **F5** to build and execute the application.

12. Click the Select Folder ... button.

13. Select a folder from the Browse for Folder dialog and click OK.

14. Verify that the selected folder path was populated into the textBox1 control.

15. Close Form1.

16. Add another Button control to Form1.

17. Set the following properties for Button2:
    - Location: 12,67 (Top = 67, Left = 12)
    - Size: 268,23 (Width = 268, Height = 23)
    - Text: Open File ...

18. In the Toolbox window, Dialogs grouping, double-click the OpenFileDialog control.

19. Select the Button2 control

20. In the Properties window, click the Events button.

21. Locate the Click event and double-click in the method selection cell.

22. Key the following code into the `Button2_Click` method:

```
// Check if the user selected OK
// on the Open File Dialog.
if (openFileDialog1.ShowDialog() ==
    DialogResult.OK)
    // The user selected OK, assign the selected
    // file name to the TextBox.
    textBox1.Text = openFileDialog1.FileName;
```

23. Press **F5** to build and execute the application.

24. Click the Open File ... button.

25. Select a file from the Open dialog and click OK.

26. Verify that the selected file, with path, was populated into the textBox1 control.

27. Close Form1.

28. Add another Button control to Form1.

29. Set the following properties for Button3:
    - Location: 12,96 (Top = 96, Left = 12)
    - Size: 268,23 (Width = 268, Height = 23)
    - Text: Save File ...

30. In the Toolbox window, Dialogs grouping, double-click the SaveFileDialog control.

31. Set the following properties for saveDialog1:
    - CreatePrompt: True
    - DefaultExt: txt

32. Select the Button3 control.

33. In the Properties window, click the Events button.

34. Locate the Click event and double-click in the method selection cell.

35. Key the following code into the `Button3_Click` method:

```
// Check if the user selected OK on
// the Save File Dialog.
if (saveFileDialog1.ShowDialog() ==
    DialogResult.OK)
    // The user selected OK, assign the
    // file name to the TextBox.
textBox1.Text = saveFileDialog1.FileName;
```

36. Press **F5** to build and execute the application.

37. Click the Save File ... button.

38. Key **TestFile** into the Name field and click **OK.**

39. Verify that the Save As prompt appears asking if you want to create the file; click Yes.

40. Verify that the TestFile name, with path and default extension, was populated into the textBox1 control.

41. Close Form1.

STOP. Save or discard the solution. It will not be used again for another exercise.

<table>
<tr><td>

CERTIFICATION READY
Can you create Windows Forms Applications by using Visual Studio?
2.1

</td><td>

You have just created a FolderBrowserDialog, an OpenFileDialog and a SaveFileDialog control. You added these controls to a Windows Form and used them to get file and folder names. Using the folder and file dialogs does not constitute the creation or changing of any files. The folder and file dialogs only provide user interfaces into the selection of folder or file names.

</td></tr>
</table>

Creating Custom Windows Forms Controls

↓
THE BOTTOM LINE

Visual Studio comes standard with a number of default controls that you use to create your Windows Forms Application. You can also purchase controls from third-party vendors, like Infragistics or ComponentOne, but you may also need to create your own custom controls or inherit from an already existing control using control inheritance.

Creating a Custom Control Library

When creating a custom control that is not inherited from another control, you will want to use the Windows Forms Control Library Template. Once you have your custom control created, you create properties and methods to give your custom control functionality.

You use the Windows Forms Control Library Template to create a default custom control. The *Windows Forms Control Library* creates a default custom control with a blank control area and the inherited properties and methods from the Windows.Forms.UserControl class. You will need to add more properties and methods to give your custom control more functionality.

→ **USE THE WINDOWS FORMS CONTROL LIBRARY TEMPLATE**

GET READY. Before you begin these steps, be sure to launch Microsoft Visual Studio.

1. From the Start Page, click Create Project to display the New Project Dialog (Figure 3-20).

Figure 3-20

New Project dialog

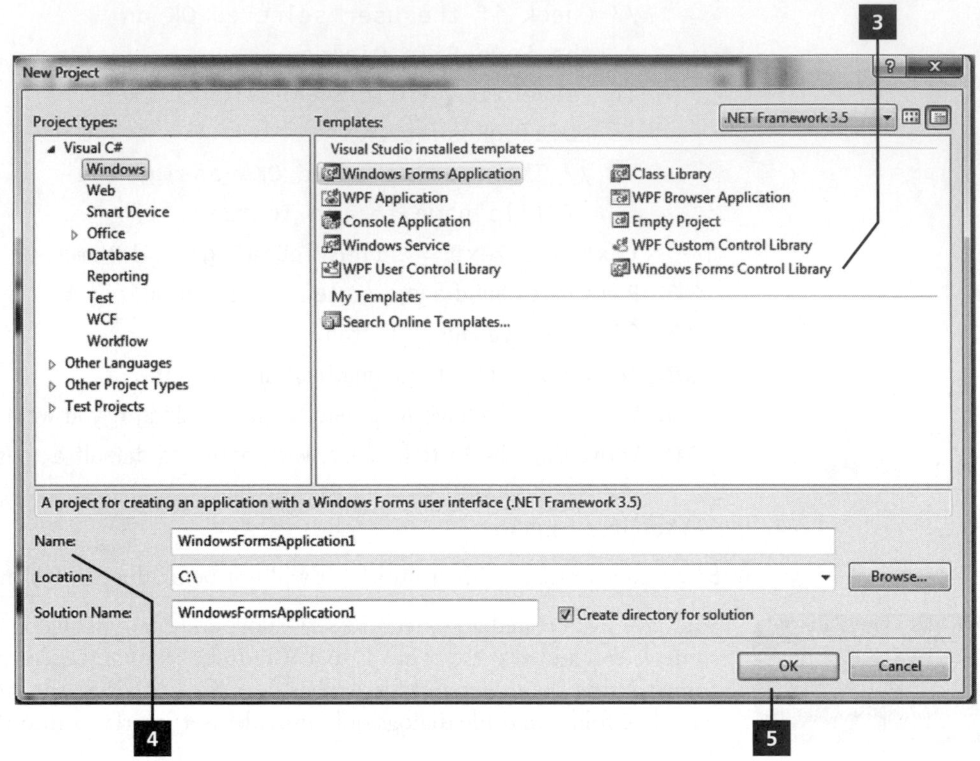

2. In Project types, select Windows.
3. In Templates, select Windows Forms Control Library.
4. Change the Name field to ucMyUserControl.
5. Click OK.
6. Select the userControl1.
7. In the Properties window, locate the Size property and key **243, 26** (Width = 243, Height = 26).
8. In the Toolbox window, double-click the MaskedTextBox control.
9. Set the following properties for maskedTextBox1:
   - Size: 35, 20 (Width = 35, Height = 20)
   - Mask: 990
10. In the Toolbox window, double-click the Label control.
11. Set the following properties for label1:
    - Location: 41,6 (Left = 41, Top = 6)
    - Text: +
12. Add another MaskedTextBox control.
13. Set the following properties for maskedTextBox2:
    - Location: 60,3 (Left = 60, Top = 3)
    - Size: 35, 20 (Width = 35, Height = 20)
    - Mask: 990

TAKE NOTE*

The Mask property uses the character 9 to represent a nonrequired number and a character 0 to represent a required number. For example, a 990 Mask means that the first two characters are numbers but they are not required, but the last character is a number that is required.

14. Add another Label control.

15. Set the following properties for label2:
- Location: 101,6 (Left = 101, Top = 6)
- Text: =

16. In the Toolbox window, double-click the TextBox control.

17. Set the following properties for textBox1:
- Location: 120,3(Left = 120, Top = 3)
- Size: 39, 20 (Width = 39, Height = 20)
- Locked: True

18. In the Toolbox window, double-click the Button control.

19. Set the following properties for Button1:
- Location: 165, 1(Left = 165, Top = 1)
- Text: Add

20. In the Toolbox window, click the Events button.

21. Locate the Click event and double-click in the method selection cell.

22. Replace the button1_Click method with the following code:

TAKE NOTE *

You will need to change the `button1_Click` event declaration to include the **protected virtual** definitions.

```
// button1_Click Event Method
// This method has been made virtual such that
// it can be overridden by inherited classes.
protected virtual void button1_Click(
    object sender, EventArgs e)
{
        // Check if both MaskedTextBoxes have a value.
        if (!string.IsNullOrEmpty(maskedTextBox1.Text) &&
            !string.IsNullOrEmpty(maskedTextBox2.Text))
                // Both MaskedTextBoxes have values, append
                // the two values into a string in TextBox1.
                textBox1.Text = (int.Parse(maskedTextBox1.Text) +
        int.Parse(maskedTextBox2.Text)).ToString();
}
```

23. Press **F5** to build and test the user control.

24. Verify that the user control is loaded into the UserControl TestContainer window (Figure 3-21).

Figure 3-21

UserControl TestContainer
window

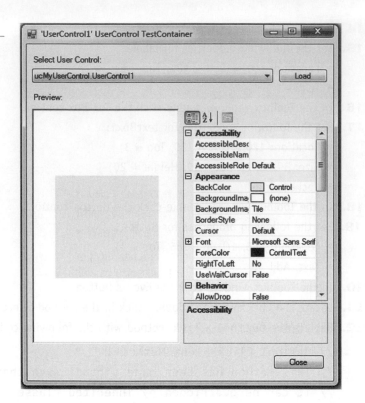

25. Select the maskedTextBox1control and key **30**

26. Press **Tab**.

27. Select the maskedTextBox2 control and key **40**

28. Click Add.

29. Verify that the textBox1 now shows the value 70.

30. Click Close.

PAUSE. Leave the solution open to use in the next exercise.

You have just created a custom user control. Your user control is comprised of six other controls. You organized the controls on the user control to create the user interface's functionality. You added a protected virtual method with a base set of processing.

Earlier in this lesson, you used the Properties window to set a control's properties. Your new custom user control needs to be extended to create its own properties.

➔ **USE WINDOWS FORMS CONTROL LIBRARY PROPERTIES**

USE the project you created in the previous exercise.

1. Just above the UserControl1 constructor, key the following code:

```
// Local variable
private int m_Threshold = 0;
// Public property
public int Threshold
{
    get { return m_Threshold; }
    set { m_Threshold = value; }
}
```

2. Replace the code in the `button1_Click` method with the following:

```
// Check if both MaskedTextBoxes have values.
if (!string.IsNullOrEmpty(maskedTextBox1.Text) &&
!string.IsNullOrEmpty(maskedTextBox2.Text))
{
        // Append both MaskedTextBoxes together
        // and assign to TextBox1.
        textBox1.Text = (int.Parse(maskedTextBox1.Text)
          + int.Parse(maskedTextBox2.Text)).ToString();

        // Check if TextBox is greater than the threshold.
        if (int.Parse(textBox1.Text) > m_Threshold)
                // Over the threshold, change the
                // TextBox1 font color.
                textBox1.ForeColor = Color.Red;
        else
                // Below the threshold, change the
                // TextBox1 font color.
                textBox1.ForeColor = Color.Black;
}
```

3. Press **F5** to build and test the user control.
4. In the Properties List on the right-hand side of the User Control Test Container dialog, locate the Threshold property and key **100**
5. Key two numbers into the User Control whose sum is greater than 100 but less than 1000.
6. Click Add.
7. Verify that the sum in textBox1 now has a ForeColor of red.
8. Locate the Threshold property and key **2000**
9. Click Add.
10. Verify that the sum in textBox1 now has a ForeColor of black.
11. Close the UserControl TestContainer dialog.

PAUSE. Leave the solution open to use in the next exercise.

You have just created a custom user control property called Threshold. You created a local variable to save the Threshold value, and a property method to get and set the local variable's value. When your user control is used in an application, the Threshold property is visible and editable to the end user. You changed the Threshold property's value in the Properties window that then affected the user control's functionality.

Rather than creating a custom user control from a blank user control, use inheritance to derive a new custom user control from an already built control.

Inheriting a Custom Control Library

New custom user controls can be created from existing controls by using inheritance. When you create a custom user control based on an already existing control, you can extend the base control to create a new custom user control.

Custom user controls support standard inheritance declarations. Depending on how the base control was declared and created, a new customer user control can override or extend existing functionality. In the first exercise for this lesson, you created a method with a protected virtual declaration. You can now use the Inherited User Control template to create a new user control based on an existing control. You can also override the virtual declaration with new functionality.

 INHERIT A CONTROL LIBRARY

USE the project you created in the previous exercise.

1. Select Project→Add User Control and the Add New Item dialog appears (Figure 3-22).

Figure 3-22

Add New Item dialog

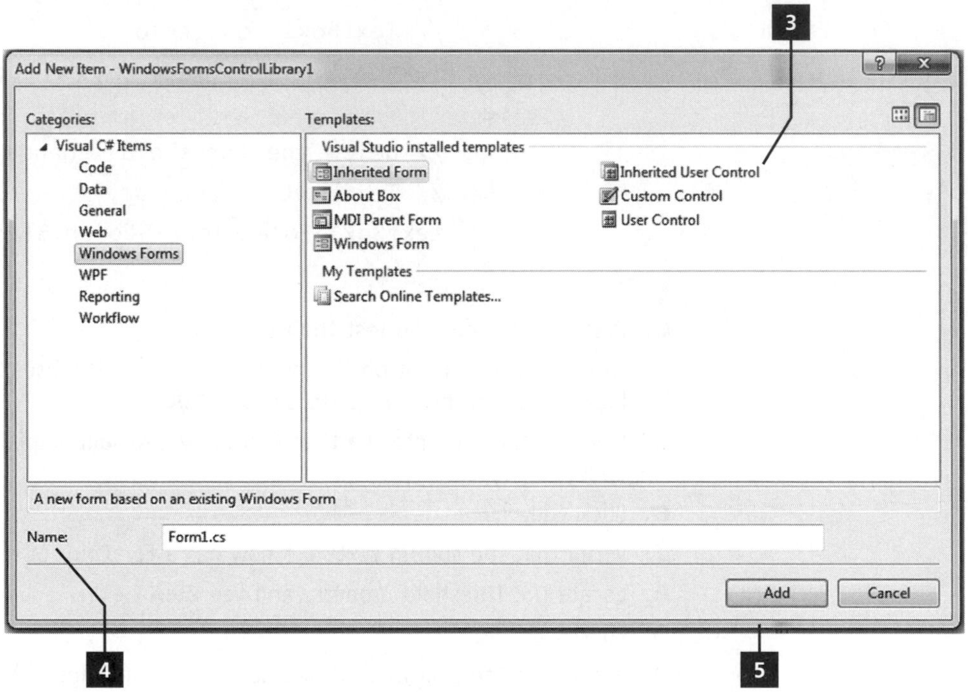

3

| Add New Item - WindowsFormsControlLibrary1 | ? X |

Categories: Templates: ⊞ ▢

▲ Visual C# Items   Visual Studio installed templates
    Code   🗋 Inherited Form   🗋 Inherited User Control
    Data   🗋 About Box   ✓ Custom Control
    General   🗋 MDI Parent Form   🗋 User Control
    Web   🗋 Windows Form
    Windows Forms   My Templates
    WPF   🗋 Search Online Templates...
    Reporting
    Workflow

A new form based on an existing Windows Form

Name: Form1.cs

                                                                    Add   Cancel

4   **5**

2. Select Windows Forms in the Categories list.
3. Select Inherited User Control in the Templates list.
4. In the Name field key **iucMyControl**
5. Click Add and the Inheritance Picker dialog appears (Figure 3-23).

Figure 3-23

Inheritance Picker dialog

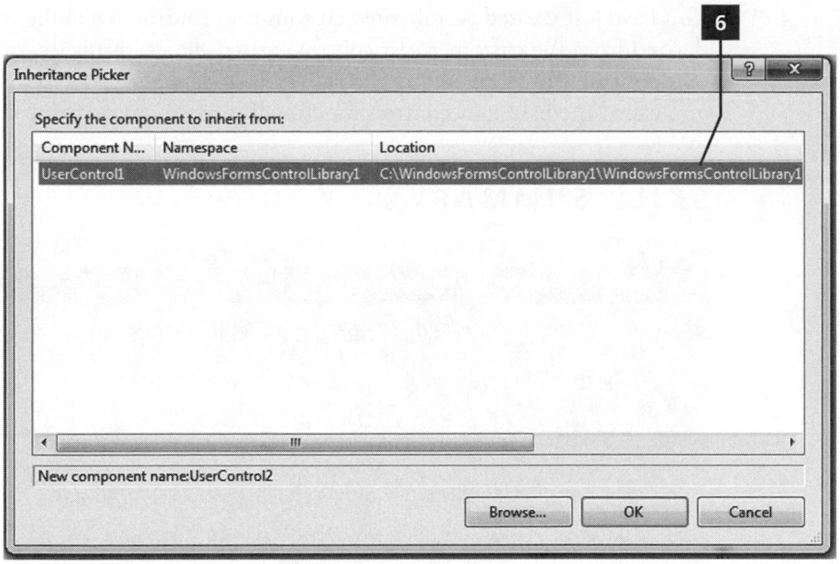

6. Select UserControl1 and click OK.
7. In Solution Explorer, locate the iucMyControl.cs item, right-click to display the Solution Explorer pop-up menu and select the View Code menu item.
8. Select the iucMyControl.cs tab.
9. Just after the iucMyControl constructor, key the following code:

```
// This method overrides the button1_Click event
// in the base class.
protected override void button1_Click(
    object sender, EventArgs e)
{
    //Check to see if the threshold is greater than 0.
    if (this.Threshold > 0)
        // Call the base class button1_Click event.
        base.button1_Click(sender, e);
}
```

10. Press **F5** to build and test the user control.
11. In the Select User Control field, ensure that the UserControl2 is selected.
12. In the first masked textbox, key **10**
13. Press **Tab.**
14. Key **10**
15. Click Add.
16. Observe that sum field does not change.
17. Locate the Threshold property and key **10**
18. Click Add.
19. Verify that the sum field has the value 20 and the ForeColor is Red.
20. Click Close.

CERTIFICATION READY
Do you know how to create Custom Windows Forms Controls?
2.3

STOP. Save or discard the solution. It will not be used again for another exercise.

You have just created an inherited custom user control. The inherited custom user control was derived from the customer user control created earlier in this lesson. You modified the derived user control's functionality by overriding the `button1_click` event. In the overridden method, you called the base user controls functionality after you performed your own functionality.

SKILL SUMMARY

IN THIS LESSON YOU LEARNED HOW TO:

- Create a Windows Forms Application and modify its properties using the Properties window.

- Inherit a Windows Form based on another Windows Form.

- Create a Windows Forms control, arrange the Windows Forms control on the Windows Forms area using the Properties window and the Design View editor, and modify various Windows Forms controls properties and methods to demonstrate most controls' functionality.

- Create a Custom User Control and add other controls to create a new control.

- Inherit a Custom User Control and override the derived controls' functionality.

■ Knowledge Assessment

Fill in the Blank

Complete the following sentences by writing the correct word or words in the blanks provided.

1. A Windows Forms Application where the Windows Forms operate independently of each other is called a _____.

2. You use the _____ declaration in the base class method when you want to allow a change in the methods behavior in a derived class.

3. The _____ property on a ToolStripStatusItem allows the control to grow and shrink based on the StatusStrip controls contents.

4. A Windows Forms Application where the Windows Forms are encompassed into a parent Windows Form is called a _____.

5. The _____ property on a MaskedEditBox control determines how and what will be entered into the control.

6. You use the _____ declaration in the derived class method when you want to change the methods behavior in the base class.

7. The _____ template enables you to create a custom user control based on an existing control.

8. A control that can hold other controls is called a _____.

9. The _____ property on a Basic Input control determines how the control will move or resize when the Windows Form is resized.

10. The _____ template enables you to create a blank custom user control.

Multiple Choice

Circle the letter that corresponds to the best answer.

1. Which of the following controls is a component control?
   a. ErrorHelper
   b. ProcessWorker
   c. MaskedEditBox
   d. MediaPlayer

2. Which of the following ways is NOT a method for setting Windows Forms properties?
   a. Design View editor
   b. Toolbox window
   c. Properties window
   d. Code View editor

3. What Windows Forms property is set to True to convert a Windows Form into a Multiple Document Windows Form?
   a. MdiContainer
   b. ParentContainer
   c. ContainsChildForms
   d. IsMdiContainer

4. Which of the following methods creates an inherited Windows Form?
   a. Add New Item
   b. Code
   c. Add New Windows Form
   d. All of the above

5. Which of the following is NOT a Container control?
   a. TabControl
   b. PanelControl
   c. GroupControl
   d. TreeViewControl

6. Which of the following control types can a ToolStripMenuItem or a ToolStripButtonItem be converted to?
   a. ListBox
   b. ProgressBar
   c. ComboBox
   d. ListView

7. Which of the following methods is NOT supported by the ListBox Items collection?
   a. Add ( )
   b. Clear ( )
   c. Delete ( )
   d. Remove ( )

8. Which of the following Dialog controls interacts only with file folders?
   a. SaveDialog
   b. OpenDialog
   c. FolderBroswerDialog
   d. OpenFolderDialog

9. Which of the following steps is required to create a property for a Windows Forms User Control?
   a. Declare a local variable to hold the property value.
   b. Declare get and set methods.
   c. Declare a public variable.
   d. All of the above

10. How many controls can a *user control* contain?
   a. One
   b. Two
   c. Ten
   d. Unlimited

■ Competency Assessment

Scenario 3-1: Contact Information

You have been given the Use Case requirement to have your application provide a mechanism to gather a user's contact information. Create a Windows Forms Application with one Windows Form. On your Windows Form include a way to gather a user's full address, phone number, and e-mail address. Make sure to take into account correct data formatting, control layout, and resizing.

Scenario 3-2: Error Messages

You showed your supervisor the contact information prototype and he/she asked where the error message would be displayed to indicate if the e-mail address did not have a "@" symbol. Enhance your contact information form to include an error provider for the e-mail address field.

■ Proficiency Assessment

Scenario 3-3: File Browsing

After reviewing the contact information prototype with users, the Use Case requirements were updated to include an area to capture a contact's photo. Enhance your contact information form to include a place to display a photo and provide a button to browse the user's computer for the contact's picture. Make sure to take into account your already existing controls layout and resizing properties when adding the new controls.

Scenario 3-4: Multiple Contact Information Forms

Your supervisor has reviewed your single-form prototype and asked to see what a multiple-form prototype would look like. The users have only asked for one contact to be open at a time, but your supervisor would like to present them with both options to help them understand the difference. Convert your single-document Windows Forms Application into a default multiple-document Windows Forms Application where multiple contact information forms can be displayed at one time. Provide a menu or toolbar navigation control to launch multiple forms. Each form's appearance and functionality should be exactly the same, except that the name of each contact should be appended to the form's caption.

Scenario 3-5: Custom Picture Control

The users really liked the multiple-document prototype, but during the demonstration they observed that the contact's picture was an empty space until a picture was loaded. The Use Case requirements were updated to have the contact's picture show "Not Available" until a picture is loaded. Create a custom control library that combines the picture control with a label to demonstrate this new requirement. Replace your existing picture control with your new custom control library.

Controlling Application Execution

LESSON SKILL MATRIX

SKILLS/CONCEPTS	MTA EXAM OBJECTIVE	MTA EXAM OBJECTIVE NUMBER
Working with Events in Windows Forms	Create and handle events.	2.1
Working with Events in WPF	Supplemental	
Working with Windows Service Applications	Create a Windows Service application.	3.1
Debugging Windows Service Applications	Debug a Windows-based application.	2.5
Working with Windows Service Applications	Install a Windows Service application.	3.2

KEY TERMS

Attach Process

Breakpoint

Bubbling Routed events

Direct Routed events

event handler

Event Handler method

events

Handled property

Property Changed Events

raising events method

Routed events

ServiceBase class

Tunneling Routed events

Your organization chose to create three different applications to meet very specific needs. You have completed the prototype UIs. Now they want to see some of the basic functionality. Your Windows Forms Application and WPF application will need to implement functionality that interacts with the operating system, input devices like a mouse or keyboard, and property changes inside the application. Your Windows Service application will also need to implement the basic Services Control Management (SCM) functionality. In addition, your organization would like a demonstration of how you plan to debug the application's functionality to ensure that the finished product will operate within specifications.

Working with Events in Windows Forms

↓
THE BOTTOM LINE
Throughout a Windows Forms Application's life cycle, it is constantly responding to device inputs and operating system actions called events. Your Windows Forms Application will process and respond to events by implementing event handlers. When needed, you can also raise your own events in response to application functionality.

Creating Windows Forms Events

To respond to and process Windows Forms events, you will implement event handlers by associating an event method. Event methods can be associated with multiple events and can be created through the Visual Studio development environment or in code.

Whenever a Windows Forms Application is executed, the operating system begins to put the Windows Forms Application into an executable life cycle. During the Windows Forms Application lifecycle, the Windows Forms Application will receive *events*, which are notifications about the executable action or about input device actions. Table 4-1 lists some of the common Windows Forms operating system and input device events and identifies the initiator for that event.

Table 4-1

Common Windows Forms Events

Event	Initiator	Description
Load	Operating System	Initiated by the operating system when the Windows Form is first being brought into memory. Use the Load event to initialize variables and perform tasks that need to occur before the Windows Form is displayed to the user.
Shown	Operating System	Initiated by the operating system just after the Windows Form is displayed to the user. Use this event as the last place to set variables and perform tasks once the Windows Form is displayed but before the user can interact with the UI.
FormClosing	Operating System	Initiated by the operating system when the Windows Form is about to be removed from the operating system's memory. Use this event to clean up variables, prompt the user if he/she really wants to close, or cancel the closing if the form is not ready.
FormClosed	Operating System	Initiated by the operating system when the Windows Form has been removed from memory. Use this event to finish any cleanup.
Click	Input Device	Initiated by an input device when the input device performs a click action. Use this event to perform any operations that depend on the input device's click action.

Table 4-1 (*continued*)

Event	Initiator	Description
DoubleClick	Input Device	Initiated by an input device when the input device performs a double-click action. Use this event to perform any operations that depend on the input device's double-click action.
Enter	Input Device	Initiated by an input device when the input device is over the form's area. Use this event to determine when the user has placed an input device over the form.
Leave	Input Device	Initiated by an input device when the input device exits the form's area. Use this event to determine when the user has removed the input device from the form's area.
KeyPress	Input Device	Initiated by an input device when the input device performs a keypress action. Use this event to determine what key(s) were pressed.
Resize	Operating System	Initiated by the operating system when the Windows Form changes dimensions. Use this event to change child control properties or adjust UI attributes that depend on the Windows Form's size property.

To enable your Windows Forms Application to react to operating system and input device actions you implement event handlers (Figure 4-1). An *event handler* is a delegate method used to process the information provided by the event. A delegate is a class that can reference a method with a predefined parameter signature. A Windows Forms Application has the EventHandler class that subscribes events with event handler methods. All event handler methods must have the following parameter declarations:

```
(object sender, EventArgs e)
```

When you use Visual Studio, event methods with the correct parameter declarations are automatically generated. You can write your own event methods and still use the Visual Studio Properties window to associate your event methods to events. The advantage of creating your own event methods is that you can group similar functionality into one event method and then associate the event method with multiple events.

Event handlers are defined by using the Properties window or by implementing code in the Form.Designer.cs file's design generated code area. When using Visual Studios WYSIWYG Design Editor and Properties window, you can generate event methods and event handler associations automatically. You can also manually code your event methods and event handler associations by changing the code in the Form.Designer.cs file.

TAKE NOTE*

Changing code in the Form.Designer.cs file is not the preferred method for editing event handlers. You will find that removing event handler references in the Properties window does not always automatically update the Form.Designer.cs file. When this occurs, you will have errors that can only be fixed by editing the Form.Designer.cs file directly.

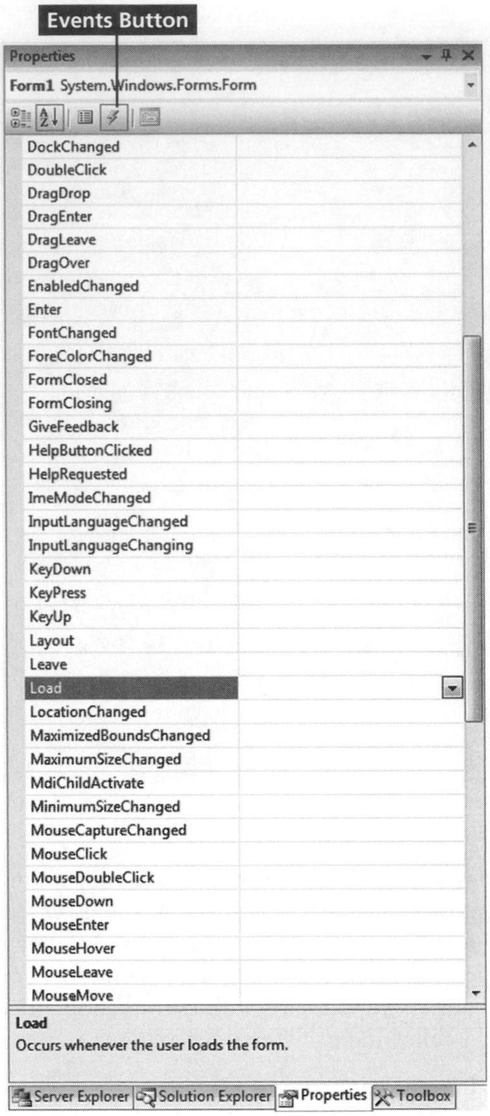

Figure 4-1

Properties window showing events

Events Button

⚠️ **WARNING** Visual Studio is designed to automatically manage event handlers. Thus if you manage event handlers manually, you risk creating a conflict between Visual Studio and your manual code. It is better to allow Visual Studio to manage your event handlers.

TAKE NOTE*

Table 4-2 shows some of the Property Changed events for a Windows Form, but some of these same events are also on other controls.

In addition to operating system and input device events, Visual Studio also provides a set of events that react to class property changes. A **Property Changed event** is an event that is generated when the value of a Windows Form or control property (for example, the background or size property) changes. Table 4-2 lists some of the common Windows Forms Property Changed events.

Table 4-2

Common Windows Forms Property Changed Events

EVENT	DESCRIPTION
SizeChanged	Initiated when the Windows Forms Width or Height property values change. Use this event much like the Resize event to manipulate controls when the Windows Form changes size.
VisibilityChanged	Initiated when the Visibility property value changes. Use this event to determine when the Windows Form is being displayed or hidden from the user.
TextChanged	Initiated when the Text property value changes. Use this event to monitor when the title of the Windows Form is being changed.
LocationChanged	Initiated when the Top and/or Left property values change. Use this event to determine if the Windows Form is being moved from one location to another.

→ USE WINDOWS FORMS EVENTS

If you are unable to find the Properties window or the Events button on the Properties window toolbar, please see Figure 4-1 or the Properties Window section in Lesson 3, "Creating a Windows Forms User Interface."

X REF

GET READY. Before you begin these steps, be sure to launch Microsoft Visual Studio and create a new Windows Forms Application named wfaEvents.

1. Select the Form1.cs [Design] tab and click on the Form1 Window.
2. Locate and select the Properties window.
3. Click on the Events button in the Properties window toolbar.
4. Locate the Load event and click the down arrow on the event selection cell.
5. Verify that the event selection list is currently empty.
6. Double-click inside of the event selection cell to automatically create a Load event.
7. Verify that the Form1.cs tab is selected, and that the cursor is inside of the private void Form1_Load(object sender, EventArgs e) method.
8. Key the following code inside of the Form1_Load method:

   ```
   // Set the form's caption to a title
   // and the current date/time.
   Text = "My Events Application - " + DateTime.Now;
   ```

9. Press **F5** to build and execute the application.
10. Verify that the Windows Forms Application has the title My Events Application, plus the current date and time.
11. Close the My Events Application window.
12. In the Solution Explorer, locate the Form1.cs item and expand the node.
13. Double click on the Form1.Designer.cs item to open the Form1.Designer.cs tab.
14. Locate the Windows Form Designer generated code region and expand the region to show the generated code.
15. Locate the following line of code where the delegate Form1_Load is subscribing to the Load event:

    ```
    Load += new System.EventHandler(Form1_Load);
    ```

16. Verify that the Form's Load event has been subscribed with the Form1_Load delegate as a new event handler.
17. Immediately below the code in step 14, key the following code:

    ```
    // Manually adding my own event handler,
    // for demonstration only, use the Properties window.
    Click += new System.EventHandler(Form1_Load);
    ```

18. Press **F5** to build and execute the application.
19. Verify that the My Events Application window has the date and time in the title.
20. Click in the My Events Application window.
21. Verify that the My Events Application window's title changes to a different date and time.
22. Close My Events Application.
23. Select the Form1.cs [Design] tab and select the Form1.
24. In the Properties window, verify that the Click event shows the Form1_Load method.
25. Select the Form1.cs tab.

TAKE NOTE ✱

Adding code directly into the Form.Designer.cs file is not good coding practice. You should use the Properties Window Event List to map the Form1_Load method to the Click event. This step is strictly used to show you what Visual Studio is automatically generating.

TAKE NOTE ✱

You may need to resize the My Events Application window to see the full date and time value.

26. Immediate following the Form1_Load method, key the following code:

```
// Create a common event handler method.
private void UpdateFormTitleWithDateAndTime (
    object sender, EventArgs e)
{
    // Change the form's caption to a title
    // and the current date/time.
    Text = "My Events Application - " + DateTime.Now;
}
```

27. Select the Form1.cs [Design] tab and select the Form1.
28. In the Properties window, locate the Click event and click the drop-down arrow in the event selection cell.
29. Verify that the UpdateFormTitleWithDateAndTime method is now displayed in the drop-down list.
30. Select the UpdateFormTitleWithDateAndTime method.
31. Locate the Load event and select the UpdateFormTitleWithDateAndTime method.
32. Press **F5** to build and execute the application.
33. Verify that the My Events Application window has the date and time in the title.
34. Click in the My Events Application window.
35. Verify that the My Events Application window's title changes to a different date and time.
36. Close My Events Application.

STOP. Save or discard the solution. It will not be used again for another exercise.

CERTIFICATION READY
Do you know how to create and handle events?
2.1

You have just created two new event handlers for your Windows Forms Application. You used the Properties window to place the first event handler on the Windows Form Load event. You then used code to add your second event handler to the Windows Form Click event. Because the Load event and the Click event were performing the same operation, you created a new shared Event Handler method with the correct event handler class parameters to centralize your functionality and set the Windows Forms event handlers to the new Event Handler method.

The operating system and input devices are not the only things that can initiate an event. Because your event methods are simply methods with a defined parameter list, they can be called just like any other method.

Raising Windows Forms Events

There will be times when you need to simulate activities within your application as if you were the user. The process of initiating event handlers without using the operating system or an input device is called *raising events*.

For each event that a Windows Forms Application wants to handle, an Event Handler method is created to process the object and its arguments. An Event Handler method is simply a method with predefined parameters; thus an Event Handler method can be called like any other method in your application. To call an Event Handler method outside of an event handler, make a method call just like any other method call. The following code demonstrates how to call an Event Handler method from within another method:

```
private void ResetForm()
{

        EventArgs e = null;
        // Calling an Event Handler from a method
        this.Form1_Load (this, e);
}
private void Form1_Load(object sender, EventArgs e)
{

        //...

}
```

Although this book provides examples using the C# programming language, it should be mentioned that VB .NET has a RaiseEvent method that is not defined in C#. The RaiseEvent method is used to raise any Event Handler method in the application. In the .NET Framework there are several Control RaiseXXXEvent methods where the XXX stands for mouse, key, or drag actions. According to the .NET Framework documentation, these methods support the .NET infrastructure and are not intended for direct use.

■ Working with Events in WPF

THE BOTTOM LINE

Much like a Windows Forms Application, a WPF application also receives events from the operating system and input device actions, but WPF introduces the concept of *Routed* events. ***Routed events*** have the capability of being handled by more than one event method called listeners. WPF also supports Attached, Changed Property, and Life cycle events.

Creating Routed Events

There are three types of Routed events: Bubbling, Direct, and Tunneling (Figure 4-2). The way in which you want to process your WPF events dictates which type of Routed event you will implement. Table 4-3 describes the types of Routed events.

Figure 4-2

WPF Routed events

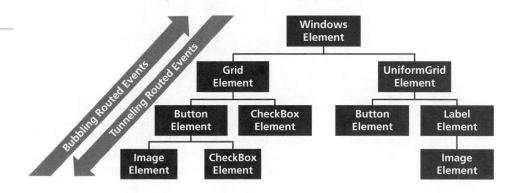

Table 4-3

Routed Event Types

TYPE	DESCRIPTION
Bubbling	Start with the event source and move to the parent of each control in the application control hierarchy, processing the same event at each level as the event bubbles up the control hierarchy. An example of using Bubbling Routed events would be if you had a Window, with a Grid inside the Window, with a Button inside the Grid, with a Label inside the Button, and you double-clicked on the Label. The DoubleClick event method for the Label would receive the event and process the information, and then WPF would pass the event up the control hierarchy to the Button control. The DoubleClick event method for the Button would receive the event, process the information, and then WPF would pass the event up the control hierarchy to the Window. The Grid control does not support the DoubleClick event; thus WPF passes the event up the control hierarchy to the next control that supports the event. The DoubleClick event method for the Window would receive the event and process the information, and the event would be done. Use Bubbling Routed events when you want to allow parent controls to receive the same event notifications as their child controls.
Tunneling	Start with the highest parent of the event source in the control hierarchy and then move down the hierarchy to each child control that is a parent control of the event source. An example of using Tunneling would be if you had a Window, with a Grid inside the Window, with a Button inside the Gird, with a Label inside the Button, and you double-clicked on the Label. The Preview DoubleClick event method for the Window would receive the event and process the information, and then WPF would pass the event down the control hierarchy to the Button. The Grid control does not support the Preview DoubleClick event, and thus WPF passed the event down the hierarchy to the next control. The Preview DoubleClick event method for the Button would receive the event and process the information, and then WPF would pass the event down the control hierarchy to the Label. The DoubleClick event method for the Label would receive the event and process the information and the event would be done. Use Tunneling Routed events when you want to allow parent controls to receive events before the source. When implementing a centralized event processing design, you will use Tunneling Routed events to capture events at the highest control hierarchy possible.
Direct	Start with the event source and move nowhere else. Neither the parent controls nor child controls are passed the event information. Direct Routed events is the same way that Windows Forms handle events.

When implementing Routed events you will control which level in the hierarchy of controls terminates the event processing by using the Handled property. The ***Handled property*** is a member of the EventArgs parameter for all events that notifies WPF if the event should be passed to the next control. If an event wants to stop the Bubbling or Tunneling of the event, the event will set the Handled property to True and WPF will stop passing the event to the next control.

To add a Routed event to a control, you will use the XAML declaration for the event handler. For Bubbling Routed events, use the non-Preview (regular) event handlers, and for Tunneling

Routed events, use the Preview event handlers. The Routed event handlers will have the value of the method in code that implements the Routed Event Handlers method. The following is an example of a bubbling Routed event handler XAML declaration:

```
<Button MouseDoubleClick="Button_MouseDoubleClick">
```

You can also use the style element called EventSetter to set an event on all controls of a certain type. The following is an example of an EventSetter XAML declaration:

```
<Style TargetType="{x:Type Button}">
    <EventSetter Event="Click" Handler="Button_Click"/>
</Style>
```

→ USE WPF ROUTED EVENTS

GET READY. Before you begin these steps, be sure to launch Microsoft Visual Studio and create a new WPF application named wpfRoutedEvents.

1. Select the Window1.xaml tab, then select the XAML tab.
2. Locate the Grid XAML declaration and place your cursor between the opening and closing elements.
3. Key the following XAML code:

```
<!-- Create a button with two event handlers for
  the mouse double-click (bubbling event) and
  preview mouse double-click (tunneling event).-->
<Button
  MouseDoubleClick="Button_MouseDoubleClick"
  PreviewMouseDoubleClick=
  "Button_PreviewMouseDoubleClick">
      <!-- Create a label with one event handler
          for the mouse double-click. -->
      <Label
        MouseDoubleClick="Label_MouseDoubleClick">
        Double-click Me ... </Label>
</Button>
```

4. Locate the following line of XAML code:

```
Title="Window1" Height="300" Width="300"
```

The Height and Width values may be different from the code sample.

5. Immediately following the XAML code in step 4, key the following Tunneling Routed event XAML code:

```
PreviewMouseDoubleClick=
```

6. Verify that when you keyed the equals sign you see the New Event Handler pop-up menu (Figure 4-3).

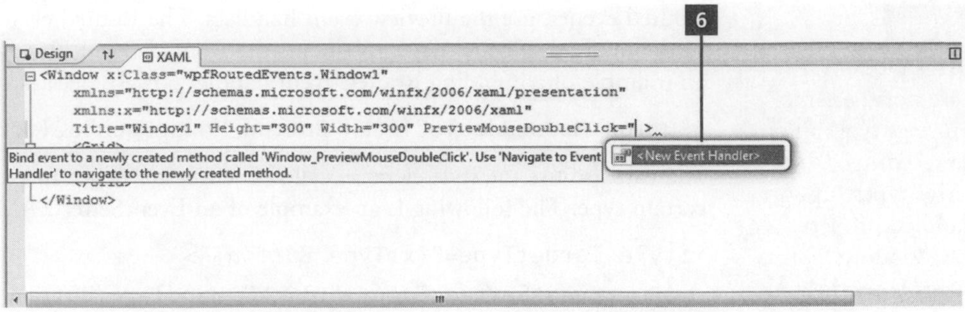

Figure 4-3

New Event Handler pop-up menu

7. Select New Event Handler.

8. Verify that your line of XAML code is the same as the following XAML code:

   Title="Window1" Height="300" Width="300"

   PreviewMouseDoubleClick=

   "Window_PreviewMouseDoubleClick">

9. Place your cursor over the Label_MouseDoubleClick XAML code and right-click to display the XAML Editor pop-up menu.

10. Select Navigate to Event Handler.

11. Inside the Label_MouseDoubleClick method, key the following code:

    // Change the form's caption to show which
    // event handler is being processed.
    this.Title = "Label Event Handler";

12. Inside the Button_MouseDoubleClick method, key the following code:

    // Change the form's caption to show which
    // event handler is being processed.
    this.Title = "Button Event Handler";

13. Locate the Button_PreviewMouseDoubleClick method and inside the method, key the following code:

    // Change the form's caption to show which
    // event handler is being processed.
    this.Title = "Button Preview Event Handler";

14. Inside the Window_PreviewMouseDoubleClick method, key the following code:

    // Change the form's caption to show which
    // event handler is being processed.
    this.Title = "Window Preview Event Handler";

15. Press **F5** to build and execute the application.

16. Double-click the Double Click Me label.

17. Verify that the Window title changed to Button Event Handler. The DoubleClick event started tunneling at the Window Preview event, went to the Button Preview event, went to the Label event, then starting bubbling by going to the Button event.

18. Close Window1.

19. At the end of the Button_PreviewMouseDoubleClick method, add the following code:

    // Event has been handled.
    e.Handled = true;

TAKE NOTE*

Tunneling events occur first. The Bubbling events begin after Tunneling events are done.

20. Press **F5** to build and execute the application.

21. Double-click the Double Click Me label.

22. Verify that the Window title changed to Button Preview Event Handler. The DoubleClick event started tunneling at the Window Preview event, went to the Button Preview event, and the Handled property was set to True; thus no more events were processed.

23. Close Window1.

24. Delete the code added in step 19.

25. Locate the `Button_MouseDoubleClick` method and at the end of this method add the following code:

```
// Event has been handled.
e.Handled = true;
```

26. Press **F5** to build and execute the application.

27. Double-click the Double Click Me label.

28. Verify that the Window title changed to Button Event Handler.

29. Close Window1.

STOP. Save or discard the solution. It will not be used again for another exercise.

You just created both Tunneling and Bubbling Routed events. You used the Handled property to notify WPF when to stop passing the events up or down the control hierarchy. In addition to Routed events, WPF also supports Attached events, Life cycle events, and Property Change events.

An Attached event is an event handler for a specific event, but the event handler is associated with an arbitrary element rather than an actual element. An example of an Attached event in WPF is the Mouse.MouseDown event. The mouse input device does not really exist. When a new input device is added, this event is attached to the new real element. Using Attached events in this type of scenario allows generic event creation for future expansion. Attached events are generally not used and only serve a WPF architectural purpose.

Most WPF elements support the same set of life cycle events. Table 4-4 lists the common WPF element life cycle events with a description.

Table 4-4

Common WPF Element Life cycle Events

Event	Description
Activated	Applies to most WPF elements and indicates when the element has the foremost position on the screen. Use this event to know when the user is paying attention to the element so that you can now update or present current information.
Closing	Applies to the Window element and indicates when the Window is being shut down and is closing. Use this event to clean up variables and to check to make sure that the application wants to close.
Deactivated	Applies to most WPF elements and indicates when the element loses the foremost position on the screen. Use this event to know when the user's attention has turned to another part of the application or to another application, so that you stop updating or presenting current information because the user is not paying attention.
Loaded	Applies to most WPF elements and indicates when the element has been loaded into memory. Use this event to set initialization information.
Unloaded	Applies to most WPF elements and indicates when the element has been removed from memory. Use this event to clean up any variables or functionality.

Much like Windows Forms Property Changed events, WPF defines several events that are raised when a Property's value changes. WPF Property Changed events can be either a Routed event or a Direct event, depending on its usage and whether the event needs to be routed through the element hierarchy.

Working with Windows Service Applications

THE BOTTOM LINE

Up to this point, we have not looked at Windows Service applications because they typically do not have a UI. To work with Windows Service applications, you need to understand the ServiceBase class, understand the Main method, and be able to override the service methods.

Understanding the Windows Service Applications

A Windows Service application consists of two parts, the application executable and services derived from the ServiceBase class. In the application executable, you implement the Main method to control the applications services. To create any Windows Service application, you must have a class derived from the ServiceBase class. The *ServiceBase class* implements virtual methods for functionality required by the Service Control Manager (SCM).

A Windows Service application is different from a Windows Forms and WPF application. Not only does a Windows Service application not have a UI, a Windows Service application has the following characteristics:

- It is designed to run for a very long time.
- The execution of the Windows Service application is separate from the services execution and functionality.
- You start and stop the Windows Service application executable independently of starting and stopping the service.
- A Windows Service application can run without a user being logged on to the machine.
- Typically, a Windows Service application runs under the System Account, but a specific account can be provided.

All of these characteristics are controlled and implemented in the base Service class called ServiceBase.

Once a Windows Service application is installed, the Service Control Manager (SCM) executes the application and the Main method is run. The Main method performs any application initialization code and then creates the services within the executable. The following code is a default Main method declaration:

```
static void Main()
{
    ServiceBase[] ServicesToRun;
    ServicesToRun = new ServiceBase[]
    {
        new Service1()
    };
    ServiceBase.Run(ServicesToRun);
}
```

The application executable Main method creates an array of ServiceBase classes, assigns the services to the array, and then runs all of the services in the array. The application executable is now running and cannot be stopped unless the machine is powered off; thus a Windows Service application's executable is always running. Now that the application is running and the service is created, the SCM calls the service's Run method to make any initializations.

Although the executable may always be running, the service can be stopped, started, paused, or continued. The SCM uses the ServiceBase class's OnStop, OnStart, OnPause, OnContinue, and OnShutdown (of the machine) methods to control the service's behavior. The service can also set property values like CanStop, CanPauseAndContinue, and CanShutdown to inform the SCM which methods are supported. Table 4-5 lists the common ServiceBase class properties and methods used by the SCM with a description.

Table 4-5

Common ServiceBase class Properties and Methods

PROPERTY/METHOD	DESCRIPTION
AutoLog	Determines if the Service Logs Start, Stop, Pause, and Continue commands to the Event Log. Use this property to keep track of what your service is doing. This property can be useful when trying to debug or monitor your service.
CanPauseAndContinue	Determines if the service can be Paused and then Continued. Use this property to tell the SCM if your service supports the OnPause and OnContinue methods. If you do not implement the OnPause and/or OnContinue methods, you will set this property to False.
CanShutdown	Determines if the service can be shut down. Use this property to tell the SCM if your service supports the OnShutdown method. If you do not implement the OnShutdown method, you will set this property to False.
CanStop	Determines if the service can be stopped. Use this property to tell the SCM if your service supports the OnStop method. If you do not implement the OnStop method, you will set this property to False.
ExitCode	Reports the service's exit code when the service is stopped. An exit code is a number reported back to the application to indicate if the service stopped correctly or an error occurred. Typically an exit code of 0 (zero) means that the service exited without an error. Anything other than 0 (zero) typically indicates the error number that occurred. Use the ExitCode method to notify the application of errors.
OnContinue ( )	Called when the SCM sends the service a continue command. Use the OnContinue method to resume the service's functionality, reset any variables, or set flags to indicate that the service has been removed off pause.
OnCustomCommand ( )	Called when the SCM sends the service a custom command. A custom command is any command other than Start, Stop, Pause, Continue, or Shutdown. The SCM does not check to see if the service supports the custom command; it only calls the OnCustomCommand method to handle the custom command. Thus if you do not implement an OnCustomCommand method, your service will return an unsupported command error. Use the OnCustomCommand method to create special functionality not handled by the Start, Stop, Pause, Continue, or Shutdown commands.
OnPause ( )	Called when the SCM sends the service a pause command. Use the OnPause method to temporarily stop the service's functionality, which might include pausing any processing or setting flags to keep functionality from executing while paused.
OnShutdown ( )	Called when the SCM sends the service a shutdown command. Use the OnShutdown method to perform any special processing because the Windows Service application is about to be stopped. The OnShutdown method differs from the OnStop method because the Windows Service application is still running during an OnStop method, but the Windows Service application stops running after an OnShutdown method.

(continued)

Table 4-5 (continued)

PROPERTY/METHOD	DESCRIPTION
OnStart ( )	Called when the SCM sends the service a start command. Use the OnStart method to initialize variables and restart the service's functionality after an OnStop method processing.
OnStop ( )	Called when the SCM sends the service a stop command. Use the OnStop method to clean up any variables or process any functionality that needs to stop while the service is turned off.
Run ( )	Called by the SCM when the Windows Service application starts and the services are first loaded. Use the Run method to perform any first-time initialization.
Stop ( )	Stops the service. Use the Stop method when you want to programmatically stop your service.

⚠ **WARNING** You cannot execute your Windows Service application from within Visual Studio. Your Windows Service application will display an error message if you attempt to F5 build and execute your application or try to double-click the exe from the file folder.

The ServiceBase class only has one event, the Dispose event. This event is initiated when the service has been unloaded from memory.

The ServiceBase class provides default definitions for the OnStart, OnStop, OnPause, and OnContinue methods, but these methods were designed to be overridden to provide custom functionality to your Windows Service application. To override the default methods, use the Override keyword when declaring the derived methods.

To execute a Visual Studio Windows Service application, you must first install the application using an installer. Once installed, your service is listed in the Windows Management console in the services section.

To get your Windows Service application installed, you must first add a service installer. You add a service installer to your Windows Service project by right-clicking in the Service.cs [Design] tab to display the Service Designer pop-up menu and then selecting Add Installer (Figure 4-4).

Figure 4-4

Service Designer pop-up menu

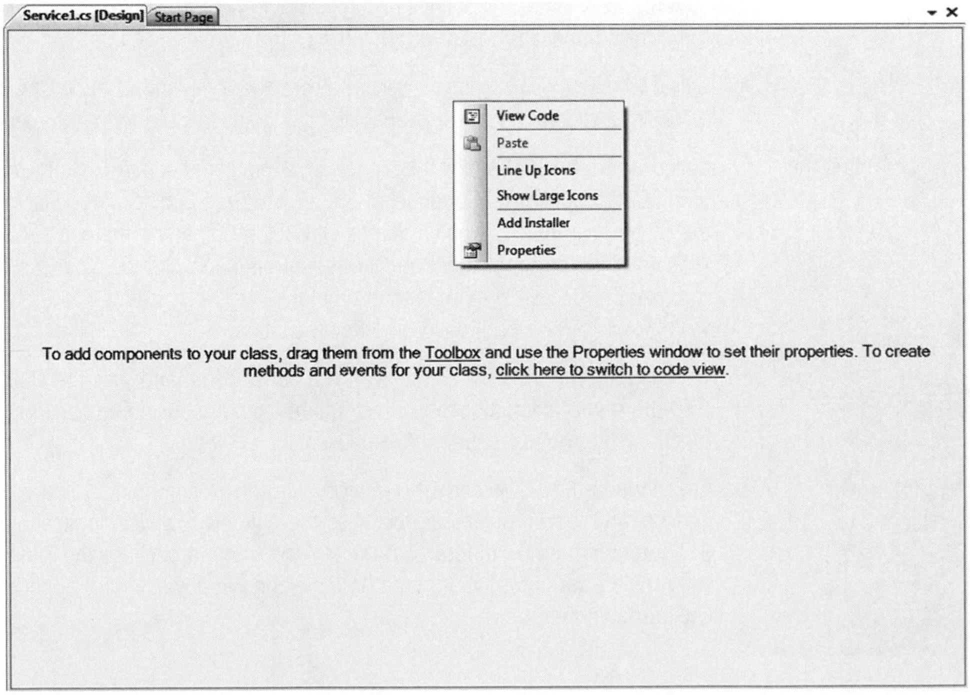

You will then configure your service installer and build the project. Once built, there are two ways to get your Windows Service application installed. You can use the Visual Studio Command Prompt to execute the InstallUtil.exe application or you can create a Setup and Deployment Setup project. When you need to modify your Windows Service application, you will need to uninstall by using the /U command with the InstallUtil.exe or use the Add or Remove Programs window.

➔ OVERRIDE THE SERVICEBASE CLASS METHODS

GET READY. Before you begin these steps, be sure to launch Microsoft Visual Studio and create a new Windows Service named wsaOverride.

1. On the Service1.cs [Design] tab, right-click to display the Service Designer pop-up menu.
2. Select Add Installer.
3. Select the ProjectInstaller.cs [Design] tab.
4. Select the serviceProcessIntaller1 icon and locate the Properties window.
5. Locate the Account property and select the LocalService option to change the service execution privileges to run as a local service rather than a specific user.
6. On the ProjectInstaller.cs [Design] tab, select the serviceInstaller1 icon and locate the Properties window.
7. Verify that the ServiceName property is Service1.

> **TAKE NOTE**＊ The serviceInstaller's ServiceName property must match the service's ServiceName property. You should always make sure that these two property values are the same.

8. Select the Service1.cs [Design] tab.
9. Locate the Toolbox window, expand the Components grouping, and double-click EventLog.
10. In the Solution Explorer (Figure 4-5), locate the Service1.cs item and click the View Code button on the Solution Explorer toolbar.

Figure 4-5

Solution Explorer toolbar

11. Immediately following the Service1 constructor inside of the OnStart method, key the following code:

    ```
    // Write a message to the event log.
    this.eventLog1.WriteEntry("My Service OnStart");
    ```

12. Press **F5** to build and execute the application.
13. Verify that the Windows Service application execution error message is displayed stating that you must first install.
14. Click OK.
15. Select Start→All Programs→Visual Studio XXXX→Visual Studio Tools→Visual Studio Command Prompt, where the XXXX is the version (2005, 2008) of Visual Studio you currently have installed (Figure 4-6).

Administrator: Visual Studio 2008 Command Prompt
Setting environment for using Microsoft Visual Studio 2008 x86 tools.
C:\Program Files\Microsoft Visual Studio 9.0\VC>

Figure 4-6

Visual Studio command prompt window

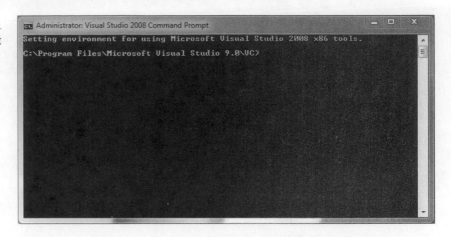

16. Key **InstallUtil <Full Path to Service executable>**. Your service executable is located in the \bin\Debug folder where you saved your project files.

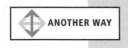

ANOTHER WAY

Instead of keying the full path to your service executable, you can open Windows Explorer, click on the executable file, and then drag and drop the executable into the Command Prompt window. This will automatically add a quoted full path to the Command Prompt line.

X REF

To create a Setup and Deployment project see Lesson 7, "Packaging and Deploying Windows Applications."

17. Press **Enter**.
18. Verify that the installer executes and that the final line of output states:

```
The Commit phase completed successfully.
The transacted install has completed.
```

19. Locate in the Start menu My Computer and right-click to display the pop-up menu (Figure 4-7).

Open
Open folder location
Manage
Map network drive...
Disconnect network drive...
Restore previous versions
Send to
Cut
Copy
Create shortcut
Delete
Rename
Properties

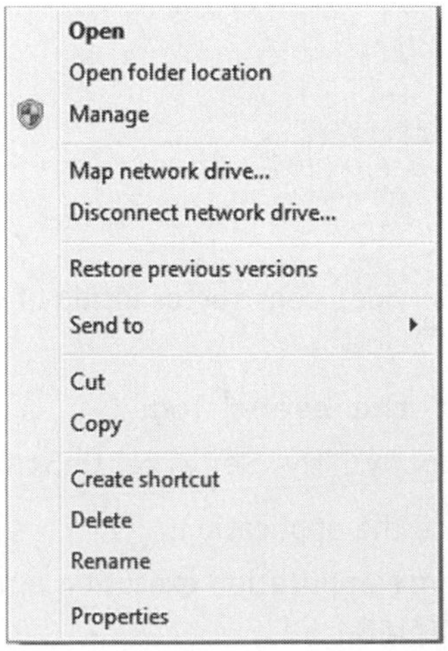

Figure 4-7

My Computer pop-up menu

20. Select Manage to display the Computer Management console (Figure 4-8).

Figure 4-8

Computer Management console

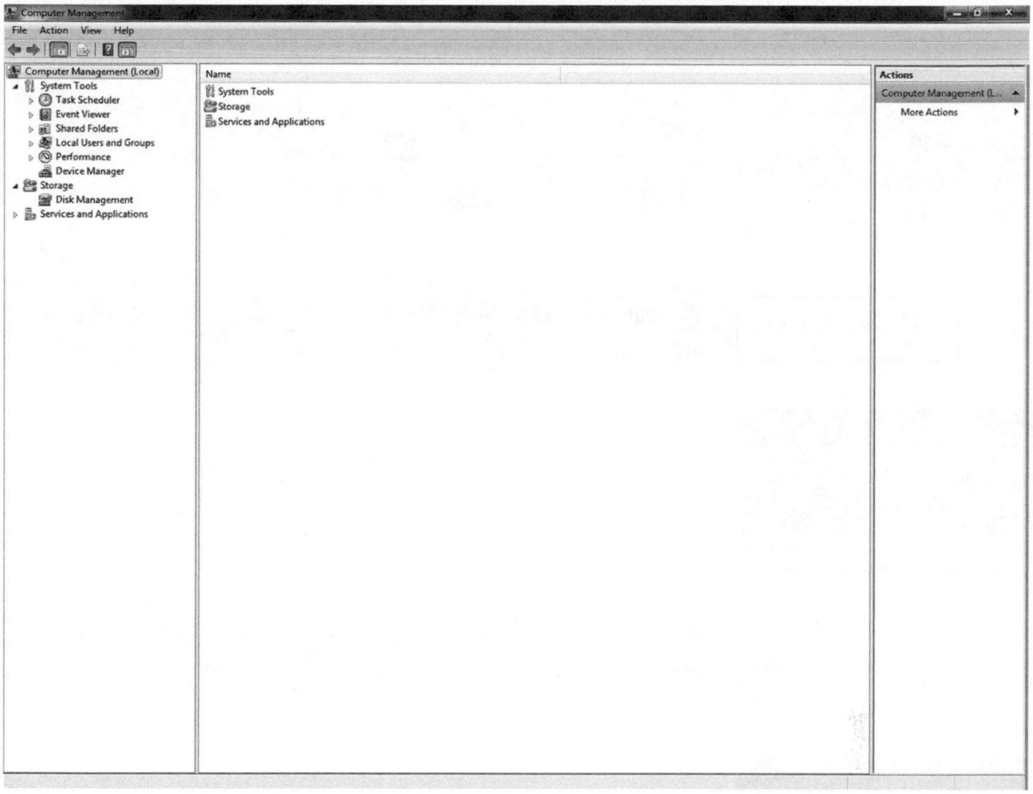

21. Locate and view the services section (Figure 4-9).

Figure 4-9

Computer Management console services

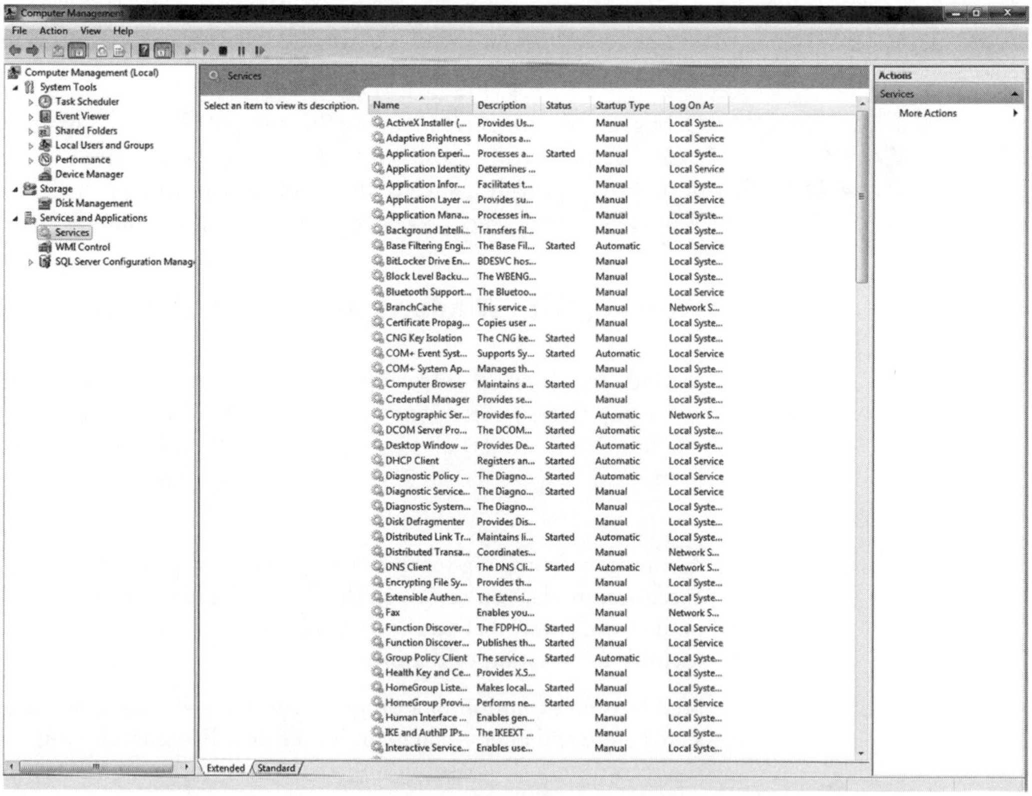

22. Locate Service1 and verify that its status is blank.

23. Select the Start button from the Computer Management console toolbar (Figure 4-10).

Figure 4-10

Computer Management console toolbar

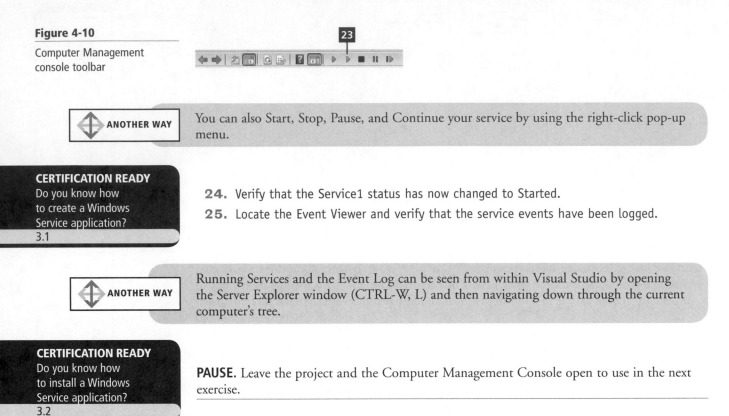

ANOTHER WAY

You can also Start, Stop, Pause, and Continue your service by using the right-click pop-up menu.

CERTIFICATION READY
Do you know how to create a Windows Service application?
3.1

24. Verify that the Service1 status has now changed to Started.

25. Locate the Event Viewer and verify that the service events have been logged.

ANOTHER WAY

Running Services and the Event Log can be seen from within Visual Studio by opening the Server Explorer window (CTRL-W, L) and then navigating down through the current computer's tree.

CERTIFICATION READY
Do you know how to install a Windows Service application?
3.2

PAUSE. Leave the project and the Computer Management Console open to use in the next exercise.

■ Debugging Windows Service Applications

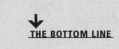

THE BOTTOM LINE

Debugging is a process of finding the cause of errors in a program, locating the lines of code that are causing those errors, and fixing those errors. Visual Studio provides a number of tools that provide a streamlined approach to debugging all kind of applications such as Windows Forms, Windows Service, and Console applications.

Working with Windows Application Debugging

Understanding the execution of any Windows application is imperative for controlling the application execution. Visual Studio provides several debugging mechanisms that allow you to understand how your application is executing and where problem areas may exist.

A common debugging technique is to execute a program step by step. By using the step execution mode, you can track the flow to logic to verify if the program is following the same path of execution that you expected it to follow. If there is a difference, you can immediately identify the location of the problem.

Step-by-step execution of a program also gives you an opportunity to monitor the program's state before and after a statement is executed. For example, you can check the value of variables, the records in a database, and other changes in the environment. Visual Studio provides several debugging tools and techniques. Table 4-6 lists the common Debugging mechanisms within Visual Studio with a description.

Table 4-6

Common Debugging Mechanisms

DEBUGGING MECHANISM	DESCRIPTION
Breakpoint	A marker inserted into source code that tells Visual Studio to pause execution at the indicated line of code. You can breakpoint at a line of code, when a condition changes, or at a function declaration. Use **breakpoints** continually when debugging your Windows application because they enable you to understand what is happening when executing.
Quick Watch Window	An immediate and temporary variable evaluation window. When the Quick Watch window is open, you cannot switch back to the code editor and continue debugging. You must close the Quick Watch window before you can continue your debugging activities. To display the Quick Watch window, you select a variable in the code editor during a breakpoint, then perform a right-click to display the code editor pop-up menu, and select Quick Watch. The Quick Watch window will appear and you can browse the current variables properties and values. Notice that as you browse various properties, the Quick Watch Expression field's value will change. You can also type an Express directly into the Express field's value, but you will need to click the Reevaluate button to see the properties area update. You can use the Expression field's value to understand how to get to different variable's properties. If you want to monitor a variable's value over the long term, you can click the Add Watch button to add the expression to the Watch window's list of monitored expressions. When you are done using the Quick Watch window, you will need to click the Close button.
Watch Window	A real-time long-term monitor area of variables and expressions. You can display the Watch window at any time using the Debug→Windows→Watch menu or by using the right-click pop-up menu Add Watch item. The Watch window is a free-floating window that can be docked anywhere within the Visual Studio environment. When open, the Watch window contains a list of all variables and expressions being watched with their current values. When available, you can edit the expression values to affect application execution.
Output Window	Used by both Visual Studio and your application to display a message. Visual Studio uses the Output window during the build process to notify you about build messages. You can use the Output window to save debug information or display debug messages. Use the `Console.Write` method to send messages to the Output window.
Immediate Window	Used to perform real-time variable evaluations or to execute ad-hoc lines of code. The Immediate window is just like a real-time code evaluator: you can key code and then have the code evaluated immediately. You can display the Immediate window by selecting Debug→Windows→Immediate menu.
Locals Window	Displays all of the presently loaded local variables. Use the Locals window to see the value of all variables currently loaded into memory.
Call Stack Window	Displays the current list of methods called and the order in which they were called. Use the Call Stack window to understand which method is calling other methods and where you are in your application when the breakpoint is encountered.
Threads Window	Displays the current list of application threads. Because Windows applications can be multithreaded, Visual Studio provides a window to see what threads are currently executing. Use the Threads window to make sure that your threads are being created and deleted correctly.
Memory Window	Displays the current state of the application memory as it is stored in the operating system's memory addresses. Use the Memory window to perform low-level debugging of memory allocations and references.

→ **USE THE DEBUGGER TO STEP THROUGH A WINDOWS APPLICATION**

USE the project wfaEvents that you created previously in this lesson.

1. Select Debug→Step Into. The program pauses for execution at the first executable statement and shows the statement highlighted. An arrow appears in the left margin of the code that points at the next statement to be executed.

2. Press F11 to proceed to the next step in code execution.

3. Select Debug→Window→Locals to open the Locals Window. You use the Locals window to see the value of all variables currently loaded into memory.

4. Select Debug→Stop Debugging to end the debugging mode.

Debugging a Window's Service Application

A Windows Service application is always executing with one or more services running internally. To debug, you must first attach to the Windows Service application, then you will have the standard Visual Studio debugging tools available.

The *Attach Process* is the procedure used by Visual Studio to monitor an already running executable and allow debugging. To attach to an executing Windows Service application, use the Attach to Process Editor (Figure 4-11).

Figure 4-11

Attach to Process editor

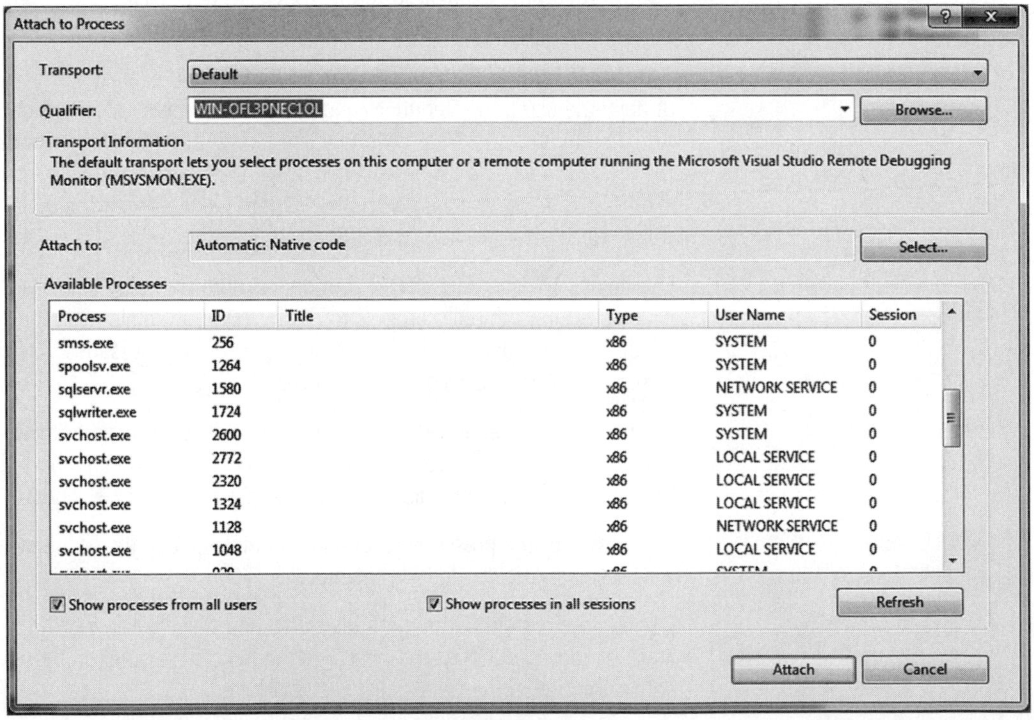

The Attach to Process Editor can be opened from the Debug→Attach to Process menu. Once the Attach to Process Editor is open, you will locate your service and select the Attach button. If you do not see your service listed, try selecting the Show Processes from the all users checkbox. When your service is executing under the LocalService, LocalSystem, or NetworkService accounts, you will need to select the Show Processes from the all users checkbox.

Once attached, your service project is now in Debug mode. You will notice that the toolbars and menu all change to reflect available debug functionality. Since your Windows Service application and services are all managed by the SCM, you will need to go back to the SCM to initiate debugging activities.

→ USE THE ATTACH TO PROCESS EDITOR

USE the project you created in the previous exercise.

1. Select Debug→Attach Process.
2. Select the Show Processes from all users.
3. In the Available Processes, locate Service1 and select the process.
4. Click Attach.
5. Select the Service1.cs tab.
6. Locate the code line entered in step 11 on page 119.
7. Select Debug→Toggle Breakpoint.
8. Locate the Computer Management Console and select Service1.
9. Select Stop from the Computer Management Console toolbar.
10. Select Start from the Computer Management Console toolbar.
11. Verify that your service breaks into the Visual Studio environment at the breakpoint inserted.
12. Select Debug→Stop Debugging.

STOP. Save or discard the solution. It will not be used again for another exercise.

CERTIFICATION READY
Do you know how to debug a Windows Service application?
2.5

SKILL SUMMARY

IN THIS LESSON YOU LEARNED HOW TO:

- Create a Windows Form event and some of the common Windows Form events and how to handle a Raised event.

- Create a WPF event; the differences among a bubbled, tunneled, and direct WPF event; and how to handle a Raised event throughout the control hierarchy.

- Understand the Windows Service application, the ServiceBase class, and how to override the ServiceBase class default methods.

- Debug Windows Service applications using the Attach Process Editor and the common debugging window mechanisms.

■ Knowledge Assessment

Fill in the Blank

Complete the following sentences by writing the correct word or words in the blanks provided.

1. A _____ is a marker inserted into source code that tells Visual Studio to pause execution at the indicated line of code.

2. All Windows Service applications must have one class derived from the _____.

3. An _____ processes an operating system or input device action.

4. The _____ event is initiated when the Windows Forms Width or Height property values change.

5. An event that is initiated when a property changes value is called a _____.

6. The process of initiating an event in code is called _____.

7. The _____ event is initiated by the operating system when the Windows Form is first being brought into memory.

8. An _____ is an operating system or input device action.

9. To debug a Windows Service application, you must use the _____ functionality.

10. The _____ property reports the Services exit code when the Service is stopped.

Multiple Choice

Circle the letter that corresponds to the best answer.

1. Which one of the following is NOT a Windows application debugging window?
   a. Output Window
   b. Locals Window
   c. Globals Window
   d. Watch Window

2. Which of the following events is initiated by the operating system when the Windows Form has been removed from memory?
   a. FormClosed
   b. Form closing
   c. Shown
   d. Leave

3. You need to detect when a Windows Form is moved around on the screen. Which of the following events should you subscribe to?
   a. SizeChanged
   b. VisibilityChanged
   c. TextChanged
   d. LocationChanged

4. You are debugging a Windows application in Visual Studio. You need to monitor the current value of an expression at each step of the debugging process. Which Visual Studio windows should you use to accomplish this task with least effort?
   a. Watch Window
   b. Immediate Window
   c. Locals Window
   d. Call Stack Window

5. Which of the following is NOT a ServiceBase class method?
   a. OnStart
   b. OnStop
   c. OnError
   d. OnPause

6. Because a Windows Service application is always running, what must be created to enable debugging?
   a. Watch Code
   b. Debugger application
   c. An Installer
   d. None of the above; you can debug right from Visual Studio without any other actions.

7. Which of the following is NOT a common Windows Forms event?
   a. Load
   b. Click
   c. FormClosing
   d. FormOpening

8. Which of the following is NOT a common WPF element life cycle event?
   a. Shown
   b. Closing
   c. Loaded
   d. UnLoaded

9. Which of the following debugging mechanisms temporarily stops your application's execution?
   a. Locals window
   b. Memory window
   c. Breakpoint
   d. Output window

10. You are debugging a Windows application in Visual Studio. You need to understand which method is calling other methods and where in your application when the breakpoint was encountered. Which Visual Studio windows should you use to accomplish this task with least effort?
    a. Memory Window
    b. Threads Window
    c. Breakpoints window
    d. Call Stack Window

■ Competency Assessment

Scenario 4-1: Windows Forms Login

You have been assigned to create a Windows Forms Login screen comparable that has two textboxes for entering the Username and Password. The Login screen will have three buttons, an OK, Clear, and Cancel. When your Username is blank, you want the OK button to be disabled. When the user presses the Clear button you will remove all text from the Username and Password fields.

Scenario 4-2: WPF Telephone Dialing Pad

You have been assigned to create a telephone dialing pad using Windows Forms. Your window will have a textbox at the top to display clicked buttons that represent the telephone numbers, laid out just like a telephone dialing pad. When a telephone button is pressed, you will add the number to the textbox. Each button should handle its own event.

Scenario 4-3: Windows Forms Login Enhanced

Your supervisor has reviewed your Windows Forms Login screen, but noticed that you can leave the Password blank and still press the OK button. The organization reviewed this requirement and decided to make sure that both the Username and Password are not blank before the user can press the OK button. Be as efficient as possible by using only one Event Handler method to perform your check.

Scenario 4-4: Memory Performance Monitor

You are concerned about the amount of memory all of the applications might be taking. You want to monitor memory consumption every minute and have the total amount of available memory written to the Event Log. You want your monitoring application to run all the time, so you will implement it as a Windows Service. The only time you want the Windows Service to stop running is when it is paused from the SCM. Once you are done, your supervisor has asked to see a running demo, so you will need to install and start the service.

Validating User Input

LESSON SKILL MATRIX

SKILLS/CONCEPTS	MTA EXAM OBJECTIVE	MTA EXAM OBJECTIVE NUMBER
Understanding the Windows User Input Model	Validate and implement user input.	2.4
Handling Input Device User Inputs	Supplemental	
Handling Exceptions	Supplemental	

KEY TERMS

control action

device action

Exception

Form/Window action

You have completed your prototype's implementation that provides basic control and execution flow, but once you allowed users to evaluate the user interface they were constantly crashing or able to input invalid data. You need to implement several levels of user input validation to reduce the evaluation user's frustration. You will also need to implement an error-trapping mechanism to make sure that the prototype stops crashing.

■ Understanding the Windows User Input Model

THE BOTTOM LINE

Windows Forms and WPF applications are constantly receiving user inputs from the keyboard, mouse, and stylus. Knowing when to handle user input events will enable the application to maintain performance and provide a better user experience.

Analyzing User Input Needs

Windows applications are designed to interact with an end user through their UI. Analyzing when, where, and how to process user input events can be done by looking at user input processing levels.

When the application is executing, you have a finite amount of processing power and machine resources to react to the user's inputs. As the user performs keyboard actions, mouse actions, and/or stylus actions, the application has the capability to process every individual action generated by each input device. If you were to respond to every action, you might overwhelm the machine's resources and degrade the application's performance. Thus, when analyzing the application requirements and designing your Form/Window UI, you need to consider at what level you want to handle each user input device action being generated. Table 5-1 summarizes the various user input processing levels.

Table 5-1

User Input Processing Levels

PROCESS LEVEL	DESCRIPTION
Device Action	This is where the application handles individual user input device actions. For each user input control in a Windows application, a user input device can generate individual actions based on what the user input device supports. For example, a keyboard generates a KeyDown event when the user presses down on a key. When the user lets go of that key and the key rises, the keyboard generates a KeyUp event. Processing each user input device action is the lowest level of user input device processing. Implement the device action level of user input processing when you want full control over user input. When you use the device action processing level, you can evaluate, accept, or reject and process each action as it occurs. Although the device action processing level gives you the greatest control, it is also the most resource intensive in terms of processing power. The more individual user input device actions you choose to process, the more processing power the application will need to process the event, which may possibly degrade the user experience. For example, take the action of entering a username. If you process the KeyDown event for each character as it is typed into the textbox and then check to see if the user exists with a partial username, your check for a valid username will be slower than the user can type. Thus, there will be a visible delay. This could cause the user to enter extra characters, or get impatient and start deleting and re-entering their username multiple times.
Control Action	The application handles user input device actions when control level events occur. For example, when the user clicks inside of a textbox, the textbox control generates a GotFocus event. Since focus has now been placed on the textbox, you can check its value and perform processing based on the current value. In the control action level of user input device processing, you are not concerned with each individual user input device action. When processing control level events you will only look at the current value of the control. The user input device events leading up to the building of the controls value is not important. Unlike the device action level, the control action level does not have control over the building of the control value as it happens, but because the control action level waits until the entire value is built it has much better performance. The control action level can make sure that the current value is acceptable before the user moves on to the next control for editing. For example, as the user is entering the username, the control action level does not process the individual input device actions. When the user presses the tab key to move to the next control, a LostFocus event is generated. The application now has time to take the entire username value and perform a username

Table 5-1 (*continued*)

Process Level	Description
	check. If the username does not exist, the application can return the user to the username control for editing, or the application could allow the user to move to the next control and allow additional editing until the Login button is pressed. Use the control action level when you have multiple controls with dependent information. When the editing of one control has an effect on another control's value or selection of values, you want to make sure that each control's value is correct before moving to the next control for editing.
Form/Window Action	The application allows the user to enter multiple control values and then all controls are evaluated at one time. Typically the Form/Window action level of user input device processing occurs at a Form/Window event, but Form/Window action level processing can also occur when a user presses a button that takes some action, like saving, against the current Form/Window control values. Form/Window action level processing delays all control value processing until one event, which saves processing time as the user is entering control values, but does take longer to validate all of the user inputs at one time. You would not want to use the Form/Window action level of processing if you have interdependent controls. Entering all of the control values and then discovering that half of what you entered was wrong would cause user frustration. Form/Window action processing should be used in conjunction with device action and control action levels to provide that last phase of checking before saving or closing the Form/Window.

CERTIFICATION READY
Can you validate and implement user input for a Windows application?
2.4

■ Handling Input Device User Inputs

↓ **THE BOTTOM LINE**

Windows applications currently support three types of input devices—the keyboard, the mouse, and the stylus. As a user interacts with an input device, actions are generated and your Windows application can implement event handlers.

Working with Keyboard User Inputs

Although both Windows Forms and WPF applications support keyboard user inputs, they have different events to support keyboard user input processing.

Table 5-2 lists the common keyboard user input events with a description.

Table 5-2

Common Keyboard User Input Events

Event	Application Type	Action Level	Description
KeyDown	Windows Forms/WPF	Device	Event is raised when the user pushes down a keyboard key. Use the **KeyEventArgs e** to determine which key was pressed and if the ALT, CTRL, or SHIFT keys were also being held. You can also suppress the key down value if the key that was pressed is invalid.

(*continued*)

Table 5-2 (*continued*)

EVENT	APPLICATION TYPE	ACTION LEVEL	DESCRIPTION
KeyUp	Windows Forms/WPF	Device	Event is raised when the user releases a keyboard key that was previously pushed down. Use the **KeyEventArgs** e to determine which key was released and if the ALT, CTRL, or SHIFT keys were also being held. You can also suppress the key-up value if the key that was released is invalid.
PreviewKeyDown	Windows Forms/WPF	Device	Event is raised when the user presses a keyboard key. This event is handled before the KeyDown event. Use the **PreviewKeyDownEventArgs** e to determine which key was pressed and if the ALT, CTRL, or SHIFT keys were also being held. You cannot suppress the key-down value from this event. This is the only Preview event supported by Windows Forms applications.
PreviewKeyUp	WPF	Device	Event is raised when the user releases a keyboard key that was previously pushed down. This event is handled before the KeyUp event. Use the **PreviewKeyDown EventArgs** e to determine which key was released and if the ALT, CTRL, or SHIFT keys were also being held. You cannot suppress the key-up value from this event. A WPF application supports a Preview event for the entire list of WPF keyboard events, although they are not all listed in this table.
KeyPress	Windows Forms	Device	Event is raised when the user presses and then releases a keyboard key. Use the **KeyEventArgs** e to determine which key was released and if the ALT, CTRL, or SHIFT keys were also being held. You can also suppress the key value if the key that was pressed and released is invalid.
GotKeyboardFocus	WPF	Control and Form/Window	Event is raised when the user uses the keyboard to transition from one field to another. Typically this can be accomplished by pressing the tab key, but this event is raised any time a keyboard key navigates between controls. Use the **KeyboardFocusChangedEventArgs** e to determine the control that had focus before this control and the timestamp that the control got focus. Use this event to determine where the user is as he/she navigates between controls via the keyboard.
LostKeyboard Focus	WPF	Control and Form/Window	Event is raised when the user uses the keyboard to transition away from the control. Typically this can be accomplished by pressing the tab key, but this event is raised any time a keyboard key navigates between controls. Use the **KeyboardFocusChangedEventArgs** e to determine the control that is getting focus after this control and the timestamp when the control lost focus. Use this event to determine where the user is going next as he/she navigates between controls via the keyboard.

USE KEYBOARD USER INPUT EVENTS

GET READY. Before you begin these steps, be sure to launch Microsoft Visual Studio and create a new Windows Forms application named wfaKeyboardInput.

1. Add a Label and TextBox control to Form1.
   a. Locate the Toolbox window and expand the Common Controls grouping.
   b. Double-click the Label item.
   c. Double-click the TextBox item.
   d. Select the Label and locate the Properties window.
   e. Key the following property values:
      - Text: Telephone
      - Location: 12,6
   f. Select the TextBox and locate the Properties window.
   g. Key the following property values:
      - Location: 79,6

2. Select the Events button on the Properties window toolbar and locate the KeyDown event.

3. Double-click in the KeyDown property event selection cell to display the Form1.cs tab in the textBox1_KeyDown method.

4. Key the following code inside the textBox1_KeyDown method:

```
// Show a message box with all of the EventArgs
// parameter e's properties.
MessageBox.Show("You pressed key (Code, Value, "
+ "Data, Alt, Shift, Ctrl) "
+ e.KeyCode.ToString() + ", "
+ e.KeyValue.ToString() + ", "
+ e.KeyData.ToString() + ", "
+ e.Alt.ToString() + ", "
+ e.Shift.ToString() + ", "
+ e.Control.ToString());
```

5. Press **F5** to build and execute the application.
6. Press any key.
7. Verify that a message box appears and displays the code, value, data, and a true/false indicating if the Alt, Shift, and/or Ctrl keys were pressed.
8. Close Form1.
9. Select Form1.cs and comment out the code keyed in step 4.
10. Key the following code immediately following the code commented out in step 9:

```
// Check if the EventArgs parameter, e's property
// has the control key pressed.
if (e.Control)
    e.SuppressKeyPress = true;
```

XREF

For more information about events and how to create events handlers, please see Lesson 4 "Controlling Application Execution."

TAKE NOTE*

To comment out code in C#, use the double backslash (//).

CERTIFICATION READY
Can you validate and implement user input for a Windows application?
2.4

11. Press **F5** to build and execute the application.

12. Press any key.

13. Verify that the character appeared in the textbox.

14. Press **CTRL** and any other key at the same time.

15. Verify that the character did not appear in the textbox.

16. Close Form1.

PAUSE. Leave the solution open to use in the next exercise.

You just created a new Windows Forms Application where you placed a textbox on the form. You used the KeyDown event from the keyboard to see what key was being pressed and if the ALT, CTRL, and/or SHIFT keys were being pressed. You then checked for the CTRL key and suppressed the character being typed when the CTRL key was pressed.

Next you will look at the mouse user inputs and the events that handle the mouse actions.

Working with Mouse User Inputs

Both Windows Forms and WPF applications support mouse user inputs. Although they both support mouse user inputs, they have different events to support mouse user input processing.

Table 5-3 lists the common mouse user input events with a description.

Table 5-3

Common Mouse User Inputs

Event	Application Type	Action Level	Description
MouseUp	Windows Forms/WPF	Device	Event is raised when the user releases any of the buttons on the mouse that were previously pressed. Use the `MouseEventArgs e` to determine which button was released, how many clicks were pressed, how much the wheel was moved, and the location of the mouse pointer.
MouseDown	Windows Forms/WPF	Device	Event is raised when the user presses any of the buttons. Use the `MouseEventArgs e` to determine which button was pressed, how many clicks were pressed, how much the wheel was moved, and the location of the mouse pointer.
MouseEnter	Windows Forms/WPF	Control	Event is raised when the mouse cursor enters the control area when it was previously not over the control area. The MouseEnter event uses the `EventArgs e` as the parameter that does not include any information about the cursor position or mouse actions. Use the MouseEnter event strictly to know when the user has placed the cursor over the control. Typically this is used to change the look of the control, for example highlight or change the color, when the cursor is moved over the control to show that the control is about to be selected.

EVENT	APPLICATION TYPE	ACTION LEVEL	DESCRIPTION
MouseLeave	Windows Forms/WPF	Control	Event is raised when the mouse cursor leaves the control area. The MouseLeave event uses the `EventArgs e` as the parameter that does not include any information about the cursor position or mouse actions. Use the MouseLeave event strictly to know when the user has moved the cursor away from the control. Typically this is used to change the look of the control, for example highlight or change the color, when the cursor is moved off the control to show that the control is no longer selected.
MouseMove	Windows Forms/WPF	Device	Event is raised any time the mouse moves while it is over the control. Use the `MouseEventArgs e` to determine which button was pressed, how many clicks were pressed, how much the wheel was moved, and the location of the mouse pointer. Use this event to keep track of where the mouse is positioned within the control.
GotMouseCapture	WPF	Device	Event is raised when the mouse is first captured. The mouse is captured when it can receive mouse inputs even when the mouse is not over the control. Use the `MouseEventArgs e` to determine which button was pressed, how many clicks were pressed, how much the wheel was moved, and the location of the mouse pointer. Use this event when performing a drag-and-drop operation to indicate when the drag begins.
LostMouse Capture	WPF	Device	Event is raised when the mouse is released from the previous capture. The mouse is released when it no longer can receive mouse inputs. Use the `MouseEventArgs e` to determine which button was pressed, how many clicks were pressed, how much the wheel was moved, and the location of the mouse pointer. Use this event when performing a drag-and-drop operation to indicate when the drag ends.
WheelMove	WPF	Device	Event is raised when the mouse wheel is turned. Use the `MouseEventArgs e` to determine which button was pressed, how many clicks were pressed, how much the wheel was moved, and the location of the mouse pointer. Use the WheelMove event to determine when to scroll content in a scrollable control.
MouseClick	Windows	Device	Event is raised when the user presses and releases any of the buttons once. Use the `MouseEventArgs e` to determine which button was pressed, how many clicks were pressed, how much the wheel was moved, and the location of the mouse pointer.
MouseDoubleClick	Windows Forms/WPF	Device	Event is raised when the user presses and releases any of the buttons twice. Use the `MouseEventArgs e` to determine which button was pressed, how many clicks were pressed, how much the wheel was moved, and the location of the mouse pointer.

→ **USE MOUSE USER INPUT EVENTS**

USE the project you created in the previous exercise.

1. Select the Form1.cs [Design] tab and select textBox1.
2. In the Properties window, select the Events button from the Properties toolbar and locate the MouseEnter event.
3. Double-click the event selection cell to display the Form1.cs tab.
4. Inside the textBox1_MouseEnter method, key the following code:

   ```
   // Set the textbox's background color to yellow
   // to show that the mouse entered.
   textBox1.BackColor = Color.Yellow;
   ```

5. Select the Form1.cs [Design] tab and select textBox1.
6. In the Properties window, select the Events button from the Properties toolbar and locate the MouseLeave event.
7. Double-click the event selection cell to display the Form1.cs tab.
8. Inside the textBox1_MouseLeave method, key the following code:

   ```
   // Clear the textbox's background color back to
   // white to show that the mouse has left.
   textBox1.BackColor = Color.White;
   ```

9. Press **F5** to build and execute the application.
10. Move your cursor over the textBox1 control and verify that the background color changes to yellow.
11. Move your cursor off of the textBox1control and verify that the background color changes to white.
12. Close Form1.

CERTIFICATION READY
Can you validate and implement user input for a Windows application?
2.4

PAUSE. Leave the solution open to use in the next exercise.

You have just created two mouse Event Handler methods to process the MouseEnter and MouseLeave events. Within your Event Handler methods, you added code to change the color of the control to indicate that the control was under the mouse.

New to WPF applications is the default support for the stylus input device. With the advent of the Tablet PC and touch screens, more applications are requiring the user to interact with stylus input devices. By default, Windows Forms do not support stylus input devices, but you can download the Table PC Software Development Kit (SDK) to integrate stylus support into your Windows Forms Application.

Working with Stylus User Inputs

By default, only WPF supports stylus user inputs. Many of the same events for the keyboard and mouse are supported for the stylus.

Table 5-4 lists the common stylus user input events with a description.

Table 5-4

Common Stylus User Inputs

EVENT	APPLICATION TYPE	ACTION LEVEL	DESCRIPTION
StylusButtonUp	WPF	Device	Event is raised when the user releases a stylus button that was previously pressed. Use the `StylusButtonEventArgs e` to determine which button was pressed, what type of stylus was used, if the stylus was in air when the event occurred, and the location of the mouse pointer.
StylusButtonDown	WPF	Device	Event is raised when the user presses a stylus button. Use the `StylusButtonEventArgs e` to determine which button was pressed, what type of stylus was used, if the stylus was in air when the event occurred, and the location of the mouse pointer.
StylusUp	WPF	Device	Event is raised when the user lifts the stylus off the surface of the screen. When the stylus is lifted up, the stylus is considered in air. Use the `StylusEventArgs e` to determine what type of stylus was used, if the stylus was in air when the event occurred, and the location of the mouse pointer.
StylusDown	WPF	Device	Event is raised when the user places the stylus back onto the screen after an in air event. Use the `StylusEventArgs e` to determine what type of stylus was used, if the stylus was in air when the event occurred, and the location of the mouse pointer.
StylusMove	WPF	Device	Event is raised when the user moves the stylus across the screen while the stylus is touching the screen. Use the `StylusEventArgs e` to determine what type of stylus was used, if the stylus was in air when the event occurred, and the location of the mouse pointer.
StylusInAirMove	WPF	Control	Event is raised when the user moves the stylus and the stylus is not touching the screen. Use the `StylusEventArgs e` to determine what type of stylus was used, if the stylus was in air when the event occurred, and the location of the mouse pointer.
StylusOutOfRange	WPF	Control	Event is raised when the user moves the stylus too far away from the screen, and the screen and the stylus lose communications. Because a stylus is not attached to the machine, it can be moved far away from the screen and lose communications. Use this event to notify the user that the stylus is no longer communicating with the application.
StylusInRange	WPF	Control	Event is raised when the user moves the stylus closer to the screen and communication is reestablished after the stylus had been too far away and communication had been lost. Use this event to notify the user that the stylus is communicating with the application again.

To see how the stylus events work, you need to have hardware and an operating system that supports stylus input devices. When the stylus is present, you can implement stylus Event Handler methods to react to the stylus actions.

There are several events that only operate at the control action and/or Form/Window level. These events are not device specific and could be raised by any number of input device types.

Working with Control User Inputs

Not all user input device events are generated by a specific type of input device. Some user input device events are generated by a variety of device types and handled by the Control and/or Form/Window.

Table 5-5 lists the common Control and/or Form/Window user input events with a description.

Table 5-5

Common Control User Inputs

EVENT	APPLICATION TYPE	ACTION LEVEL	DESCRIPTION
Click	Windows Forms	Control and Form/Window	Only supported in Windows Forms. In WPF use the MouseDown/MouseUp event and the e.ClickCount property to determine how many clicks the user initiated. The Click event is raised when the user presses and then releases the mouse button once. Use this event to determine when the user performed a single click, but the EventArgs e does not provide information on where the user clicked or with what buttons.
DoubleClick	Windows Forms/WPF	Control and Form/Window	Supported in both Windows Forms and WPF, even though you can still use the MouseDown/MouseUp event and the e.ClickCount property to determine how many clicks the user initiated. The DoubleClick event is raised when the user presses and then releases the mouse button twice. Use this event to determine when the user performed a double-click, but the EventArgs e does not provide information on where the user clicked or with what buttons.
GotFocus	Windows Forms/WPF	Control and Form/Window	Event is raised when a control receives the focus from a user input device action. The GotFocus event uses the EventArgs e parameter, so that which type of user input device initiated the action or which control had the focus previously is not known. Use this event to determine when the application has received focus.
LostFocus	Windows Forms/WPF	Control and Form/Window	Event is raised when focus moves away from the control. The LostFocus event uses the EventArgs e parameter, so that which type of user input device initiated the action or which control is getting focus next is not known. Use this event to determine when the application no longer has focus.

EVENT	APPLICATION TYPE	ACTION LEVEL	DESCRIPTION
Validating	Windows Forms	Control and Form/Window	Event is raised on any control derived from the Control class. When controls gain and lose focus, they progress through the control focus life cycle: • Enter • GotFocus • Leave • Validating • Validated • LostFocus When the user wants to leave a control, the Validating event is raised when the control's CauseValidation property is set to true. Use this event to perform any value validation before indicating to the user that this control's value is a valid input. You will commonly use this event with the ErrorProvider control. If your validation process fails, use the e.Cancel property of the `CancelEventArgs e` parameter to keep the Validated event from being raised.
Validated	Windows Forms	Control and Form/Window	Event is raised when the Validating event's e.Cancel property is false. Use this event to clear any error messages, say on an ErrorProvider control, perform any clean-up activities, and/or set interdependent control values based on the validated control value.

USE CONTROL LEVEL USER INPUT EVENTS

USE the project you created in the previous exercise.

1. Select the Form1.cs [Design] tab and select textBox1.
2. In the Properties window, select the Events button from the Properties toolbar and locate the Click event.
3. Double-click the event selection cell to display the Form1.cs tab.
4. Inside the textBox1_Click method key the following code:

```
// Show a message box to display what text has
// been highlighted.
MessageBox.Show("textBox1's highlighted text is:"
+ textBox1.SelectedText);
```

5. Press **F5** to build and execute the application.
6. Key **Hello World.**
7. Click in between the two L's in Hello. Make sure to press down and release your mouse button to complete the entire Click event.
8. Verify that the message box appears and the highlighted value is blank.
9. Place your cursor in between the words Hello and World.
10. Press down the mouse button and drag the mouse to the right until you have highlighted to the end of textBox1.
11. Release the mouse button.

12. Verify that the message box appears and the highlighted value is World.

13. Close Form1.

PAUSE. Leave the solution open to use in the next exercise.

You have just implemented an Event Handler method for the textBox Click event. The Click event is raised when the mouse is pressed down and then released; thus in the first part of the exercise you raised the Click event with nothing highlighted because the mouse did not move. In the second part of the exercise, you raised the Click event with text highlighted because you moved the mouse between the mouse down and mouse up.

In addition to Control level user input events, you also have Form/Windows level user input events. The Form/Window level user input events are both reactions to user input devices and to validation processing.

USE FORM/WINDOW LEVEL USER INPUT EVENTS

USE the project you created in the previous exercise.

1. Select the Form1.cs tab and locate the Click and DoubleClick Event Handler methods.

2. Comment out the lines of code inside of the Click Event Handler method.

3. Select the Form1.cs [Design] tab.

4. Locate the Toolbox window and expand the Common Controls grouping.

5. Double-click the Button item.

6. Select the Button and locate the Properties window.

7. Key the following property values:

Location: 185,4

Text: Push Me

8. Select the Form1.cs [Design] tab and select textBox1.

9. In the Properties window, select the Events button from the Properties toolbar and locate the Validating event.

10. Double-click the event selection cell to display the Form1.cs tab.

11. Inside the textBox1_Validating method, key the following code:

```
// Check to see if the textbox's text content
// has a length of 7 or less.
if (textBox1.Text.Length < 7)
        // The text content is not too long, set the
        // textbox's font color to black.
        textBox1.ForeColor = Color.Black;
else
{
        // The text content is too long; set the
        // textbox's font color
        // to red to indicate there is an issue.
        textBox1.ForeColor = Color.Red;
}
```

12. Press **F5** to build and execute the application.

13. Key **Hello** and press **Tab**.

14. Verify that the textBox font color is still black.

15. Select the textBox and key **Hello World**.

16. Press **Tab**.

17. Verify that the textBox font color is now red.

18. Close Form1

19. Select the Form1.cs [Design] tab and select the textBox1 control.

20. In the Properties window, locate the Validated event.

21. Double-click the event selection cell to display the Form1.cs tab.

22. Inside of the textBox1_Validated method key the following code:

```
// Display a message box to indicate that the
// Validated event was processed. Typically,
// you would not display a message if a value
// is correct; this is for demonstration
// purposes only.
MessageBox.Show("TextBox is Valid.");
```

23. Locate the following code inside of the textBox1_Validating method:

```
// Change the textbox's font color to red,
// indicating that an error
// has occurred. You could also display a
// message box.
textBox1.ForeColor = Color.Red;
```

24. Immediately following the code in step 23, key:

```
// Cancel the validation. This sets focus back
// to the textbox allow
// the user to fix the issue.
e.Cancel = true;
```

25. Press **F5** to build and execute the application.

26. Key **Hello** and press **Tab**.

27. Verify that the textBox font color is still black and that the message box appears stating that the textbox is valid.

28. Select OK.

29. Select the textBox and key **Hello World**.

30. Press **Tab**.

31. Verify that the textBox font color is now red and that the message box is not shown because the Validated event is not raised.

32. Close Form1.

33. Verify that you cannot close Form1. Because your form has been marked as not valid, you will not be able to close the form until you have processed the Validation event without a cancellation.

34. Select the textBox, key **Hello** and then press **Tab**.

35. Close Form1

CERTIFICATION READY
Can you validate and implement user input for a Windows application?
2.4

PAUSE. Leave the solution open to use in the next exercise.

You have just created Validating and Validated Event Handler methods to respond to the lost focus user input life cycle. You validated that the textbox's contents were less than seven characters long and changed the font color based on your validation. You then added additional validation code to cancel the Validated event when validation failed.

During the validation process, you will encounter situations where the user has entered text into a number field or entered a decimal number into an integer field. When you try to validate these types of situations, Visual Studio will encounter an error and throw an Exception.

■ Handling Exceptions

↓ **THE BOTTOM LINE**   When processing user inputs, it is common for values to be in the wrong format or data type. Attempting to process invalid formatting or data types will cause Exceptions.

Understanding the Exception Class

An *Exception* is a run-time error that will halt the execution of the application unless handled. Understanding when an Exception is generated and what type of information the Exception provides will help you to respond correctly.

The Exception class is a part of the System namespace and handles all run-time error handling. When an Exception occurs, the error is handled either by the System Exception Handler or by a specific application Exception Handler. Exception handling can be categorized into two basic types:

- Common Language Runtime (CLR) Exceptions: This type of Exception is usually generated from data-type conversion errors, assignment errors, or invalid property or method functionality.
- User-Defined Exceptions: You will define these Exceptions yourself. Use user-defined Exceptions to notify various parts of the application that another part of the application has experienced an error.

Table 5-6 lists the common properties of the Exception class with a description.

Table 5-6

Common Exception Class Properties

PROPERTY/EVENT	DESCRIPTION
HelpLink	Clickable text that launches the help system for the Exception. Use this property to launch the help topic associated with the Exception where you can get additional information not contained in the Message property.
Message	A short textual description explaining the Exception error. Use this property to quickly identify what Exception was raised. When working with user-defined Exceptions, make this property as descriptive and meaningful as possible without being too verbose.
Source	The control, method, or object that generated the Exception. Use this property to identify where the Exception is coming from.
StackTrace	A complete capture of the call stack when the Exception occurred. Use this property to debug where and why the Exception was raised. Although the StackTrace output can look ominous and formidable, it can be your best source of information when trying to identify why an Exception was raised. If you start at the top of the StackTrace output and spend the time to work call by call down through the provided information, you will find where and why the Exception was thrown.

When an Exception is raised it halts all application execution. If unhandled, the default Visual Studio Exception handler will be used to display the Exception dialog (Figure 5-1).

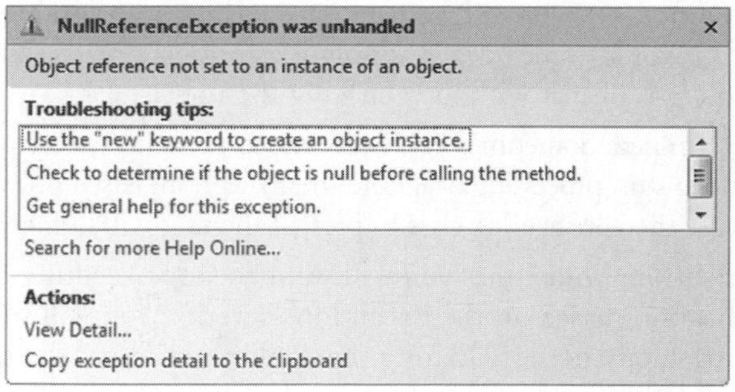

Figure 5-1

Visual Studio default Exception handler

Allowing the default Visual Studio Exception handler to take care of all your Exceptions is not a best practice and will cause the application to exit execution any time an unhandled Exception is raised. It is a best practice to implement your own Exception handling routines.

Trapping Exceptions

To implement a best-practice Exception handling routine, you first need to trap your Exceptions. Exceptions are trapped in Visual Studio using the Try-Catch-Finally statement.

The following code represents the try-catch-finally code statement syntax:

```
try
{
    // Try to perform some processing . . .
}
catch (Exception ex)
{
    // Process exception
}
finally
{
    // No matter what, these are the things
    // I still want to perform
}
```

The Try block is where the application is trying to process functionality. An example of some processing that might occur in the Try block would be the action of creating a new file on the hard drive. There are a number of errors that could occur when the application tries to create a file: the file path could be wrong, you could run out of disk space, you could have insufficient permission to the folder where you want to save the file, and so forth. Any one of the errors mentioned above would cause the action of saving your file to generate an Exception.

Once the Exception is raised, the Catch block begins to execute. In the Catch block, you will try to figure out which Exception has occurred and what to do with the Exception. There are several actions you can take when you encounter an Exception in the Catch block:

- Ignore: Sometimes you will want to ignore the Exception by doing nothing in the Catch block. You would want to ignore only Exceptions that you know will not cause the application to crash or exit without notifying the user.

- User Determined: Sometimes you will want to present the Exception to the user for input. You may want to stop processing or ignore the Exception, based on what you want to accomplish. You can use the MessageBox class to present the user with a message for processing.

- Halt Execution: Sometimes you will want to stop executing the application or even exit the application, based on the Exception's severity. You will want to exit the application only if absolutely needed. Exiting the application leaves the user wondering what happened and how to resolve the issue. It is better to notify the user of the issue, present him/her with options, and then process the Exception accordingly.

The Exception class is the base class for creating derived Exception classes. There are over 50 derived Exception classes in the System namespace, with more Exception classes in other .NET Framework namespaces that handle very specific types of Exceptions.

Table 5-7 lists some of the common derived System Namespace Exception classes with a description.

Table 5-7

Common Derived System Namespace Exception Classes

EXCEPTION CLASS	DESCRIPTION
AccessViolationException	Event is raised when you attempt to access random-access memory that you do not have permission for or that is protected.
ApplicationException	Event is raised when a nonfatal Exception occurs within the application. A nonfatal Exception means that the application does not exist without notice.
ArgumentException	Event is raised when you try to pass a parameter to a method and the parameter is the wrong format or type.
ArithmeticException	Event is raised when a mathematical error has occurred. There is also a DivideByZeroException that catches division expressions where the denominator is a zero. For all other conversion or math casts, the ArithmeticException is raised.
DllNotFoundException	Event is raised when the application tries to gain a reference to a DLL but cannot find the DLL at the specified path.
IndexOutOfRangeException	Event is raised when you try to access an array item and the index for the item is not within the upper and lower array limits.
InsufficientMemoryException	Event is raised when the operating system notifies the application that it has run out of physical memory to allocate to the application.
NullReferenceException	Event is raised any time you try to assign or evaluate a variable and the variable has a null value. This is one of the most common Exceptions you will encounter.
OverflowException	Event is raised when you try to assign a value to a variable and the variable cannot hold the value. This Exception is most commonly seen when incrementing a counter and you exceed the highest number the counter variable can hold.
StackOverflowException	Event is raised when the stack that keeps track of the method calls grows too large and overflows the maximum number of method calls that can be tracked. This Exception usually occurs when you implement recursive methods and you are in an infinite loop.

When the Try block is executing, different derived Exception classes may raise an Exception that you want to handle. To handle multiple types of Exception classes, declare multiple Catch blocks. You can also have a Catch block that catches all Exception classes by using the Exception class or no Exception class declaration at all:

```
try
{
    // Try to perform some processing . . .
}
catch (StackOverflowException exStack)
{
    // Process exception handling for stack overflow
    // exceptions
}
catch (NullReferenceException exNull)
{
    // Process exception handling for null exceptions
}
catch
{
    // Process all other exceptions
}
finally
{
    // No matter what, these are the things I still
    // want to perform
}
```

Once the Catch block has completed its exception handling, the Finally block is executed. The Finally block is optional, but when it is present, it is always executed. Even if an Exception is not raised, the Finally block will still be executed. Use the Finally block to complete any cleanup.

USE THE TRY-CATCH-FINALLY EXCEPTION HANDLER

USE the project you created in the previous exercise.

1. Select the Form1.cs tab and locate the `textBox1_Validating` method.
2. Replace the current `textBox1_Validating` method's code with the following code:

```
// Initialize
string testText = null;
// Validate the text content and convert the text
// to all uppercase characters.
try
{
    // Check to see if the textbox's text content
    // has a length of 7 // or less.
    if (textBox1.Text.Length < 7)
```

```
                {
                    // The text content is not too long,
                    // set the textbox's
                    // font color to black.
                    textBox1.ForeColor = Color.Black;
                    // Causes an exception
                    testText = testText.ToString()
                            .ToUpper();
                }
                else
                {
                    // The text content is too long, set
                    // the textbox's font
                    // color to red to indicate there is an issue.
                    textBox1.ForeColor = Color.Red;
                    // Cancel the validation navigation and
                    // keep focus on
                    // the textbox control.
                    e.Cancel = true;
                }
            }
            // Check for a null reference exception
            catch (NullReferenceException exNull)
            {
                    // Trapped the exception, now handle the
                    // exception by displaying
                    // a message box notifying the user.
                    MessageBox.Show("Exception: (" +
                        exNull.GetType().ToString()
                        + ") - " + exNull.Message);
            }
            // Check for another type of exception
            catch (Exception ex)
            {
                    // Leave the exception unhandled.
            }
            finally
            {
                    // Display a message to show how the finally
                    // part of the try-catch code block works.
                    // Typically you would not annoy
                    // the user with a message, only perform code
                    // that needs to be performed after the execution
```

```
                            // of the try-catch.
                    MessageBox.Show("I am always executed.");
        }
```

3. Press **F5** to build and execute the application.

4. Key **Hello** and press **Tab**.

5. Verify that a message box appears that states that an Exception has occurred, the Exception is a NullReferenceException, and that the message states that the object reference is not set to an object.

6. Click OK.

7. Verify that a message box is displayed that shows the "I am always executed." message.

8. Click OK.

9. Click OK when the Valid message box appears.

10. Place the cursor at the end of the text entered in step 4 and key **SPACE** and **World**.

11. Press **Tab.**

12. Verify that a message box is displayed that shows the "I am always executed." message. The Finally block is always run, even when an Exception is not raised.

13. Click OK.

14. Click OK when the Valid message box appears.

15. Click OK when the "I am always executed." message box appears.

16. Close Form1.

CERTIFICATION READY
Can you validate and implement user input for a Windows application?
2.4

PAUSE. Leave the solution open to use in the next exercise.

You have just introduced a NullReferenceException error into you application code to see how the Try-Catch-Finally block operates. When you tried to convert a null value to an uppercase value, the ToUpper method raised a NullReferenceException. You caught and handled the NullReferenceException and presented a message to the user. When the Catch block was complete, the Finally block was executed.

You can respond to System Exceptions or you can raise your own custom Exceptions.

Throwing Exceptions

In addition to System Exceptions, you can create your own Exception classes and/or you can raise your own Exceptions based on the base Exception class.

Much like any other class in the .NET Framework, the Exception class can be derived and extended to perform custom Exception handling. Some derived classes like the OutOfMemoryException can also be inherited and extended, but other derived classes like the StackOverflowException cannot be inherited. Check the .NET Framework documentation to understand which derived Exception classes are inheritable.

If you want to raise a custom Exception without creating a derived Exception class, you can use the Throw method. The Throw method can also be used to re-raise an Exception that was previously trapped. The following code is an example of throwing a nonderived Exception:

```
throw new Exception("Custom Exception...");
```

⊙ THROW CUSTOM EXCEPTIONS

USE the project you created in the previous exercise.

1. Select the Form1.cs tab and locate the `textBox1_Validating` method.

2. Replace the current `textBox1_Validating` method's code with the following code:

```csharp
    // Try to validate the textbox contents.
    try
    {
        // Call the validateProcessing method. This method
        // will trap for the Null Reference Exception.
        validateProcessing();
        // If an exception is not thrown from
        // within the validateProcessing method
        // then this line of code is
        // executed to make sure that the validation
        // navigation continues.
        e.Cancel = false;
    }
    // Trap for a Null Reference Exception.
    catch (NullReferenceException exNull)
    {
        // Display a message box to show that a
        // Null Reference Exception occurred.
        MessageBox.Show("Exception: (" +
        exNull.GetType().ToString() + ") - "
        + exNull.Message);
        // Cancel validation navigation.
        e.Cancel = true;
    }
    // Trap for any other exception.
    catch (Exception ex)
    {
        // Display a message box to show that an
        // exception occurred.
        MessageBox.Show("Exception: (" +
        ex.GetType().ToString() + ") - " + ex.Message);
        // Cancel validation navigation.
        e.Cancel = true;
    }
    // Always execute . . .
    finally
    {
        // Display a message to show how the finally
        // part of the try-catch code block works.
        // Typically you would not annoy
        // the user with a message, only perform code
        // that needs to be performed after the execution
        // of the try-catch.
        MessageBox.Show("I am always executed.");
    }
```

3. Immediately following the textBox1_Validating method, key the following code:

```
// Create the validateProcess method.
// This method checks the length of the textBox1
// text contents and
// converts the text contents to all uppercase.
private void validateProcessing()
{
    // Validate the text content and convert the
    // text to all uppercase characters.
    try
    {
        // Check to see if the textbox's text content
        // has a length of 7 or less.
        if (textBox1.Text.Length < 7)
        {
            // The text content is not too long,
            // set the textbox's font color to black.
            textBox1.ForeColor = Color.Black;
            // Causes an exception
            testText = testText.ToString().ToUpper();
        }
        else
        {
            // The text content is too long, set
            // the textbox's font color to red
            // to indicate there is an issue.
            textBox1.ForeColor = Color.Red;
            // Cancel the validation navigation and keep
            // focus on the textbox control.
            e.Cancel = true;
        }
    }
    // Check for a null reference exception
    catch (NullReferenceException exNull)
    {
        // Throw a new exception with a custom message.
        // This exception will be trapped a general
        // exception in the calling method.
        throw new Exception("Custom Exception...");
    }
}
```

4. Press **F5** to build and execute the application.
5. Key **Hello** and press **Tab**.

6. Verify that a message box appears that states that an Exception has occurred, the Exception is a System.Exception, and that the message shows your Customer Exception . . . message.

7. Click OK.

8. Verify that a message box is displayed that shows the "I am always executed" message.

9. Click OK.

10. Click OK when the Valid message box appears.

11. Place the cursor at the end of the text entered in step 5 and key **SPACE** and **World**.

12. Press **Tab**.

13. Verify that a message box is displayed that shows the "I am always executed" message.

14. Click OK.

15. Click OK when the Valid message box appears.

16. Close Form1.

STOP. Save or discard the solution. It will not be used again for another exercise.

CERTIFICATION READY
Can you validate and implement user input for a Windows application?
2.4

You have just created a new method to perform your validation processing where you are trapping for the NullReferenceException, but when the Exception is raised, you handle the Exception by throwing your own custom Exception. In the `validateProcessing` method, you are still checking for an Exception, but now the generic Exception block is trapping and handling the message.

SKILL SUMMARY

IN THIS LESSON YOU LEARNED HOW TO:

- Understand the Windows User Input Model and the various device input action levels.
- Understand Keyboard, Mouse, and Stylus events and their device input action level.
- Create Keyboard, Mouse, and Stylus Event Handler methods.
- Understand the Exception class and various derived Exception classes.
- Handle various Exceptions and raise a custom Exception.

■ Knowledge Assessment

Fill in the Blank

Complete the following sentences by writing the correct word or words in the blanks provided.

1. The _____ event is raised when a mouse button is pressed.

2. A _____ is raised from an individual action on an input device.

3. The _____ event is raised when the user presses and then releases a keyboard key.

4. The _____ class is the base class for all derived Exception Handler classes.

5. A _____ is raised when an input device action is handled on a per-control basis.

6. The _____ event is raised when a keyboard key is released.

7. A _____ event is raised when a mouse button is pressed down and then released all as one event.

8. A _____ event is raised as part of the control focus life cycle to check a control's value.

9. A _____ is raised when an input device action is handled on a per-Form/Window basis.

10. The _____ Exception class property contains a list of all the methods called before the Exception is raised.

Multiple Choice

Circle the letter that corresponds to the best answer.

1. Which of the following events is NOT a mouse device action event?
   a. MouseUp
   b. MouseClick
   c. MouseDown
   d. MouseLeave

2. Which of the following events is NOT a keyboard device action event?
   a. KeyPress
   b. KeyUp
   c. KeyDown
   d. KeyClick

3. Which of the following is NOT a derived System Exception class?
   a. ExecutableNotFoundException
   b. NullReferenceException
   c. DivideByZeroException
   d. DllNotFoundException

4. Which of the following code syntax is NOT used to handle an Exception?
   a. Catch
   b. Catch (Exception ex)
   c. Finish
   d. Try

5. Which of the following code syntax is NOT used to throw a custom Exception?
   a. Raise
   b. New
   c. Throw
   d. Exception

6. Which Mouse event do you use to handle the user spinning the wheel?
   a. MouseSpin
   b. MouseWheel
   c. MouseMove
   d. MouseTurn

7. Which property of the CancelEventArgs on the Validating event causes the Validated event NOT to be raised?
   a. Valid
   b. Cancel
   c. Stop
   d. Error

8. Which of the following events is raised when a control becomes the current input selection?
   a. Focus
   b. Focused
   c. FocusChanged
   d. GotFocus

9. Which of the following input devices is NOT supported in a Windows Forms Application without an additional SDK?
   a. Keyboard
   b. Stylus
   c. Mouse
   d. None of the above

10. Which action level would you use if you wanted to validate each character before it was displayed to the user?
    a. Form/Window
    b. Control
    c. Device
    d. All of the above

■ Competency Assessment

Scenario 5-1: Navigation Indicators

You have been assigned the task to prototype the new navigation features for the data entry screen for the Human Resources (HR) department. You will need to collect personal information for each employee including full name, full address, home and work telephone numbers, and an e-mail address. The HR department does not want to use the mouse once they start entering data and wants to easily be able to determine which field they are currently working with. The HR department does not like the MaskedTextBox control; thus do not use it in your prototype.

Scenario 5-2: Required Fields

You now need to extend your HR data entry screen to provide some basic value validation. All of the fields on this screen are required. When the user moves from one control to the next, validate that a value was entered. If a value is not entered, notify the user that the field is required.

■ Proficiency Assessment

Scenario 5-3: Custom Telephone Mask

After the first review of the HR data entry screen, your test users said that they did not like that the telephone controls were not formatted correctly. Implement a centralized Event Handler to ensure that your telephone controls follow the format "X.(XXX).XXXX", where X is a number only. Make sure to handle the Backspace and Delete key. Remember, the HR department does not like the MaskedTextBox control; thus do not use it in your prototype.

Scenario 5-4: Cryptic Exception Messages

Another complaint from your prototype users was that the application would exit after displaying a cryptic Exception message. Implement an Exception trapping process that ensures that, no matter what, the application will never show an Exception message. Once implemented, create a custom Exception that is raised when a non-number key is pressed inside the telephone control.

Integrating Data

LESSON SKILL MATRIX

SKILLS/CONCEPTS	MTA EXAM OBJECTIVE	MTA EXAM OBJECTIVE NUMBER
Understanding Data in Windows Applications	Understand data access methods for a Windows application.	4.1
Working with Data in Windows Forms	Understand databound controls.	4.2
Working with Data in WPF		

KEY TERMS

Add Connection Dialog

ADO.NET

connected

data store

DataProvider

DataSet

disconnected

Server Explorer

WPF binding

Part of the prototype requires that you interface with your organization's information technology system to read and display company information. You will be evaluating and comparing the way that Windows Forms and WPF applications implement data controls. You will be presenting at a leadership meeting the Windows Forms and WPF applications you create. You should be prepared to answer any questions about how both of the applications provide database support.

■ Understanding Data in Windows Applications

THE BOTTOM LINE When creating Windows applications with Visual Studio, you have the capability to integrate various data sources within the application. A data source enables you to save application data into a managed medium where you are not concerned about the format of the file system data, only with the format presented by the management medium.

Introducing Active Data Objects (ADO.NET)

The Microsoft .NET Framework provides consistent access to various data sources through the *Active Data Objects (ADO.NET)* set of classes in the System.Data namespace.

As you develop Windows applications, your need to store data long term or to interact with large amounts of data at one time requires you to use a data store. A ***data store*** is a data file and a management engine that provides access into the data file. Microsoft Access and Microsoft SQL Server are both examples of data stores. Data store interactions are handled through the use of the .NET Framework System.Data (ADO.NET) and System.XML namespaces (Figure 6-1). Microsoft has developed these two namespaces to provide you with the ability to have both connected and disconnected data objects. ***Connected*** is when you can read/write directly with a data source. ***Disconnected*** is when you can read/write temporarily to an XML file until connected again.

Figure 6-1

ADO.NET architecture

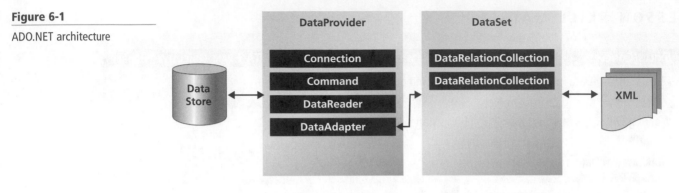

There are two major components to the ADO.NET architecture, the ***DataProvider*** and the ***DataSet***. Table 6-1 summarizes the two ADO.NET major components and their subcomponents.

Table 6-1

ADO.NET Components and Subcomponents

COMPONENTS	SUBCOMPONENTS	DESCRIPTION
DataProvider		A fast forward-only, read-only data manipulation interface to a data store. Each DataProvider is explicitly designed to communicate with only one type of data store.
	Connection	How the DataProvider talks with the data store. The Connection component is established first and is used by the other DataProvider components to perform operations.
	Command	How the DataProvider gets and changes data, as well as runs stored procedures against the data store. The Command component uses the Connection component to talk with the data store and usually has a return value to indicate whether the command was successful.
	DataReader	Provides high-performance streams of information from the data store. The DataReader is high performance because it is forward-only and read-only, thus limiting the number of transactions and speeding up the processing. The DataReader uses the Connection component to talk with the data store.
	DataAdapter	Provides the ability to execute SQL commands against the data store and synchronizes changes between the DataSet and the data store. The DataAdapter uses the Connection component to talk with the data store and the Command component to define the SelectCommand, InsertCommand, DeleteCommand, or UpdateCommand. A DataAdapter can also populate a DataSet.
DataSet		A collection of tables, with rows and columns, primary keys, foreign keys, and constraints, and the relationships between the tables. The DataSet was designed to be the key component for disconnected operations. Because the DataSet can hold information from various data stores and save directly to XML, data can be manipulated and saved back to a connected data store or to a disconnected XML file.

Table 6-1 (*continued*)

Components	Subcomponents	Description
	DataTableCollection	Consists of multiple DataTable objects where each DataTable consists of columns, rows, primary keys, foreign keys, and constraints. Use DataTableCollection most often to locate and manipulate your data. Use the DataColumnCollection with its DataColumn object to access a table's columns. Use the DataRowCollection with its DataRow object to access a table's rows.
	DataRelationCollection	Consists of multiple DataRelation objects where each DataRelation consists of a relationship between two DataTable objects. Use the DataRelationCollection to enforce integrity constraints on your data while it is disconnected from the data store.

The .NET Framework provides several built-in Data Providers. Data Providers can be developed by anyone who needs to interface with a data store, but are typically produced by the data store's manufacture. Table 6-2 summarizes the .NET Framework built-in Data Providers.

Table 6-2

.NET Framework Data Providers

Data Provider	Description
SQL Server	Designed to work best with the SQL Server database application. If you need to access data from a SQL Server version 7.0 or later or a Microsoft Data Engine (MSDE) database, use the SQL Server Data Provider. The SQL Server Data Provider is preferred over the SQL OLE DB Data Provider, except when you are accessing a SQL Server version 6.5 or earlier, where you are required to use the SQL OLE DB Data Provider.
Object Linking and Embedding (OLE) Database (DB)	The Object Linking and Embedding (OLE) Database (DB) Data Provider is a generic data-access provider for data stores that support the OLE DB interface. OLE DB was designed to be a replacement for the ODBC interface and provides a wider range of support for non-relational data stores. Use the OLE DB Data Provider when your data store does not have its own unique Data Provider.. The OLE DB Provider is the preferred method of connecting to a Microsoft Access database and should be used over any ODBC Data Providers.
ODBC	The most generic data-access provider for data stores that support the ODBC interface. An ODBC Data Provider should only be used when no other Data Provider is available. Although the most generic of all the Data Providers, the ODBC Data Provider is also the most supported among the data stores. You will usually be able to find an ODBC Data Provider for almost any data store available.
Oracle	Designed to work specifically with the Oracle database application. If you need to access data from an Oracle database 8.1.7 or later, it is best to use the Oracle Data Provider, for which you will need to reference both the System.Data and System.Data.OracleClient namespaces.

To connect to a data store from within the Visual Studio environment, use the Server Explorer window and the new data source wizard.

Connecting Data to Windows Applications

TAKE NOTE*

For this lesson, you will create and manage data source functionality only. Managing and creating server connections is outside the scope of this book.

Visual Studio provides a centralized location for managing data source connections using the Server Explorer. The Server Explorer has a built-in add connection feature that provides you with the set of dialogs needed to create and test a data source connection.

The ***Server Explorer*** window is a centralized location within the Visual Studio environment where you can manage and create connections to data sources and servers. The Server Explorer provides a data source connection feature that provides a set of dialogs to configure and test data source connections.

To create a data source connection, you need to open and locate the Server Explorer window (Figure 6-2). To open the Server Explorer window, use the View➔Server Explorer menu or the CTRL-W, L accelerator keys.

Figure 6-2

Server Explorer window

On the Server Explorer toolbar is the Connect to Database button, the third button from left on the toolbar below, which initiates the Data Connection creation process (Figure 6-3).

Figure 6-3

Server Explorer window toolbar

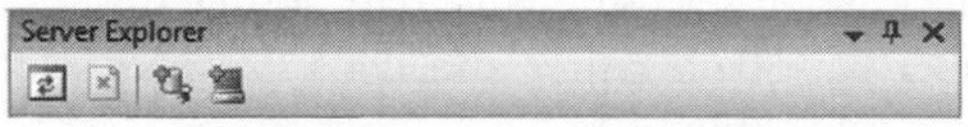

Pressing the Connect to Database button opens the ***Add Connection dialog***—a set of configurable options used to create a connection to a data store (Figure 6-4).

Figure 6-4

Add Connection dialog (Microsoft Access Database)

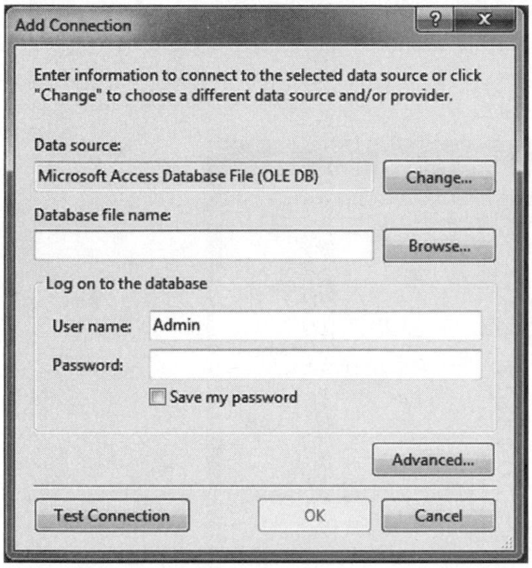

The first configuration option is the data source that is comprised of a type of database and the Data Provider used to connect to the database. You can make a different selection by using the Change . . . button that opens the Change Data Source dialog (Figure 6-5).

Figure 6-5

Change Data Source dialog

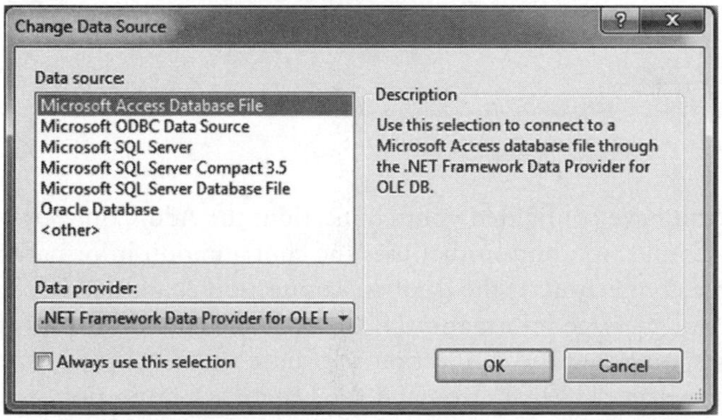

In the top portion of the Change Data Source dialog, you will set the type of database that you want to connect with. This list will grow if you install any additional third-party data providers or databases. The default list of data sources is provided by Microsoft. Beneath the Data Source selection is the Data Provider selection. You can select only one Data Provider for a data source, but a data source can have multiple Data Provider options. To see how this works, select the Microsoft SQL Server Data Source, and then use the drop-down arrow to see the list of Data Providers. A Microsoft SQL Server has both the SQL Server Data Provider and the OLE DB Data Provider. Not all data sources have more than one Data Provider, so ensure that you check when selecting your data source option. If you would like to have Visual Studio remember your data source and Data Provider selections, you can check the Always use this selection checkbox.

Depending on what type of data source you select, the Add Connection dialog will change (Figure 6-6). In Figure 6-3, you saw the Add Connection dialog configured to connect to a Microsoft Access database. The Add Connection dialog provided a control to set the file path, username, and password for the Microsoft Access database connection. If you change your data source to SQL Server with the SQL Server Data Provider, the Add Connection dialog will change to provide you with controls to select a server name, username, password, initial database, or database file name.

Figure 6-6

Add Connection dialog
(SQL Server)

Once you have configured your connection, the Add Connection dialog provides for you a Test Connection button that uses the configuration information provided to attempt a database connection. If the database connection is not possible, a message box will appear with error message information. If the database connection is completed, a message box will appear stating that the connection was successful. Once your connection was successful, you can select the OK button and the Database Connection is added to the Server Explorer (Figure 6-7).

Figure 6-7

Server Explorer window with
new Data Connection

Figure 6-8

Server Explorer window with
Data Connection expanded

A Data Connection inside of the Server Explorer has several features that you will use to interact with your database. For each Data Connection, Server Explorer adds subfolders entitled Tables, Views, Stored Procedures, and Functions. You can expand any one of these subfolders to see additional folders that expand to display database information (Figure 6-8).

The Server Explorer also has a right-click feature that enables you to view the data in a table, create a new query, and/or see the properties on a Data Connection element. By right-clicking, you will see the Server Explorer Window pop-up menu (Figure 6-9).

Figure 6-9

Server Explorer window
pop-up menu

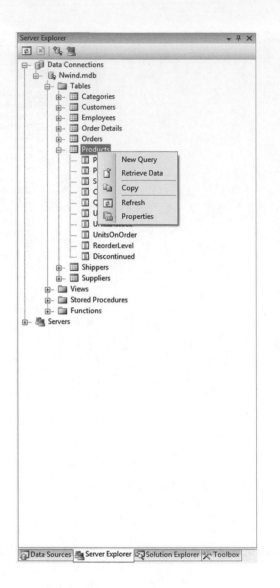

CREATE A DATA CONNECTION

GET READY. Before you begin these steps, be sure to launch Microsoft Visual Studio. A project is not needed to complete this exercise.

1. Locate the Server Explorer window.

2. On the Server Explorer window, click the Connect to Database button to display the Add Connection dialog.

3. On the Add Connection dialog, the data source should already be configured to use the Microsoft Access Database File (OLE DB) data source, but if it is not, use the following steps to set your data source to Microsoft Access Database File (OLE DB).

   a. Click the Change . . . button to display the Change Data Source dialog.

   b. In the data source list, select Microsoft Access Database File (OLE DB).

   c. In the Data Provider, select .NET Framework Data Provider for OLE DB.

   d. Click OK.

DOWNLOAD

All of the exercises in this lesson use the Microsoft Access 2000 Northwind Sample database, which can be downloaded from Microsoft at http://www.microsoft.com/downloads/details.aspx?familyid=c6661372-8dbe-422b-8676-c632d66c529c&displaylang=en

4. In the Database file name, key the path to your Nwind.mdb file or click Browse . . . to locate the file on your hard drive.

5. Click Test Connection.

6. Verify that the Test Connection Succeeded message appears.

7. Click OK to make the message disappear.

8. Click OK to add your data connection.

9. Locate the Nwind.mdb folder in your Server Explorer window.

10. Expand the Nwind.mdb folder.

11. Verify that you have Tables, View, Stored Procedures, and Functions subfolders.

12. Expand the Tables folder.

13. Verify that you have a list of tables from the Nwind.mdb database.

14. Right-click on the Customers Table to display the Server Explorer window's pop-up menu.

15. Select Retrieve Data.

16. Verify that a new tab appears with the contents of the Customer's table presented.

CERTIFICATION READY
Do you understand data access methods for a Windows application?
4.1

PAUSE. Leave Visual Studio open to use in the next exercise.

You have just created a connection to a Microsoft Access database. The connection was created using the Server Explorer, Connect to Database feature. You used the Add Connection dialog and the Change Data Source dialog to configure your connection and then tested to make sure that your connection worked. Once your connection was added to the Server Explorer window, you expanded some of the folder to see the information provided by your database.

Adding a connection to the Server Explorer is only the beginning of adding database functionality to the application. In a Windows Forms Application, you can add data-aware controls or add database functionality in code.

■ Working with Data in Windows Forms

↓ THE BOTTOM LINE

A Windows Forms Application has several data controls that can be added to the UI to provide users with data interactions without much code. If you would prefer, you can also write code to control all of your data interactions using the System.Data namespace.

Creating Windows Forms Data Controls

The .NET Framework provides several Windows Forms controls that can be used to present data store information.

Table 6-3 lists the Windows Forms controls and some of their functionality.

Table 6-3

Windows Forms Data Controls

Control	Property/Method	Description
BindingSource		This is the first control you will want to add to any Windows Form when you want to use data in the application. The BindingSource control has several features that are used by other controls to connect with a data store. The BindingSource control defines the data source and Data Provider for the data connection. When adding a BindingSource control to your Windows Form, you will automatically get a DataSet that represents the selected information defined in the BindingSource control's DataSource property.
	AllowEdit	Determines if the BindingSource will allow the data source content data to be changed. You set this property to True when you want to allow the users to edit the data in the data store.
	AllowNew	Determines if the BindingSource will allow new items to be added to the data source content data. You set this property to True when you want to allow the users to add new items to the data store.
	AllowRemove	Determines if the BindingSource will allow items to be deleted from the data source content data. You set this property to True when you want to allow the users to delete items from the data store.
	DataMember	Further defines the list of data for the DataBinding control. The DataMember requires that the DataSource be set first. Once the DataSource has been defined, the DataMemeber further refines and selects an individual list within the DataSource as the single list for data. Use the DataMember when you want your DataBinding control to interact with only a single list within your DataSource.
	DataSource	Defines the type of data the connector is bound with. There are several types of data that a DataSource can be bound with, for example, a non-list, an array, or an enumerable data type. The DataSource is the first property you should set when adding a DataBinding control.
	Filter	Defines an expression that hides data from the current selection. The Filter property does not remove the hidden data from the DataSource; the remaining data is merely a subset of the entire data available. Use the Filter property to reduce the amount of data you want available for editing. To remove a filter, set the Filter property to Null.
	Position	Identifies where you are in the DataSource data. Use this property to get your current numeric placement. You can use this property with the Item property to get an Item at a certain position.
	Sort	Defines how the data is to be ordered. Use this property to organize your data after it has already been read.
	AddNew (object)	Adds a new item to the data. Use this method when you want to save your data.
	CancelEdit ( )	Cancels any edits since the last save or EndEdit method calls. Use this method to throw away any edits the user may have made if he/she presses a cancel button or closes a form without pressing a save button.

Table 6-3   *(continued)*

CONTROL	PROPERTY/METHOD	DESCRIPTION
	EndEdit ( )	Causes the DataBinding control to commit the current changes to the data store. Use this method when you are ready to save any data that has changed, or when the user presses a save button in his/her UI.
	Find (object description)	Searches for items in the data source. The Find method has two overrides. One Find method moves to the item found by the Find criteria. The other Find method returns the index of the item found by the Find criteria. Use this method to search for items.
	Insert (index, object)	Adds a new item at the index provided. Use this method to add a new item at a specific location when you are trying to keep your data organized.
	MoveFirst ( )	Moves the Position property to the first item in the data source. Use this method when you want to reset to first item.
	MoveLast ( )	Moves the Position property to the last item in the data source. Use this method when you want to fast forward to last item.
	MoveNext ( )	Moves the Position property to the next item in the data source. Use this method when you want to navigate one item forward.
	MovePrevious ( )	Moves the Position property to the previous item in the data source. Use this method when you want to navigate one item backward.
	Remove (object)	Deletes from the data source the item provided. Use this method to delete an item.
	RemoveAt (index)	Deletes the item from the data source at the provided index. Use this method to delete a specific item when you know the index only.
	RemoveCurrent ( )	Deletes the current positioned item from the data source. Use this method when you want to delete the item you are currently positioned on.
	RemoveFilter ( )	Clears any filters and allows all data to be visible. The RemoveFilter method has the same effect as setting the Filter property to Null.
	RemoveSort ( )	Clears any sorting and no longer organizes the data. The RemoveSort method has the same effect as setting the Sort property to Null.
	ResumeBinding ( )	Notifies any controls that are looking at the BindingSource that they should now update their values based on the current item selected. The ResumeBinding method is typically only called after a SuspendBinding method has been called. Use the ResumeBinding and SuspendBinding methods to keep your bound UI controls from trying to update values while you are browsing through the data.
	SuspendBinding ( )	Notifies any controls that are monitoring the BindingSource that they should not update their value while the BindingSource is changing.
DataSet		An easy way to get a DataSet added to the application without having to create the DataSet in code from scratch. The DataSet control has all the same functionality as the DataSet class and provides an in-memory representation of your data store content.

(continued)

Table 6-3 (*continued*)

CONTROL	PROPERTY/METHOD	DESCRIPTION
	EnforceContraints	Determines if the DataSet will ensure that any constraints defined in the DataSet are checked before an operation is performed on the data. Use this property to maintain or bypass any integrity checks that might be implemented within the data. There are times when you want to set the EnforceContraints property to False while you are fixing/cleaning up some data. You will then want to set the EnforceConstraints property back to True for future processing.
	ExtendedProperties	A collection of user-defined information stored with the DataSet. Use this property to save additional information about the DataSet that is not a part of the data contents. For example, if you wanted to store the last person who updated the data, you would use the ExtendedProperties.Add method to include a field called LastUpdatedBy with a value of the person's name that performed the update.
	DataSource	Determines which BindingSource this DataSet will be storing data for.
	Relations	A collection of DataRelations. Use the Relations property to gain access to all of the DataSet's defined relations. Use the DataRelation object to set the ChildTable, ChildKey, ParentTable, and ParentKey to define parent-child table relations.
	Tables	A collection of DataTables. Use the Tables property to gain access to all of the DataSets tables. Use the DataTables object to access the Columns and Rows properties.
	Clear ( )	Removes all data from the DataSet, but keeps the DataSet schema (data content definition). Use this method to remove all rows from all tables, but leave the tables and relations.
	Clone ( )	Makes a copy of the schema and structure of the DataSet, but leaves behind the data. Use the Clone method when you want to create an empty DataSet based on the structure of another DataSet.
	Copy ( )	Makes a new DataSet with the same schema, structure, and data as the DataSet being copied. Use this method to make an exact copy of the original DataSet.
	Merge ( )	Takes two DataSets and integrates the tables, relationships, and data into one DataSet. Use this method when you need to bring two copies of your DataSet into one. Because a DataSet can be disconnected from the data store until you are ready to update the data, you may find that you have more than one DataSet update that can all be merged into one DataSet before the update.
	ReadXML ( )	Reads the specified XML document into a DataSet. There are several overrides for the ReadXML method. The easiest to use is the ReadXML method, which requires a path to the XML document. If a schema is specified, the ReadXML method will create the DataSet based on the schema. If no schema is specified, the DataSet will infer the schema based on the XML content.
	WriteXML ( )	Saves the DataSet to an XML file. There are several overrides for the WriteXML method. The easiest to use is the WriteXML method, which requires a path to a file for writing. You can specify to save the schema with the file or not.

Table 6-3 *(continued)*

CONTROL	PROPERTY/METHOD	DESCRIPTION
BindingNavigator		An easy way to provide the users with nice move forward, back, first, last, add, and delete buttons. The BindingNavigator is a pre-configured button bar with all of the buttons needed to navigate your BindingSource. In addition to the preconfigured buttons, the BindingNavigator also has a ToolStrip control that allows you to add your own buttons for any custom operations you want to provide to the users.
	AllowItemReorder	Determines if the user will be allowed to move the buttons around on the BindingNavigators ToolStrip. Use this property if you want to allow the users to configure the BindingNavigator. Remember that if the users change the order of the buttons, you will need to handle the saving and restoring of the changed configuration.
	AddNewItem	Determines which of the ToolStripButtons will be the Add New button. Use this property to create your own custom Add New button and then associate your button with the BindingNavigator's Add New functionality.
	BindingSource	Determines which BindingSource this BindingNavigator will be navigating.
	Items	The collection of ToolStripButtons defined in the BindingNavigator. Use this property to manage the ToolStripButtons.
	MoveFirstItem	Determines which of the ToolStripButtons will be the Move First button. Use this property to create your own custom Move First button and then associate your button with the BindingNavigator's Move First functionality.
	MoveNextItem	Determines which of the ToolStripButtons will be the Move Next button. Use this property to create your own custom Move Next button and then associate your button with the BindingNavigator's Move Next functionality.
	MovePreviousItem	Determines which of the ToolStripButtons will be the Move Previous button. Use this property to create your own custom Move Previous button and then associate your button with the BindingNavigator's Move Previous functionality.
	MoveLastItem	Determines which of the ToolStripButtons will be the Move Last button. Use this property to create your own custom Move Last button and then associate your button with the BindingNavigator's Move Last functionality.
	PositionItem	Determines which of the ToolStripButtons will be the current Position indicator button. Use this property to create your own custom Position button and then associate your button with the BindingNavigator's current Position functionality.
DataGridView		A columns and rows representation of the BindingSource. Although the DataGridView does not support all of the functionality of a good spreadsheet application, it is an easy method of representing your BindingSource in a column and row configuration. Use the DataGridView when you need to display a large amount of your BindingSource to the user.

(continued)

Table 6-3 (*continued*)

CONTROL	PROPERTY/METHOD	DESCRIPTION
	AllowUserToAddRows	Determines if the user will be allowed to add rows via the DataGridView control. Use this property if you want to allow rows to be added when you are not using a BindingNavigation control.
	AllowUserToDeleteRows	Determines if the user will be allowed to remove rows via the DataGridView control. Use this property if you want to allow rows to be removed when you are not using a BindingNavigation control.
	AllowUserToOrderColumns	Determines if the user will be allowed to move columns around on the grid. Use this property to give the user more control over the Grid's column order. Remember, if you allow the user to reorder, you are responsible for saving the new column order and restore the order the next time the grid is loaded.
	AllowUserToResizeColumns	Determines if the user will be allowed to resize the width of each column. Use this property to give users more flexibility in the UI. Remember, if you allow the user to resize, you are responsible for saving the new column size and restoring the size the next time the grid is loaded.
	AllowUserToResizeRows	Determines if the user will be allowed to resize the height of each row. Use this property to give your users more flexibility in the UI. Remember, if you allow the use to resize, you are responsible for saving the new row size and restore the size the next time the grid is loaded.
	AlternatingRowsDefaultCellStyle	Used to change the style (background color, font …) of every other grid row. Use this property to give your users a visual guide that defines every other row. By alternating the background color of every other row, you create a visual effect that makes it easier for users to move across the grid without losing track of which row they are looking at.
	AutoGenerateColumns	Determines if the DataGridView control will automatically create the number of columns and the default column titles based on the data contained in the DataSource. Use this property to add data to the DataGridView at run time without having to preconfigure the DataGridView layout. You will want to pay close attention to the column names in your DataSource, given that they will become your column titles.
	AutoSizeColumnsMode	Determines if the DataGridView columns will automatically resize when the container is resized. Use this property to allow your columns to grow and shrink as the Container control grows and shrinks.
	AutoSizeRowsMode	Determines if the DataGridView rows will automatically resize when the container is resized. Use this property to allow your rows to grow and shrink as the Container control grows and shrinks.
	Columns	A collection of all the columns in the DataGridView control. Use this property to navigate and manipulate columns.

Table 6-3 *(continued)*

Control	Property/Method	Description
	CurrentCell	Determines the currently selected cell in the DataGridView. Use this property to get the value of the current cell and also to determine where (ColumnIndex and RowIndex) you are in the DataGridView.
	DataSource	Determines which BindingSource this DataGridView will be displaying.
	Rows	A collection of all the rows in the DataGridView control. Use this property to navigate and manipulate rows.
	SelectedColumns	Determines which columns the user has selected. This property is a collection of column objects. Use this property to determine if and how many columns the user has highlighted.
	SelectedRows	Determines which rows the user has selected. This property is a collection of row objects. Use this property to determine if and how many rows the user has highlighted.
	ClearSelection ( )	Removes the highlight from the current column and/or row selections. Use this property to reset the selection process.
	InvalidateColumn ( )	Marks the entire column as dirty, causing the DataGridView to refresh the column. Use this property when you have changed a value and want to ensure that the DataGridView updates the data change in the UI.
	InvalidateRow ( )	Marks the entire row as dirty, causing the DataGridView to refresh the row. Use this property when you have changed a value and want to ensure that the DataGridView updates the data change in the UI.
	Process . . . Key ( )	Supports a set of Process . . . Key methods where the... includes some keys like the Delete, Down, Left, Next, Right. Use these methods to provide the user with custom functionality when he/she presses any one of these keys. You may want to have the DataGirdView scroll 50 rows when the user presses the down key. Use the ProcessDownKey method then to move the selection 50 rows.
	Select ( )	Selects a cell within the DataGridView control. Use this method to move the current selection.
	SelectAll ( )	Selects all columns and rows within the DataGridView control. Use this method when you want to make the entire control the selection.
	Sort ( )	Adds sorting functionality in addition to BindingSource sort functionality. You typically use this method to sort your DataGridView data when you want to leave your BindingSource sort untouched.

TAKE NOTE ✱ This lesson focuses on Windows applications, but Windows Services also support the same data controls as Windows Forms. The BindingSource control can be very helpful when you need to connect data to your Windows Service application.

USE WINDOWS FORMS DATA CONTROLS

GET READY. Before you begin these steps, be sure to create a new Windows Forms project named wfaDataControls.

1. Locate the Toolbox window and expand the Data grouping (Figure 6-10).

Figure 6-10

Toolbox windows Data group

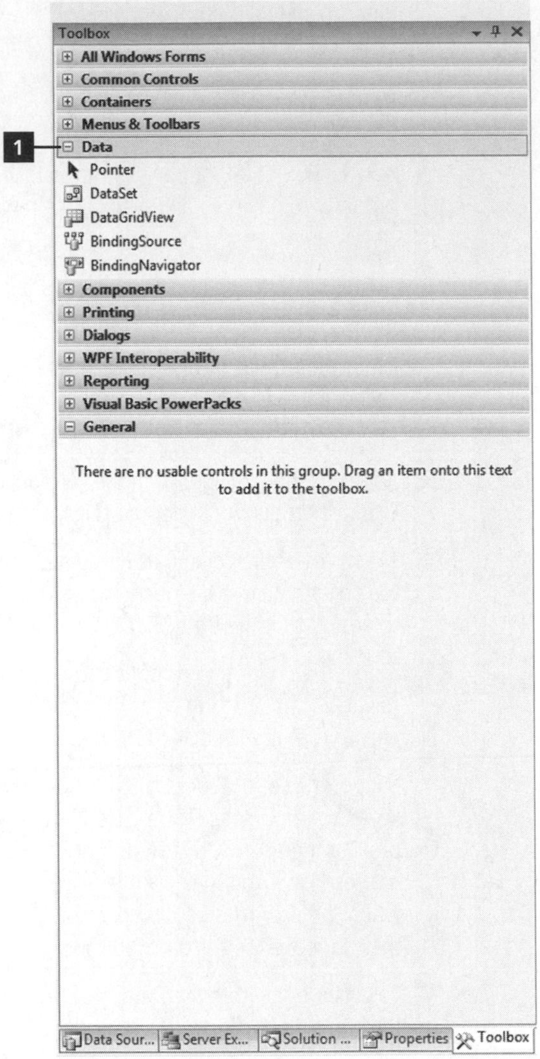

2. Locate the BindingSource control and double-click to add a BindingSource control to Form1.

TAKE NOTE*

The BindingSource control is not added to the Form's UI. You will find the BindingSource control at the bottom of the Form1.cs [Design] tab window.

3. Locate the Properties window and click in the DataSource properties value cell to display the DataSource properties editor (Figure 6-11).

Figure 6-11

BindingSource DataSource
properties editor

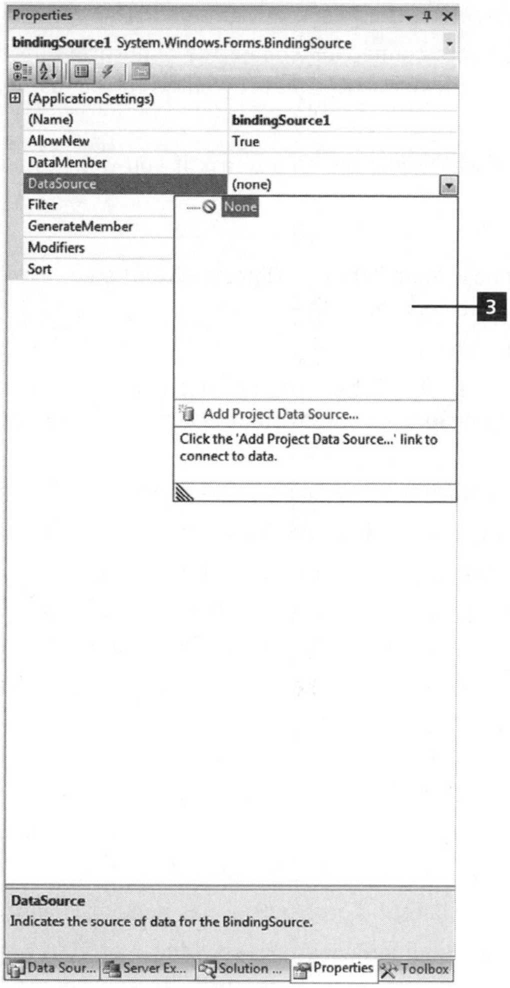

4. Click the Add Project Data Source . . . link at the bottom of the DataSource properties
editor to display the Data Source Configuration Wizard dialog (Figure 6-12).

Figure 6-12

Data Source Configuration
Wizard dialog

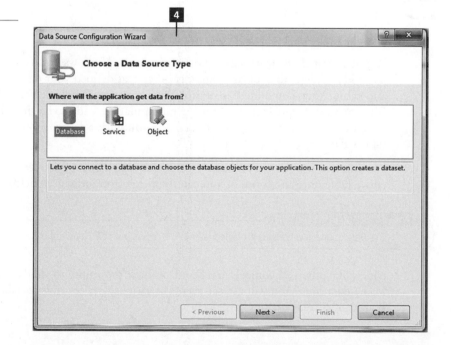

5. Select Database and click Next.

6. In the Which data connection should the application use to connect to the database? field, select the Nwind.mdb connect created in the last exercise.

7. Click Next.

8. Verify that Visual Studio prompts to ask if you want to add the file to your project, click Yes.

9. Click Next.

10. From the Choose Your Database Objects Wizard step, expand the Tables items and select the Customers table.

11. Click Finish.

12. Verify that a new DataSet control has been added to your Form1.cs [Design] tab and that the bindingSource1 controls DataSource property has the value of the DataSet control.

13. Locate the Toolbox window and double-click on the BindingNavigator control.

14. Locate the Toolbox window and double-click on the DataGridView control.

15. Select the Dock in parent container link from the DataGridView Tasks pop-up.

16. In the Properties window, locate the DataSource property and select the drop-down arrow to display the DataGridView DataSource property editor.

17. Expand the bindingSource1 item and select the Customers item.

18. Verify that a CustomersBindingSource control and a CustomersTableAdapter control were added automatically to Form1.

19. Select the bindingNavigator1 control, then locate in the Properties window the BindingSource property and select CustomersBindingSource.

20. Press **F5** to build and execute the application.

21. Verify that your DataGridView control has populated with the Customer's table's data.

22. Verify that the BindingNavigator is showing 1 of 91 rows.

23. Select row 5 and verify that BindingNavigator changes to show 5 of 91.

24. Select the Next button on the BindingNavigator toolbar and verify that the sixth row in the DataGridView is now selected.

25. Close Form1.

CERTIFICATION READY
Do you understand how to use the various databound controls?
4.2

PAUSE. Leave the project open to use in the next exercise.

You just created an entire data window using only Windows Forms data controls without any code needed. You added a BindingSource that defined your data provider, connection, and table. You then added a BindingNavigator and DataGridView that added another BindingSource and DataAdapter for manipulating and navigating the data. All of the controls then worked together to provide you with a UI to interact with the Customer table's data.

You can also use the Data Source's window to add a grid of data by dragging and dropping an entire table onto the form, or you can drag and drop individual fields.

> **➕ MORE INFORMATION**
> The Data Source's window is explained later in this lesson with WPF applications.

Much like other UI controls, data controls have the ability to validate data before it is saved to the data store. You will use the events of various data controls to validate data and determine if any concurrency issues have occurred.

Validating Data in Windows Forms

The data controls for Windows Forms support various events that allow you to validate data before and after edits have occurred.

Table 6-4 lists the some of the events used to validate data within a Windows Form and some of their functionality.

Table 6-4

Data Control Validation Events

CONTROL	EVENT	DESCRIPTION
BindingSource	AddingNew	Event raised when a new item is added to the DataSource. Use this event to determine when the user added new information. You can then validate if the information is valid.
	DataError	Event raised when concurrency-related exception is silently handled by the BindingSource. Use this event to understand if there was a concurrency issue that was handled but needs some additional attention.
	PositionChanged	Event raised when the position of the DataSource has changed. Use this event to understand when the user is moving from one item to another, so that you can decide if you want to commit any changes or not.
DataSet	MergeFailed	Event raised when a merge action is being performed and the two DataSets could not be merged. Use this event to understand if there are any conflicts when trying to merge data. Typically you will have merge issues when constraints fail or relationships conflict.
DataGridView	Cell . . .	Supports several cell events like CellEnter, CellLeave, CellClick. Use these events to validate individual cell-level activities. The most common event you will handle is the CellValueChange event. The CellValueChange event is raised when the contents of the cell change.
	DataSourceChanged	Event raised when the DataSource property value changes. Use this event to understand when the contents of the DataGridView are changing.
	RowsAdded	Event raised when new row(s) are added to the DataGridView control. This event works in conjunction with the UserAddedRow event. The RowsAdded event is raised when a row is added in code, whereas the UserAddedRow event is raised only when the add row functionality is initiated from the UI.

(continued)

Table 6-4 (*continued*)

CONTROL	EVENT	DESCRIPTION
	RowsRemoved	Event raised when existing row(s) are removed from the DataGridView control. This event works in conjunction with the UserDeletedRow event. The RowsRemoved event is raised when a row is deleted in code, whereas the UserDeletedRow event is raised only when the delete row functionality is initiated from the UI.
	RowStateChanged	Event raised when a row has transitioned from being shared to unshared, or unshared to shared. The DataGridView control has the capability of allowing you to lock and unlock the edits for rows of data. This enables you to make sure that no more than one user is editing a row of data at a time.
	RowUnshared	Event raised when a row transitions from the shared to the unshared state. Use the event to make sure that a row is locked from other users' edits while the row is unshared.
	RowValidating	Event raised while the row is being validated. Use the RowValidating event much like any of the control Validating events to perform data integrity checks. You can cancel the Row navigation process by setting the e.Cancel property to True.
	RowValidated	Event raised when the RowValidating event is completed and the e.Cancel property is False. Use this event to confirm that the row has correct data and, if desired, you can now commit the changes to the data store.
	UserAddedRow	Event raised when the add row functionality was initiated from the UI on the DataGridView control. Use this event to know when the user is adding a row versus when you might be adding a row in code or from another control. This event works in conjunction with the RowsAdded event.
	UserDeletedRow	Event raised when the delete row functionality was initiated from the UI on the DataGridView control. Use this event to know when the user is deleting a row versus when you might be deleting a row in code or from another control. This event works in conjunction with the RowsDeleted event.
	UserDeletingRow	Event raised when the delete row functionality is initiated from the UI on the DataGridView control, but has not occurred. Use this event to prompt the user to make sure that they want to delete or about any other predelete functionality.

⊕ **USE DATA CONTROL VALIDATION EVENTS**

USE the project you created in the previous exercise.

1. Select the Form1.cs [Design] tab and select the DataGridView control.
2. Locate the Properties window and click the Event button on the Properties window toolbar.
3. Locate the CellValueChanged event and double-click in the Event Handler selection cell.
4. Key the following code inside of the dataGridView1_CellValueChanged method:

```
// Check to see if the cell value that changed
// is not in the first row.
if (e.RowIndex > 0)
    // Display a message which indicates which
    // column and row
    // the cell that changed values resides.
    MessageBox.Show("Cell (" + e.ColumnIndex + ","
    + e.RowIndex + ") value has changed.");
```

5. Press **F5** to build and execute the application.
6. Scroll down in the grid to the last row that is empty, key some text, and press **Tab**.
7. Verify that a message box appeared indicating that the Cell (0,92) value has change.
8. Click OK.
9. Press **Delete** to remove the partial row you just entered. If you do not delete this row, you will see an Exception message that is going to be handled by the DataGridView control. This Exception will not stop the execution of the application. If the Exception appears, just click OK.
10. Close Form1 to stop the application from executing.
11. Select the Form1.cs [Design] tab.
12. Select the DataGridView control.
13. Locate the Properties window and locate the UserAddedRow event and double-click in the Event Handler selection cell.
14. Key the following code inside the dataGridView1_UserAddedRow method:

```
// Display a message to show that a row was added.
MessageBox.Show("User added a row...");
```

15. Locate the Properties window and locate the UserDeletedRow event and double-click in the Event Handler selection cell.
16. Key the following code inside the dataGridView1_UserDeletedRow method:

```
// Display a message to show that
// a row was deleted.
MessageBox.Show("User deleted a row...");
```

17. Press **F5** to build and execute the application.
18. Scroll down in the grid to the last row that is empty and key some text.
19. Verify that a message box appeared stating that a user added a row.
20. Click OK.
21. Press **Delete**.

CERTIFICATION READY
Do you understand
how to use the various
databound controls?
4.2

22. Verify that a message box appeared stating that a user deleted a row.
23. Click the yellow plus sign on the BindingNavigator toolbar.
24. Verify that a new row was added, but a message box did not appear.
25. Click the red "X" on the BindingNavigator toolbar.
26. Verify that the row was deleted, but a message box did not appear.
27. Close Form1.

STOP. Save or discard the solution. It will not be used again for another exercise.

You have just added validation Event Handlers to your data controls in a Windows Forms Application. You used the CellValueChanged event to determine when a change was occurring and what cell the change occurred in. You used the UserAddedRow and UserDeletedRow events to determine when the user was adding or deleting from the DataGridView control. You also observed that an add or delete action from the BindingNavigator did not raise the UserAddedRow or UserDeletedRow events, but if you wanted to handle the BindingNavigator actions, you could handle the RowsAdded or RowsDeleted events.

In a WPF application, there are no specific data controls. All controls can be bound to data. WPF introduces the ability to bind any property to any piece of data.

■ Working with Data in WPF

↓ THE BOTTOM LINE

Working with data in the WPF application is more flexible, easier, and more powerful than any previous Microsoft application development environment. WPF introduces the capability to bind anything from controls, to XML, to properties, or objects themselves.

Introducing WPF Binding

The power of the WPF is its ability to bind multiple kinds of elements to multiple kinds of data.

WPF binding is the process of associating a WPF element's property to a data source. To implement binding in WPF, you must have a target and a source. The source is where the data is coming from. A source can be a public property of any .NET Framework object including another control, XAML elements, or an ADO.NET object, including a DataSet or XML. The target is where the source data will be assigned. To support binding, the target must be derived from the DependenceyProperty class. To declare a WPF binding, use the Binding element as the following XAML code demonstrates:

```
<Binding ElementName="InputText" Path="Text"/>
```

In this example, the `ElementName` property is part of the binding source that represents the name of another element in the XAML. The `Path` property is the other part of the binding source that represents the `Text` property on the other element. This binding declaration would be assigned to a target property, as the following example shows:

```
<Label Height="24" VerticalAlignment="Top">
    <Label.Content>
        <Binding ElementName="InputText" Path="Text"/>
    </Label.Content>
</Label>
```

In the example, the Text property of the InputText element is now bound to the Content property of the label element. Any time the . . . property of the . . . element changes, the . . . property of the label element will change. Here is how the full example would appear:

```
<Label Height="24" VerticalAlignment="Top">
    <Label.Content>
        <Binding ElementName="InputText" Path="Text"/>
    </Label.Content>
</Label>
<TextBox Width="248" Height="24" Name="InputText" Text=" " />
```

This example uses the one-element-per-line binding declaration; this declaration can be shortened to the following XAML:

```
<Label Height="24" VerticalAlignment="Top" Content="{Binding
ElementName=InputText, Path=Text}"/>
<TextBox Width="248" Height="24" Name="InputText" Text=" " />
```

This example shows that as you change the text inside the textbox, the contents of the label are also updated immediately. This mode of binding is called OneWay and is the default WPF binding mode for the TextBox element. Table 6-5 summarizes the various binding modes.

Table 6-5

WPF Binding Modes

MODE	DESCRIPTION
OneWay	Continuously updates the target when the source changes. Use this binding mode when you want to ensure that the target is always synchronized with the source.
OneTime	Updates the target at the start of the application or when the DataContent property changes. The target does not listen for all changes to the source. Use this binding mode when you want to update the target at start-up or only periodically, not on every change.
OneWayToSource	Updates the source with the target's data. The OneWayToSource binding mode is opposite from the OneWay binding mode in that the value moves from the target to the source, rather than from the source to the target. The OneWayToSource binding mode account for the situation where you have a target property, but it does not support the DepenedencyProperty class. Since the target property must support the DependencyProperty class, you would make the target the source and the source the target by setting the binding mode as OneWayToSource. You have in effect switched the properties and the mode direction; thus you have been able to bind a property that does not support the DependencyProperty class.
TwoWay	Updates in both directions. When the target changes, the source changes, and vice versa. Use this binding mode when you have two elements that you want to keep updated with each other.

→ **USE SIMPLE WPF BINDING**

GET READY. Before you begin these steps, be sure to launch Microsoft Visual Studio and create a new WPF application named wpfSimpleBinding.

1. Locate the Window1.xaml tab and place your cursor inside of the <Grid> element in the XAML tab.

2. Key the following XAML code:

```
<!-- Create a stack panel element -->
<StackPanel>
    <!-- Create a label element -->
    <Label Width="248" Height="24"
    Content="Your selected color is:" />
    <!-- Create a textbox and bind the text
    property to the contents property of the
    myColors (ListBox below) element. -->
    <TextBox Width="248" Height="24" Text="{Binding
    ElementName=myColors, Path=SelectedItem.Conten}"/>
    <!-- Create a label element ->
    <Label Width="248" Height="24" Content="Colors:"/>
    <!-- Create a listbox element with the name myColors for
    use with the textbox text property. -->
    <ListBox x:Name="myColors" Width="248" Height="56">
        <!-- Create a couple of ListBox item elements -->
        <ListBoxItem Content="Aqua"/>
        <ListBoxItem Content="Red"/>
        <ListBoxItem Content="Golden"/>
        <ListBoxItem Content="Orange"/>
    </ListBox>
</StackPanel>
```

3. Press **F5** to build and execute the application.

4. Select a color and verify that text of that color appears in the textbox.

5. Close Window1.

6. Locate the following XAML code:

```
<TextBox Width="248" Height="24" Text="{Binding
ElementName=myColors, Path=SelectedItem.Content}"/>
```

7. Change the XAML code in step 6 to the following XAMl code:

```
<!-- Change the binding mode from the default
mode of OneWayToSource, to TwoWay. Now you can
change the textbox's text and have the
listbox's selected item change to match. -->
<TextBox Width="248" Height="24"
Text="{Binding ElementName=myColors,
Path=SelectedItem.Content, Mode=TwoWay}"/>
```

8. Press **F5** to build and execute the application.

9. Select a color and verify that text of that color appears in the textbox.

10. Select the textbox, delete the current color, and key **Purple**, then press **Tab**.

11. Verify that the currently selected color's text has now changed to Purple.

12. Select a different color and repeat step 10, but key a different color not already listed.

13. Verify that the currently selected color's text has now changed to the different color.

14. Close Window1.

STOP. Save or discard the solution. It will not be used again for another exercise.

You have just created a simple binding between a listbox, the source, and a textbox, the target. You bound the listbox's content selection to the textbox's text property. As you change the listbox content selection, you would see the textbox's text change. You first implemented OneWay binding between the target and the source. You then changed to TwoWay binding, which caused updates in the listbox when the textbox changed, as well as the original updates to the textbox when the listbox changed.

In the example, you saw how WPF supports binding between elements and properties. WPF also supports binding to data using the XMLDataProvider and ObjectDataProvider elements.

Using WPF Specialized Binding

WPF has two special elements that enable your WPF application to bind to data. Use the XMLDataProvider and the ObjectDataProvider to bind your XAML elements to data.

Table 6-6 lists the two data binding classes and some of their properties and methods.

Table 6-6

WPF Data Binding Classes

CLASS	METHOD/PROPERTY	DESCRIPTION
XMLDataProvider		Specifically designed to allow XAML access to XML data. Use this class when you want to bind XAML elements to XML data.
	Data	The XML data loaded into the XMLDocument from the Source property. Use this property to get direct access to the XML data itself.
	Document	A standard XMLDocument. Use this property to gain access to the underlying XMLDocument.
	Source	Determines where the XML data is coming from. The XML data can be declared in XAML or from a file.
	XPath	Determines the XPath query expression that will be used against the XML data to filter out the amount of XML data used during binding.
	InitialLoad ( )	Performs the first loading of the XML data into the Document property.

(continued)

Table 6-6 *(continued)*

CLASS	METHOD/PROPERTY	DESCRIPTION
	Refresh ( )	Reloads the XML data from the Source property into the Document property. Use this method if you know that your XML data has changed and you want to load the latest data.
ObjectDataProvider		Specifically designed to create and wrap an object for use for data binding. An object can be created in XAML, in code, like a class, or can be a DataSet. Use this class to create a binding source from a business layer class, or for a database data store.
	Data	The data of the object. Use this property to get direct access to the object data itself.
	MethodName	Determines the name of the object method that will be called to populate the Data property.
	MethodParameters	Determines the parameters that will be passed to the MethodName when called to populate the Data property.
	ObjectInstance	Determines what object is used as the binding source. Use this property to set the source object for binding.

⊙ USE THE XMLDATAPROVIDER CLASS

GET READY. Before you begin these steps, be sure to launch Microsoft Visual Studio and create a new WPF application named wpfXMLBinding.

1. Locate the Window1.xaml tab and place your cursor inside of the <Grid> element in the XAML tab.

2. Create a StackPanel XML data resource by keying the following XAML code:

```
<!-- Create a stack panel element -->
<StackPanel>
    <!-- Create a stack panel resource element-->
    <StackPanel.Resources>
      <!-- Create a XmlDataProvider element -->
     <XmlDataProvider x:Key="XmlLibraryData"
    XPath="Library/Books">
       <!-- Define some book data. -->
       <x:XData>
        <Library xmlns="">
           <Books>
              <Book Status="in">
                 <Title>Moby Dick</Title>
              </Book>
              <Book Status="out" >
                 <Title>
                   Grapes of Wrath
                 </Title>
```

```
                    </Book>
                    <Book Status="out" >
                        <Title>
                            A Christmas Carol
                        </Title>
                    </Book>
                    <Book Status="in" >
                        <Title>Tom Sawyer</Title>
                    </Book>
                </Books>
                <DVDs>
                    <DVD Status="in">
                        <Title>
                            Charles Dickens' Classics
                        </Title>
                    </DVD>
                    <DVD Status="out">
                        <Title>
                            Great American Novels
                        </Title>
                    </DVD>
                </DVDs>
            </Library>
        </x:XData>
    </XmlDataProvider>
    </StackPanel.Resources>
</StackPanel>
```

3. Bind a listbox's items to the XML data by keying the following XAML code just above the `</StackPanel>` code in step 2:

```
<!-- Create a label element -->
<Label FontSize="18" FontWeight="Bold" Margin="10"
HorizontalAlignment="Center">
    Library Books Checked-Out</Label>
<!-- Create a listbox element -->
<ListBox Height="300" Background="Linen">
    <!-- Start the definition for the binding of
    the listbox's ItemsSource property. -->
    <ListBox.ItemsSource>
      <!-- Bind the listbox's ItemSource property
      to the stackpanel resource XmlLibaryData. -->
      <Binding Source="{StaticResource XmlLibaryData}"
      XPath="*[@Status='out']"/>
```

```
                    </ListBox.ItemsSource>
                    <!-- Create an item template for the listbox.
                    The Item template defines which XmlLibraryData
                    fields will be displayed and how. -->
                    <ListBox.ItemTemplate>
                    <!-- Define a DataTemplate. -->
                    <DataTemplate>
                      <!-- Define a text block where the title tag
                      in the XmlLibraryData is bound to the text
                      block's text property. -->
                      <TextBlock>
                        <TextBlock.Text>
                          <Binding XPath="Title"/>
                        </TextBlock.Text>
                      </TextBlock>
                    </DataTemplate>
                  </ListBox.ItemTemplate>
                </ListBox>
```

4. Press **F5** to build and execute the application.

5. Verify that only the books that have a XML Status of "out" are listed in the window.

6. Close Window1.

STOP. Save or discard the solution. It will not be used again for another exercise.

You have just bound XML data to XAML elements in a WPF application. You created an inline XML document, then you bound the Title attribute of the Book tag to the ListBox's items. Alternatively, you could have defined the XML in an XML document, and then placed the path to the XML document in the Source property.

In addition to simple and specialized binding, WPF applications can bind to database data.

Using WPF Database Binding

> The Visual Studio environment provides several features that enable the binding of database information to WPF elements.

In the Windows Forms section of this lesson, you used the data controls provided by the .NET Framework to provide database functionality to the application. For WPF applications, the .NET Framework does not provide data controls; thus you use the Data Sources window to create the base classes for database interactions and then manually implement database functionality.

TAKE NOTE *

In Visual Studio 2008, WPF did not support drag and drop from the Data Sources window or a data grid. In Visual Studio 2010, WPF now supports drag and drop from the Data Sources window and a DataGrid element. Thus, in Visual Studio 2010 the Data menu and Data Sources window functionality are the same for Windows Forms and WPF applications.

USE THE WPF DATA SOURCE

GET READY. Before you begin these steps, be sure to launch Microsoft Visual Studio and create a new WPF application named wpfDatabaseBinding.

1. Select Data→Add New Data Source . . . to display the Configure New Data Source Wizard dialog.

2. Select a Database and New Connection to the Nwind.mdb file.

3. When the Choose your database objects wizard step is presented, expand the Tables item, select the Products table, and click Finish.

4. Verify that the Products table is added to the Data Sources window and that your project now has an NwindDataSet.xsd file (Figure 6-13).

Figure 6-13

Data Sources window

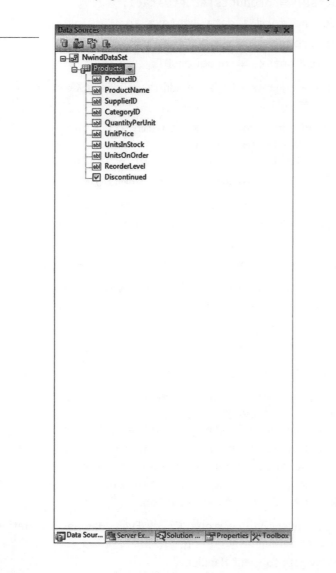

5. Select the Window1.xaml.cs tab and locate the Window1 constructor.

6. Just above the Window1 constructor, key the following code:

```
// Create a new data adapter to the dataset
// which stores the Nwind products table.
NwindDataSetTableAdapters.ProductsTableAdapter
```

```
productsTA = new NwindDataSetTableAdapters
            .ProductsTableAdapter();
// Declare a new data table which is defined
// just like the products table.
NwindDataSet.ProductsDataTable productsDT;
```

7. Locate the Window1 constructor and add the following code at the end of the method:

```
// Fill the products data table with the database
// information retrieved
// using the products data adapter.
productsDT = productsTA.GetData();
// Set the form's data context to
// the products table.
this.DataContext = productsDT;
```

8. Select the Window1.xaml tab and add the following XAML code in between the <Grid> elements:

```
<!-- Bind the ProductName column from the
Products table in the Nwind
database to the text property of a textbox. -->
<TextBox Text="{Binding ProductName}"/>
```

9. Press **F5** to build and execute the application.

10. Verify that the product name is now displayed in the textbox.

11. Close Window1.

12. Just below the code entered in step 6, key the following code:

```
// Create a collection view to display the all
// of the products in
// the products data table.
CollectionView productsView;
```

13. Just below the XAML entered in step 8, key the following XAML:

```
<!-- Create two buttons to move forwards and
backwards. Add event
handlers to each button's click event. -->
<Button Height="25" VerticalAlignment="Bottom"
Click="Previous_Click">Previous</Button>
<Button Height="25" VerticalAlignment="Bottom"
Click="Next_Click">Next</Button>
```

14. Right-click over the Previous_Click Event Handler declaration to see the XAML Editor pop-up menu.

15. Select Navigate to Event Handler.

16. Inside of the Previous_Click method, key the following code:

```
// Move back in the view.
productsView.MoveCurrentToPrevious();
```

17. Select the Windows1.xaml tab, right-click over the Next_Click Event Handler declaration to see the XAML Editor pop-up menu.

18. Select Navigate to Event Handler.

19. Inside of the Next_Click method, key the following code:

```
// Move forward in the view.
productsView.MoveCurrentToNext();
```

20. Press **F5** to build and execute the application.

21. Verify that as you click the Next and Previous buttons, the product name changes values.

22. Close Window1.

STOP. Save or discard the solution. It will not be used again for another exercise.

You have just created a WPF application using database data. You used the Data Source feature within Visual Studio to add the Products table to your project. You added a DataSet and DataAdapter to set the Window's DataContent. Setting the DataContent associated the contents of the Products table with elements within the Window. You added your WPF elements and bound them to the Product table's columns. To enable navigation, you added a CollectionView and some Button elements.

SKILL SUMMARY

IN THIS LESSON YOU LEARNED HOW TO:

- Create functionality using the ADO.NET System.Data namespaces.

- Create a connection to a data store and then use that connection to create Windows Forms and WPF applications.

- Create Windows Forms data controls and validate data manipulation actions.

- Create WPF bindings to .NET Framework objects, WPF elements, and data sources.

■ Knowledge Assessment

Fill in the Blank

Complete the following sentences by writing the correct word or words in the blanks provided.

1. When a WPF element is associated with data, it is called _____.

2. A collection of tables, with rows and columns, keys, and constraints that is disconnected from a data store is called a _____.

3. The _____ is the part of the .NET Framework that handles data store interactions.

4. When data can be exchanged directly with the data store, it is considered _____.

5. The _____ contains all of the options needed to configure a data store connection.

6. When data cannot be exchanged directly with the data store, but is instead exchanged with an XML file, it is considered _____.

7. A fast, forward-only, read-only data manipulation interface to a data store is called a _____.

8. To add a data source to the Visual Studio environment without a solution or project being loaded, you use the _____.

9. A _____ is the first Windows Forms control added to a Windows Form to provide data connectivity.

10. A file and management engine where data is persisted is called a _____.

Multiple Choice

Circle the letter that corresponds to the best answer.

1. You are developing an application that needs to print reports based on the customer data. You will sequentially access the records but will never update any data. You want to access the data as fast as possible. Which of the following classes should you use to access data?
   a. Command
   b. DataReader
   c. DataAdapter
   d. DataSet

2. Which of the following is NOT part of the ADO.NET framework?
   a. Command
   b. InterfaceAdapters
   c. DataProvider
   d. DataSet

3. Which of the follow is NOT a .NET Framework built-in DataProvider?
   a. SQL Server
   b. OLE DB
   c. ODBC
   d. MySQL

4. Which Windows Forms control would you use if you wanted to provide the users with a navigation and record manipulation toolbar?
   a. BindingSource
   b. BindingNavigator
   c. DataGridView
   d. None of the above

5. Which of the following Windows Forms DataGridView event would you use to check if the user added a new record from outside the DataGridView control?
   a. RowAdded
   b. UserAddedRow
   c. RowInserted
   d. UserInsertedRow

6. You are working with a DataGridView control. You need to take certain actions when the underlying data source is changed. Which of the following events should you use?
   a. RowStateChanged
   b. RowsAdded
   c. RowsRemoved
   d. DataSourceChanged

7. Which of the following is not a valid property name for a DataAdapter property?
   a. InsertCommand
   b. UpdateCommand
   c. DeleteCommand
   d. CreateCommand

8. Which property of the XMLDataProvider class is used to determine where inline XML data comes from?
   a. Document
   b. XPath
   c. Source
   d. Data

9. What feature within Visual Studio provides drag-and-drop data store to Windows application functionality?
   a. Data Sources Window
   b. Server Explorer
   c. Data Explorer
   d. None of the above

10. A DataSet is in what state when it is saving data to an XML file because it cannot save through the DataProvider to the data store?
    a. Transitional
    b. Connected
    c. Disconnected
    d. None of the above

Competency Assessment

Scenario 6-1: Details View

Your requirements call for a Details View of the products in your database. In a Details View, each column in your database has one individual control to display each piece of information. You may not use the DataGrid View control to display the Products information. Using the Northwinds database, create a Windows Forms application with a Details View for the Products table. There should be one control on the form for each column in the Products table. Make sure to include a navigation mechanism.

Scenario 6-2: Theme Picker

One of your requirements is that the application should allow the user to theme or select colors for various interface properties. You have been asked to provide this prototype in a WPF application to demonstrate the binding capabilities. Create a WPF application with a textbox element where the textbox's background color, font size, and whether it will allow Enter key entries are all controlled from another element.

Proficiency Assessment

Scenario 6-3: Details and Grid View

After your presentation to the senior leadership, it was suggested that you add the DataGridView to the already existing Details View. Extend the application from Scenario 6-1 to have both a DataGridView and a Details View.

Scenario 6-4: Navigation Bar

The WPF prototype was well received and functioned well, but after review, your supervisor has asked that you create a toolbar for the WPF prototype to make it look similar to the Windows Forms navigation bar. Implement a simple toolbar with Next and Previous buttons.

Packaging and Deploying Windows Applications

LESSON SKILL MATRIX

SKILLS/CONCEPTS	MTA EXAM OBJECTIVE	MTA EXAM OBJECTIVE NUMBER
Introducing Windows Application Distribution	Understand Windows application deployment methods.	5.1
Introducing Windows Application Distribution Working with Windows Application Setup and Deployment Project Templates	Create Windows setup and deployment projects.	5.2
Working with ClickOnce Deployment	Supplemental	

KEY TERMS

ClickOnce Deployment

Merge Module

Setup Project

You have reached the point where you need to start sharing your prototypes with a broader audience. Up to this point, copying your project's output to a shared location has worked okay, but management would like to see your prototypes in a real-world installation scenario. Different parts of your project have different distribution needs, and thus each part of the project needs to use its appropriate type of installation. You will be researching the different types of installation methods, determining which installation method is best for each part of the project, and then creating the installation packages.

■ Introducing Windows Application Distribution

↓ THE BOTTOM LINE

Visual Studio provides several distribution options. There are Setup and Deployment template projects, ClickOnce Deployment and the Windows Service application Installer. Depending on your distribution needs, you will need to understand which of the provided distribution options to use.

Understanding Windows Application Distribution Options

> There are five different Setup and Deployment template project types, ClickOnce Deployment, and the Windows Service application Installer that can be used to distribute the application.

At various times throughout the application development process, you will need to distribute the application to a wider audience. Although you could simply take your build folder and send it to others, this method of distribution has its drawbacks and will not work for a Windows Service application. To avoid distribution issues, Visual Studio provides five different Setup and Deployment template project types, ClickOnce Deployment, and the Windows Service application Installer. To use one of the Setup and Deployment project templates, you will need to create a new Setup Project. A Setup Project can be created within its own Visual Studio Solution using the New Project feature or added to an existing Visual Studio Solution using the Add New Project feature. Adding a Setup Project to an existing solution is the preferred method of creating a Windows Installer application. When a Setup Project is added to an existing Windows application project, the creation process is aware of your Windows application project settings and will prompt you to add various parts of the application to the Setup Project. When creating a Setup Project in its own solution, you will not be prompted, so that you will need to configure additional installation items. Table 7-1 summarizes the various Visual Studio distribution options.

Table 7-1

Visual Studio Distribution Options

Method	Description
Setup Wizard	The easiest option to create a Setup Project. The Setup Wizard has five steps that walk you through the Setup Project creation process. If you want to create a Setup Project quickly and with the most common configurations, then use the Setup Wizard template.
Setup Project	The **Setup Project** template creates a default Setup Project. Unlike the Setup Wizard template, the Setup Project template does not walk you through the creation process. You will need to manually configure each aspect of the Setup Project. The Setup Project template is a more advanced option for getting your Setup Project created, but because the Setup Project is not automatically configured, you have more control.
Merge Module Project	The Merge Module Project template creates a Setup Project that creates Windows Installer Merge Modules (MSI) files. A **Merge Module** is a setup and deployment file that can be included in other Setup Projects and does not have a UI. You create a Merge Module when you have a set of installation functionality that is common to several Setup Projects. You move the common functionality to a Merge Module, and then you can include the Merge Module in several Setup Projects. Merge Modules enable your Setup Project's output to be more modular and maintainable.
CAB Project	Creates an install for ActiveX components. An ActiveX component can be an OCX UI control or a Component Object Model (COM) DLL. The CAB Project is intended for web-server-based installations where you need to download an ActiveX component from the web server to the web browser for installation on the client machine. Previous to .NET, applications would include COM DLLs and OCX files. COM files require registration with the operating system, and thus the install would need to make sure that any COM controls were registered correctly. In .NET, DLLs do not need to be registered and any .NET DLLs should be included in your Setup Project or a Merge Module.

(continued)

Table 7-1 *(continued)*

METHOD	DESCRIPTION
Web Setup Project	An installer for web server based applications on a web server. Use the Web Setup Project when you need to install the application into a Virtual Root directory on a web server. The Web Setup Project is not for installing applications over the web or for installing web applications on a client machine.
ClickOnce Deployment	A new technology for WPF, Windows Forms, and Windows Services/Console applications that enables the creation of an application that is self-updating. Once the application is published using ClickOnce Deployment, it will check for newer versions as they become available and automatically update newer files.
Windows Service Application Installer	An installation package created for Windows Service applications. You used a Windows Services Application Installer in Lesson 4, Controlling Application Execution, to install your Windows Service into the Computer Management Console. The Windows Service Application Installer can be used only for installing Windows Service applications.

CERTIFICATION READY
Do you understand the various Windows application deployment methods?
5.1

The quickest and easiest way to get a Setup Project created is by using the Setup Wizard template.

Working with the Setup Wizard Template

The Setup Wizard template is a step-by-step process for creating a Setup Project.

Table 7-2 summarizes the five Setup Wizard steps.

Table 7-2

Setup Wizard Steps

STEPS (IN ORDER)	DESCRIPTION
Welcome	Has no functionality. It is simply an introduction to the Setup Wizard Template process. You will want to select Next to move to the next wizard step.
Choose a project type	Provides four different options to create your Setup Project. You can select: • Create a setup for a Windows application. • Create a setup for a web application. • Create a merge module for Windows Installer. • Create a downloadable CAB file. You will select the option that is most appropriate based on the application.
Choose project outputs to include	An optional step in the Setup Wizard. If you are creating a Setup Project within a solution where a Windows Forms or WPF project is not present, this step is skipped, because there are no known project

Table 7-2 *(continued)*

STEPS (IN ORDER)	DESCRIPTION
	output files to select. If you are creating a Setup Project within a solution with a Windows Form or WPF project, this setup will show you the available project outputs for your selection. You can select: • Localized resources • XML serialization assemblies • Content files • Primary output • Source files • Debug symbols • Documentation files
Choose files to include	Provides a mechanism to add additional files to your Setup Project. You can browse for your additional files and, once selected, they will be added to a list of files for inclusion. Use this step to include any help files or files that are not a part of the application project but are needed for the application to work.
Create project	A verification of your Setup Project creation selections. Use this step to ensure that you have selected the right creation options and then click Next to create the Setup Project. If any of your Setup Project creation selections are incorrect, use the Previous button to move back through the Setup Wizard and correct your selections.

USE THE SETUP WIZARD TEMPLATE

GET READY. Before you begin these steps, be sure to launch Microsoft Visual Studio and create a new Windows Forms Application named wfaSetupWizard.

1. On the Solution Explorer, locate the solution element and right-click to display the Solution Explorer pop-up window.

2. Select Add→New Project to display the New Project dialog (Figure 7-1).

Figure 7-1

New Project dialog

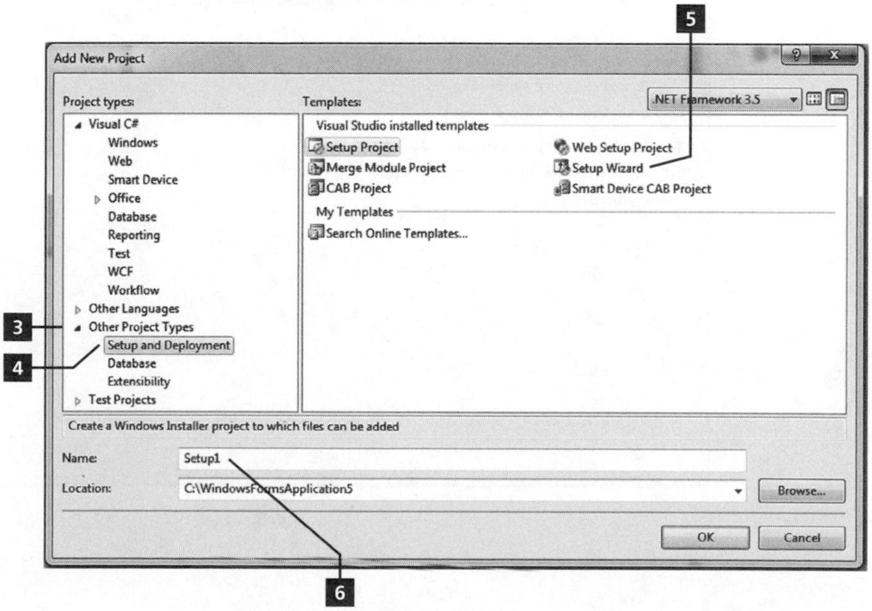

3. In the Project Types, locate the Other Project Types items and double-click to expand the item.

4. Select the Setup and Deployment item.

5. In the project templates, locate the Setup Wizard item and click.

6. In the Name field, key **MySetupProject** and click OK to display the Setup Wizard on the Welcome step (Figure 7-2).

Figure 7-2

Setup Wizard Welcome step

7. Click Next to display the Choose a project type step (Figure 7-3).

Figure 7-3

Setup Wizard Choose a project type step

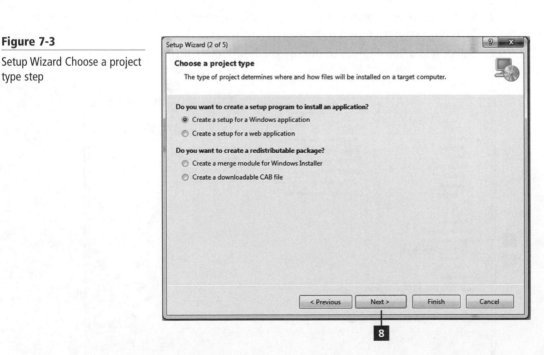

8. Select Create a setup for a Windows application and click Next to display the Choose project outputs to include step (Figure 7-4).

Figure 7-4

Setup Wizard Choose project outputs to include step

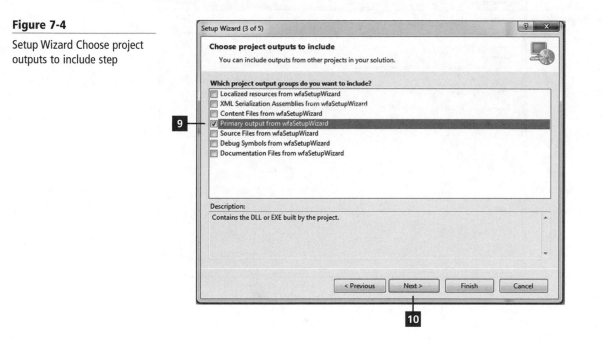

9. Click Primary output from wfaSetupWizard.

10. Click Next to display the Choose files to include step (Figure 7-5).

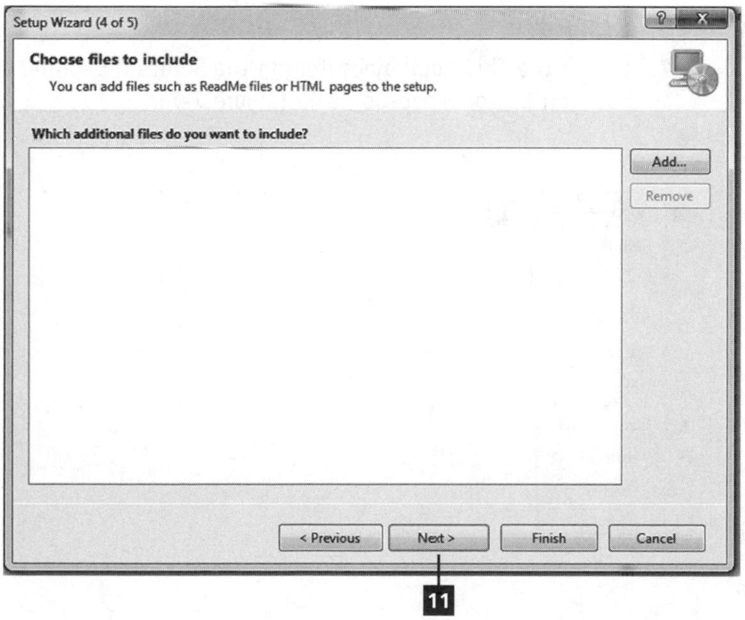

Figure 7-5

Setup Wizard Choose files to include step

11. Click Next to display the Create Project step (Figure 7-6).

Figure 7-6

Setup Wizard Create Project step

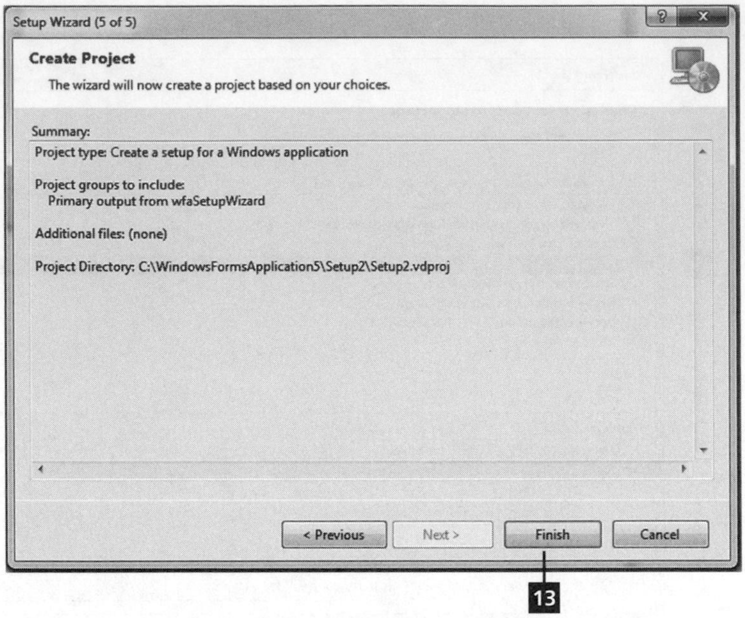

Setup Wizard (5 of 5)

Create Project

The wizard will now create a project based on your choices.

Summary:

Project type: Create a setup for a Windows application

Project groups to include:
Primary output from wfaSetupWizard

Additional files: (none)

Project Directory: C:\WindowsFormsApplication5\Setup2\Setup2.vdproj

< Previous   Next >   **Finish**   Cancel

13

12. Verify that the following settings will be used to create your Setup Project:
- Project type: Create a setup for a Windows application
- Project groups to include: Primary output from wfaSetupWizard
- Additional files: (none)
- Project Directory: Same folder as your wfaSetupWizard

13. Click Finish.

14. Locate the MySetupProject item in the Solution Explorer and right-click to display the Solution Explorer pop-up menu (Figure 7-7).

Figure 7-7

Solution Explorer Setup Project pop-up menu

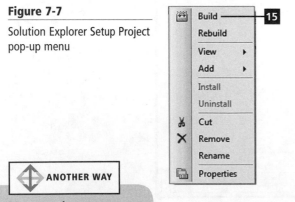

Build ——— **15**
Rebuild
View ▶
Add ▶
Install
Uninstall
Cut
Remove
Rename
Properties

ANOTHER WAY

You can also start the build process by selecting Build➔Build MyProjectSetup.

15. Select Build and wait for the Build succeeded message.

You can also start the install process by selecting Project→Install.

CERTIFICATION READY
Do you know how to create Windows setup and deployment projects?
5.2

16. Locate the MySetupProject item in the Solution Explorer and right-click to display the Solution Explorer pop-up menu.

17. Select Install and the MySetupProject setup application will start and the Welcome setup step is displayed.

18. Click Next to display the Select installation folder setup step.

19. Click Next to display the Confirmation setup step.

20. Click Next to start the setup installation process.

21. Click Close to exit the setup application.

22. Verify that this simply installed the executable into the folder selected in step 18.

23. Verify that the install did not create a Start Menu folder or desktop icons.

24. Locate the MySetupProject item in the Solution Explorer and right-mouse click to display the Solution Explorer pop-up menu.

25. Select Uninstall and wait for the MySetupProject uninstallation process to complete.

PAUSE. Leave Visual Studio open to use in the next exercise.

You have just created a setup application using the Setup Wizard Project template. You went step by step to create a Setup Project that installs the executable application into a folder in the Program Folders directory. You executed your install and then uninstalled. Your install did not install a Start menu option, a desktop icon, or any other UI functionality to access your Windows Forms Application.

By default, the Setup Wizard does not provide a step for configuring the UI of the installation process. To configure additional options in the setup application, like the UI, you will use various editors of the Setup Project.

■ Working with Windows Application Setup and Deployment Project Templates

THE BOTTOM LINE

Visual Studio provides several different Setup and Deployment project templates. You used the Setup Wizard Project Template in the last exercise. You will now work with the Setup Project and Merge Module Project.

Understanding the Windows Application Setup and Deployment Project Components

Each of the project templates creates a Setup Project with several common components. You will configure the File System, Registry, File Types, User Interface, Common Actions, and/or Launch Conditions.

Depending on which type of Setup and Deployment project templates you create, you will have some or all of the project components to configure. Table 7-3 summarizes the various Setup and Deployment project components.

Table 7-3

Setup and Deployment Project Configurable Components

CONFIGURABLE COMPONENT	DESCRIPTION
File System Editor	Configures the installation of application, help, and any support files onto the end user's machine. The File System Editor has three default locations where you can install files: • Application Folder (typically . . . \Program Files\<Application Name>) • User's Desktop • User's Programs Menu When you have a Web Setup Project, you will only have one default location: • Web Application Folder You can add additional folders, including a custom folder created by the install application, by using the Add Special Folder pop-up menu. The Add Special Folder pop-up menu provides various folders for installing files. The following is a list of the common special folders: • Fonts Folder: Use this special folder to install a font file (ttf) into the Windows font folder. • Program Files Folder/Program Files (64-bit) Folder: Typically the Program Files Folder for 32-bit applications and 64-bit applications are different. Use the correct special folder setting depending on your project output product type. • System Folder/System (64-bit) Folder: Typically the System Folder for 32-bit applications and 64-bit applications are different. Use the correct special folder setting depending on your project output product type. • User's Send To Menu: Use this special folder to add an application to the Windows Send To menu. When you right-click in the Windows Explorer there is always a Send To menu; this special folder allows you to add an item to this menu. • Global Assembly Cache Folder: Use this special folder when you want to install your .NET DLLs into the Global Assembly Cache rather than locally to the installed application. • Custom Folder: Use this special folder when you want to specify a folder that is not listed by the predefined special folders. You may have an application that needs to be executed from a folder with no spaces in the path. Use the Custom Folder to create your specific folder with no spaces, and then you can install your files within the custom folder. Once you have added your special folders, you will add files, folders, project output, and/or assemblies or create shortcuts to various files.
Registry Editor	Configures your registry settings during the installation process. The Registry Editor has five default registry locations: • HKEY_CLASSES_ROOT: Use this registry setting if you have 16-bit Windows components in the application installation. This registry key holds file name extension associations and COM registration information. • HKEY_CURRENT_USER: Use this registry setting if you want to store installation information for the currently logged in user. • HKEY_LOCAL_MACHINE: Use this registry setting if you want to store installation information for the current machine. • HKEY_USERS: Use this registry setting if you want to store installation information for all users.

Table 7-3 (*continued*)

CONFIGURABLE COMPONENT	DESCRIPTION
	• User/Machine Hive: Use this registry setting when you might have different users on the same machine with different access permissions running the installation application. Any registry keys in this registry section are automatically moved to the HKEY_CURRENT_ USER, HKEY_LOCAL_MACHINE, and/or HKEY USERS section based on permissions and installation selections.
	Each of the registry settings allows you to organize registry keys into folders and add keys with key values.
File Types Editor	Configures the file extensions that will be associated with the application and the actions that can be performed. When you select a text file from the Windows Explorer, you see a special text file icon that provides a visual clue. When you double-click on the file, it is automatically opened in the Notepad application. Use the File Types Editor to accomplish the same functionality.
	Use the Add File Type pop-up menu to add a default file association. You then use the Properties window to edit the command, file extensions, and icon. You can add an action item that associates an operating system function, like opening a document, with your file type definition to enable the application to open various file types.
User Interface Editor	Configures the step-by-step process your end users will see when running your installation application. You can use some of the prebuilt steps provided, or add your own steps based on the dialog templates. Setup Projects that support the User Interface Editor all have two types of installations: the Install, for non-administrative users, and the administrative install, for those with administrative privileges. Each install has three processing areas:
	• Start: Use to perform any user interactions before the installation process begins. You might use the Start processing area to display copyright information and prompt the user to agree before the installation begins.
	• Progress: Use to notify the user of installation progress. You might use the Progress processing area to show transitions between install application files versus help files.
	• End: Use to perform any cleanup or post-installation user interactions. You might use the End processing area to ask the user if he/she wants to check for updates or visit the application's Web site.
Common Actions Editor	Configures any applications or scripts that you want to execute as part of your installation application. By default your Setup Project will have four custom action areas:
	• Install: Use to run an application and/or script during the installation process. You might use the Install custom action area to pre-configure the machine before the installation process begins.
	• Commit: Use to run an application and/or script once the installation process has completed successfully. You might use the Commit custom action to open a browser window and navigate the product's Web site once an installation was performed correctly.
	• Rollback: Use to run an application and/or script once the installation process has completed unsuccessfully. You might use the Rollback custom action to open a browser window and navigate to the product's support page.

(*continued*)

Table 7-3 (*continued*)

CONFIGURABLE COMPONENT	DESCRIPTION
	• Uninstall: Use to run an application and/or script during the uninstall process. You might use the Uninstall custom action if you want to ask the user to take a survey on why they are uninstalling the application.
	All custom action activities must be associated with an application or script that already exists in the File System Editor area of the Setup Project. Thus, you should add the application and/or script in the File System Editor component, then use the Custom Actions Editor to associate the application and/or script with the appropriate custom actions area.
Launch Conditions Editor	Configures the prerequisites that need to be satisfied before your installation application can begin. By default your Setup Project will have a Search Target Machine configuration and a Launch Condition definitions area.
	The Search Target Machine area configures three different places on the users machine to search for the Launch Condition definitions:
	• File
	• Registry
	• Windows Installer
	For a Web Server Setup Project, the Search Target Machine area already has a predefined Registry key search for the Internet Information Services (IIS) server.
	Use the File Search to configure a search based on various file system areas and criteria by using some of the following properties:
	• FileName
	• Folder
	• MinDate
	• MaxDate
	• MinSize
	• MaxSize
	• MinVersion
	• MaxVersion
	Use the Registry Search to configure a search based on various registry key areas and values by using some of the following properties:
	• RegKey
	• Root
	• Value
	Use the Windows Installer Search to configure a search based on various components that are present or missing in the Windows Installer application.

Table 7-4 summarizes the various Setup and Deployment Project components that can be configured for each project template type.

Table 7-4

Project Template Type and Supported Configurable Components

Project Template	Supported Configurable Components
Setup Wizard/Setup Project	The Setup Wizard and Setup Project template types both support the following components: • File System Editor • Registry Editor • File Types Editor • User Interface Editor • Common Actions Editor • Launch Conditions Editor
Merge Module Project	The Merge Module Project template supports the following components: • File System Editor • Registry Editor • File Types Editor • Common Actions Editor The Merge Module Project does not have a UI; thus it does not support the User Interface Editor. In addition, you cannot launch a Merge Module as a standalone installation application, and thus you do not have the Launch Conditions Editor.
CAB Project	The CAB Project template type does not support any of the configurable components or editors. To add a project output or file to a CAB Project, you use the Solution Explorer pop-up menu Add feature.
Web Setup Project	The Web Support Project template supports the following components: • File System Editor • Registry Editor • File Types Editor • User Interface Editor • Common Actions Editor • Launch Conditions Editor The File System Editor and Launch Conditions Editor are defaulted differently from a Setup Project, but both editors still have the same functionality.

Working with a Setup Project

The Setup Project template supports all of the configurable components in an installation project. Although all components are configurable, not all components need be configured for every installation application.

Just like any other application, your installation application needs to be designed and developed based on a plan. When using a Setup Project, you have all of the configurable components available to create your installation application, but this does not mean that you need to use every configurable component. Table 7-5 lists the various configurable components and some questions that should be considered before configuring each component.

Table 7-5

Configurable Components and Plan Questions

Configurable Component	Plan Questions
File System Editor	One of the most common areas you will edit when creating your installation application. The following list of questions will help you to plan this section: • What files do you need to install? • Where do the files you need to install need to be placed on the end user's machine? • Will you install a shortcut in the Start Programs or Desktop? • If you are using a Custom Action, what files are needed by the Custom Action?
Registry Editor	Only configure when needed. For most installations, you will not need to configure the registry during installation. Most often you will interface with the registry during application execution, but the following list of questions will help you to identify if you have a need: • Do you need to initialize a set of registry keys for the application to use? • Do you need to set any flags in the registry for future installations?
File Types Editor	Typically only used when you have a document file associated with the application. The File Types Editor is used to enable the double-click open functionality, but unless you implement a command-line feature to read and open the document, configuring the File Types Editor is not as helpful. The following list of questions will help you to identify if you have a need: • Do you have any files that need to be opened by the application? • Do you have any files that are created by the application? • Is your file extension the same as another already well-known extension?
User Interface Editor	Another common area of configuration. You can modify the default dialogs or add your own dialogs. Be careful not to get too complicated. You have the ability to add an unlimited number of dialogs to your installation, but who wants to install an application if they have to click Next too many times? The following list of questions will help you to identify if you have a need: • Do you need to change any of the default instructions or text currently in the default dialogs? • Do you need to add any additional dialogs? • Do you really need to add any custom dialogs?
Custom Actions Editor	An advanced section of the installation setup process because it requires additional executable applications or scripts written in Visual Basic Scripting. Although you can create some powerful installation features, typically you will not have any Custom Actions defined. The following question will help you to identify if you have a need: • Is there any functionality not supported by the Windows Installer application?
Launch Conditions Editor	Typically only configured when you have an installation dependency. When your installation requires that another condition exist before your installation application, then you will want to define a Launch Condition. The following list of questions will help you to identify if you have a need: • Does the application depend on additional software besides the .NET Framework or IIS for web applications? • Is your installation an upgrade to an already installed application?

CONFIGURE A SETUP PROJECT

USE the project you created in the previous exercise. You are not going to create a Setup Project from scratch; the Setup Wizard from the last exercise configured the basic settings.

1. In the Solution Explorer, locate the MySetupProject item and click the File System Editor button, the second button on the Solution Explorer toolbar, to display the File System (MySetupProject) tab (Figure 7-8).

Figure 7-8

Solution Explorer Full Setup Project toolbar

> Solution Explorer - Setup2

2. Select the Application Folder item and verify that this folder contains only the Primary output from wfaSetupWizard (Active).
3. Select the Primary output from wfaSetupWizard (Active) and right-click to display the File System Editor File pop-up menu (Figure 7-9).

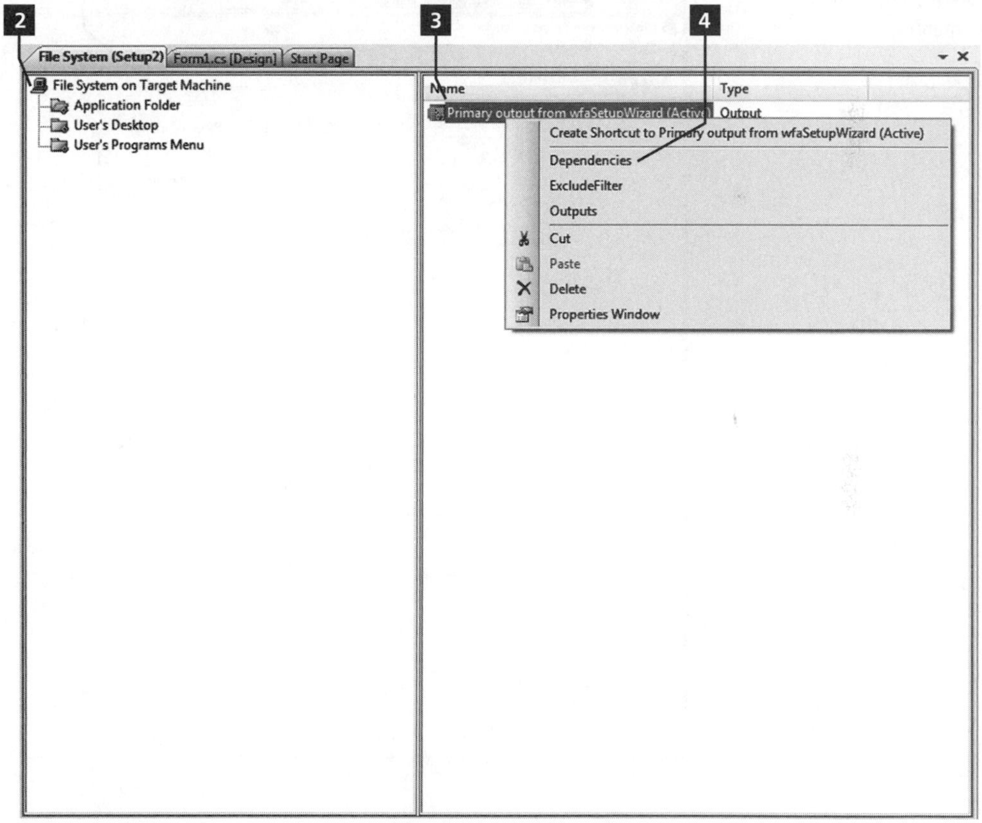

Figure 7-9

File System Editor File pop-up menu

> **File System (Setup2)** | Form1.cs [Design] | Start Page
>
> File System on Target Machine
> - Application Folder
> - User's Desktop
> - User's Programs Menu
>
> | Name | Type |
> | --- | --- |
> | Primary output from wfaSetupWizard (Active) | Output |
>
> - Create Shortcut to Primary output from wfaSetupWizard (Active)
> - Dependencies
> - ExcludeFilter
> - Outputs
> - Cut
> - Paste
> - Delete
> - Properties Window

4. Select Dependences to display the Dependences dialog.
5. Verify that your only dependency is the .NET Framework. If there were more items listed in this dialog, you would want to add a Launch Condition.
6. Click OK.
7. Select the Primary output from wfaSetupWizard (Active) and right-click to display the File System Editor File pop-up menu.
8. Select Outputs to display the Outputs dialog.

9. Verify that your only output is the wfaSetupWizard.exe application. If there were more outputs for this application, they would be listed in the Outputs dialog.

10. Click OK.

11. Select the Primary output from wfaSetupWizard (Active) and right-click to display the File System Editor File pop-up menu.

12. Select Create Shortcut to Primary output from wfaSetupWizard (Active) and verify that a Shortcut to Primary output from wfaSetupWizard (Active) was created.

13. Locate the Properties window and in the Name property key **Setup Wizard**.

14. Drag and drop the Setup Wizard item to the User's Desktop folder and verify that the Setup Wizard item is no longer listed in the Application Folder and is now listed in the User's Desktop folder.

15. Select the Application Folder and repeat steps 11 to 13.

16. Select the User's Program Menu item and right-click to display the File System Editor Folder pop-up menu (Figure 7-10).

Figure 7-10

File System Editor Folder pop-up menu

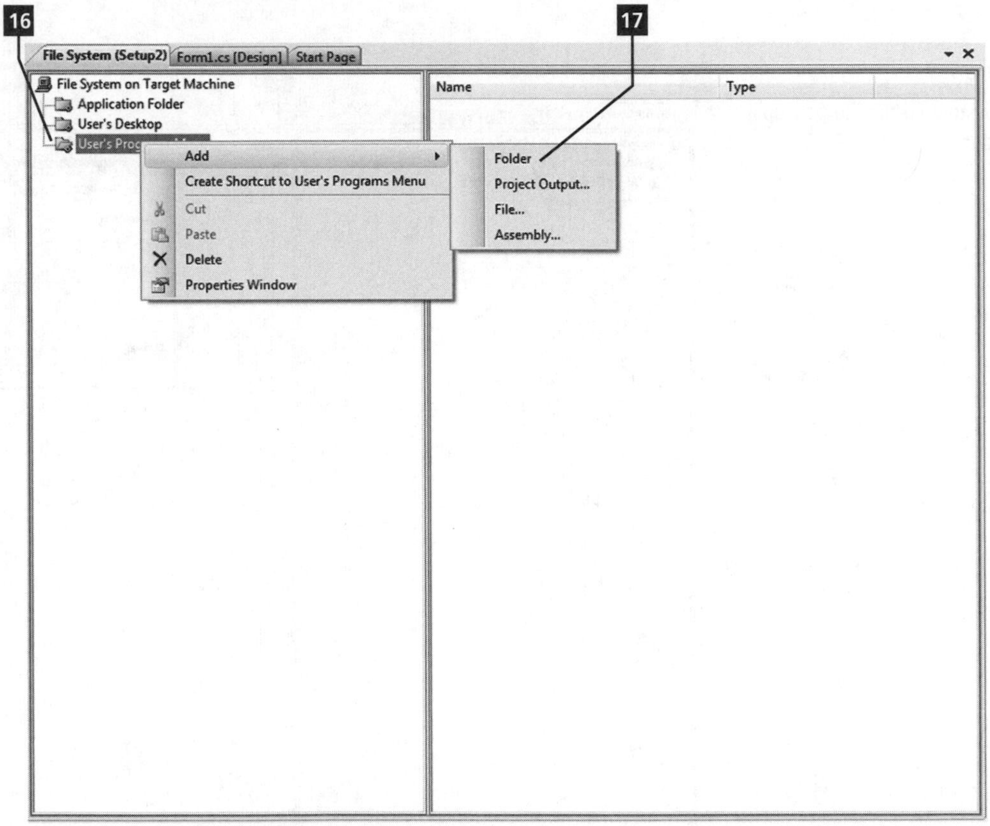

17. Select Add→Folder and verify that a new folder is added underneath the User's Program Menu folder.

18. Locate the Properties window and in the Name property key **My Application**.

19. Select the Application Folder item, then drag and drop the Setup Wizard item to the My Application folder and verify that the Setup Wizard item is no longer listed in the Application Folder and is now listed in the My Application folder.

20. In the Solution Explorer, locate the MySetupProject item and click the User Interface Editor button on the Solution Explorer toolbar to display the User Interface (MySetupProject) tab.

21. Select the Welcome item under the Install\Start item.
22. In the Properties window, locate the WelcomeText property.
23. Locate the text [ProductName] and highlight this text.
24. Key **My Application**.
25. Press **SHIFT+F6** to build the setup application.
26. Select Project→Install to display the Welcome dialog.
27. Verify that the Welcome step text shows the My Application product name.
28. Click Next to display the Select installation folder setup step.
29. Click Next to display the Confirmation setup step.
30. Click Next to start the setup installation process.
31. Click Close to exit the setup application.
32. Minimize all windows to verify that the Setup Wizard Shortcut was added to the Desktop.
33. Select Start→Programs→My Application and verify that the Setup Wizard Shortcut was added.

CERTIFICATION READY
Do you know how
to create Windows
Setup and Deployment
Projects?
5.2

PAUSE. Leave Visual Studio open to use in the next exercise.

You have just enhanced your Setup Project to create two shortcuts. One shortcut will be placed on the end user's desktop and the other shortcut will be placed in the end user's Programs menu. You did not look at the other editors because we did not have a need to configure the other editors within the installation application.

Working with a Merge Module Project

As a best practice, applications are typically developed using common files and functionality. Distributing the same files in every installation is inefficient and can cause maintenance issues. Using Merge Modules to group common installation functionality enables your install development to be as efficient as the application development.

You will not always need to create a Merge Module Project or insert a Merge Module into your Setup Project. The following is a list of questions you can use to help identify if you need to create a Merge Module Project:

• Do you have a set of files or menus in several Setup Projects that always get installed into the same System folder?

• Do you have a set of registry keys in several Setup Projects that always get set during installation?

• Do you have a Custom Action that you want to use in several different Setup Projects?

➔ USE A MERGE MODULE PROJECT

USE the project you created in the previous exercise.

1. Locate in the Solution Explorer the wfaSetupWizard Project item and right-click to display the Solution Explorer pop-up menu.
2. Select Add→New Item to display the Add New Item dialog (Figure 7-11).
3. In the Categories list, select General and in the Template list, select Text File.

Figure 7-11

Add New Item dialog

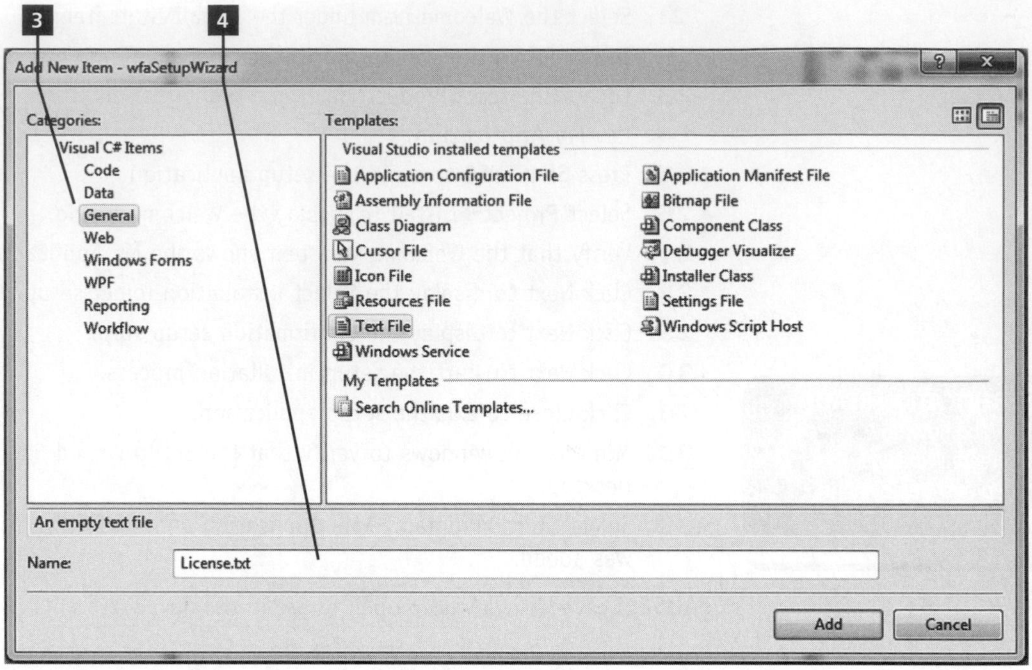

TAKE NOTE*

Remember where you save the License.txt file; you will need this path later in the exercise.

4. In the Name field, key **License.txt** and click Add.
5. Select File→New→Project to display the Add New Project dialog (Figure 7-12).

Figure 7-12

Add New Project dialog

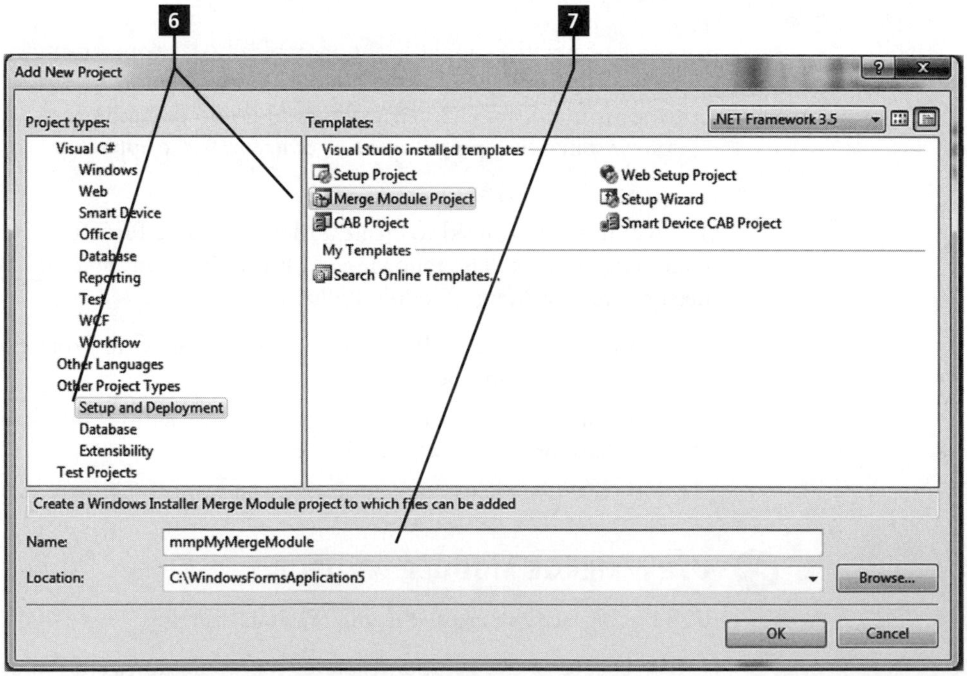

6. In the Project Types, select Other Project Types, Setup and Deployment, and in the Templates list, select Merge Module Project.
7. In the Name field, key **mmpMyMergeModule**

TAKE NOTE * Remember where you save the Merge Module Project; you will need this path later in the exercise.

8. In the Solution field, verify that the Add to Solution is selected.

9. Click OK to create a Merge Module Project in your existing project.

10. In the Solution Explorer, locate and select the mmpMyMergeModule item.

11. On the Solution Explorer toolbar, select the File System Editor button.

12. Select the File System on Target Machine item and right-click to display the File System Editor pop-up menu.

13. Select Add Special Folder (Figure 7-13).

Figure 7-13

Add Special Folder pop-up menu

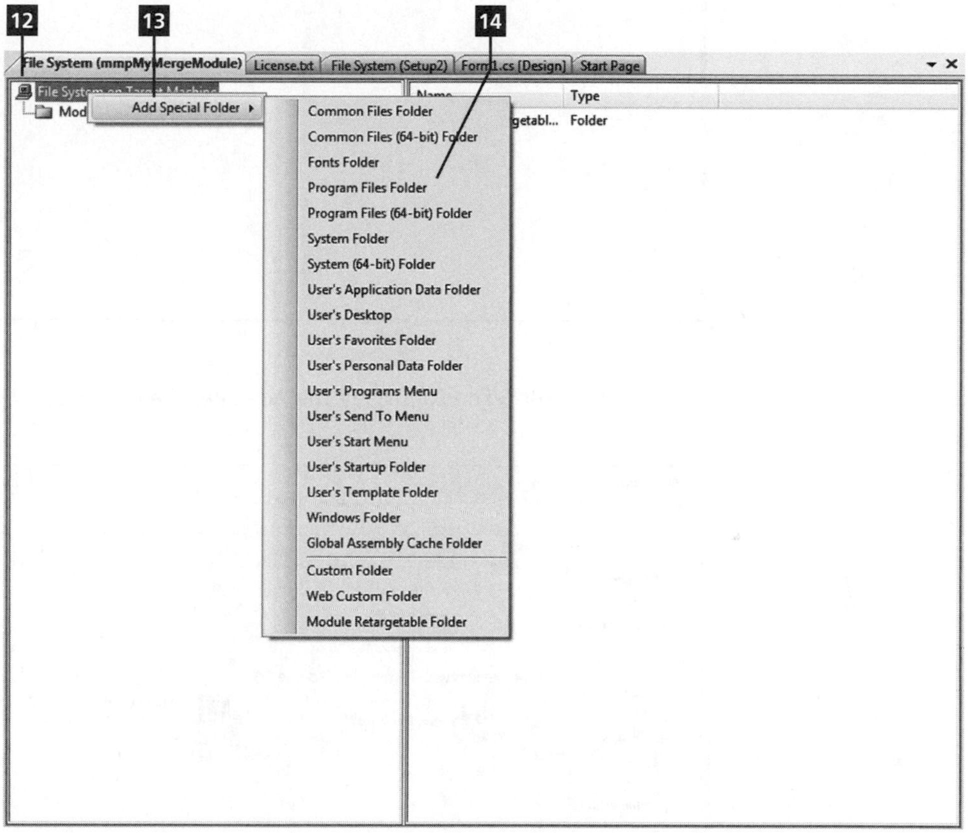

14. Select Program Files Folder.

15. Select the File System on Target Machine item and right-click to display the File System Editor pop-up menu.

16. Select Add Special Folder→User's Programs Menu.

17. In the File System Editor, select the Program Files Folder item and right-click to display the File System Editor pop-up menu (Figure 7-14).

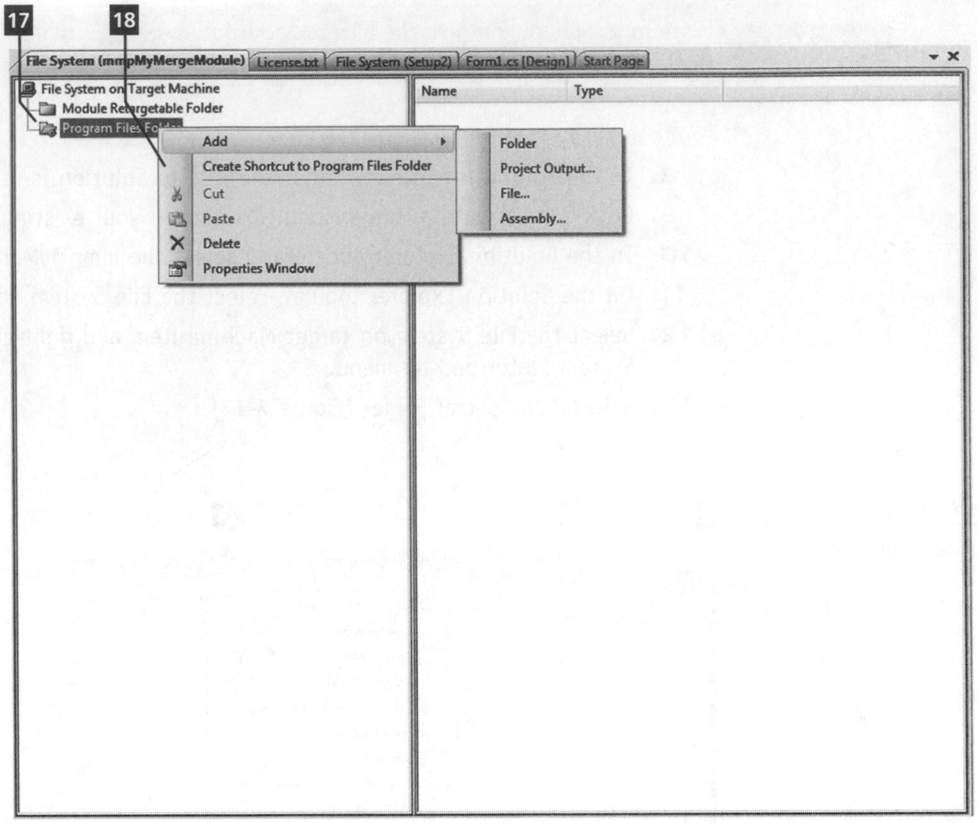

Figure 7-14

Program Files Folder pop-up
menu

File System (mmpMyMergeModule)	License.txt	File System (Setup2)	Form1.cs [Design]	Start Page		▼ ✕
🖳 File System on Target Machine	Name	Type
📁 Module Retargetable Folder		
📁 Program Files Folder		

Add ▶   Folder
Create Shortcut to Program Files Folder   Project Output...
✂ Cut   File...
📋 Paste   Assembly...
✕ Delete
🗔 Properties Window

18. Select Add→File to display the Add Files dialog (Figure 7-15).

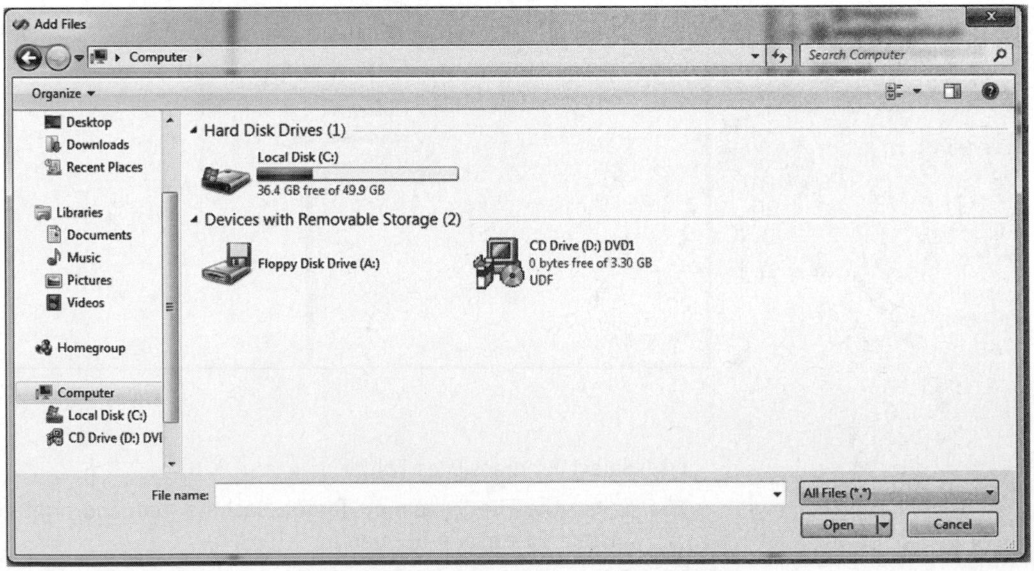

Figure 7-15

Add Files dialog

> **Add Files**
>
> ◀ ◯ ▼ 🖳 ▸ Computer ▸   ▼ ↻ | Search Computer 🔍
>
> Organize ▼   🔳 ▼ 🔲 ❓
>
> 🖥 Desktop   ▲ Hard Disk Drives (1)
> 🔽 Downloads   Local Disk (C:)
> 📍 Recent Places   36.4 GB free of 49.9 GB
>
> 📚 Libraries   ▲ Devices with Removable Storage (2)
> 📄 Documents
> 🎵 Music   Floppy Disk Drive (A:)   CD Drive (D:) DVD1
> 🖼 Pictures   0 bytes free of 3.30 GB
> 🎬 Videos   UDF
>
> 🖧 Homegroup
>
> 🖥 Computer
> 💾 Local Disk (C:)
> 💿 CD Drive (D:) DVI
>
> File name: _____ ▼   All Files (*.*) ▼
>
>   Open ▼   Cancel

19. Navigate to the folder where you created the License.txt file and select the
License.txt file.

20. Select Open to add the file to the Program Files Folder.

21. Select the License.txt item and right-click to display the File System Editor File
pop-up menu (Figure 7-16).

Figure 7-16

File System Editor File pop-up menu

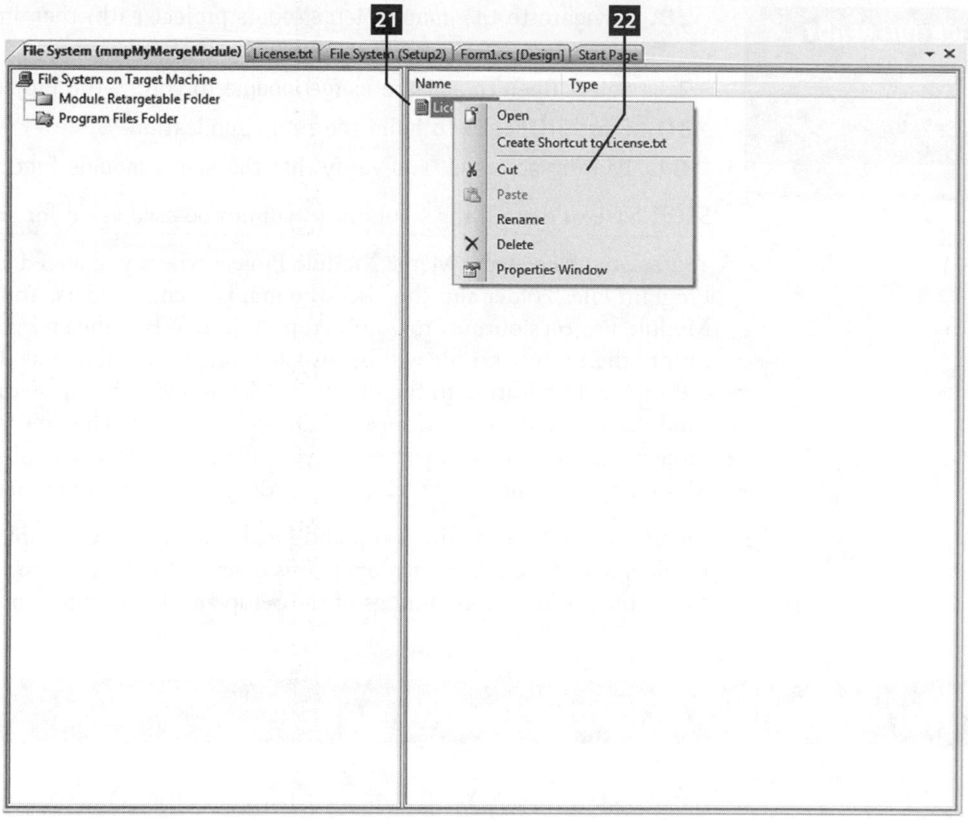

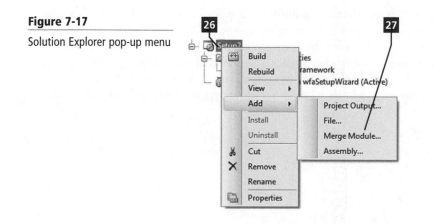

22. Select Create Shortcut to License.txt.
23. Select the Shortcut to License.txt item and drag and drop the item to the User's Programs Menu folder.
24. In the Properties window, Name field, key **End User Licenses Agreement (EULA)**
25. Press **SHIFT+F6** to build the merge module.
26. Locate the MySetupProject in the Solution Explorer and right-click to display the Solution Explorer pop-up menu (Figure 7-17).
27. Select Add→Merge Module to display the Add Modules dialog.

Figure 7-17

Solution Explorer pop-up menu

28. Navigate to the mmpMyMergeModule project path, then into the \bin\debug folder, and select the mmpMyMergeModule.msm file.

29. Select Open to add the merge module to your Setup Project.

30. Press **SHIFT+F6** to build the setup application.

31. Perform an install and verify that the merge module functionality is performed.

STOP. Save or discard the solution. It will not be used again for another exercise.

You have just created a Merge Module Project where you added a License.txt file to the Program Files Folder and the User's Programs Menus folders. You then added your Merge Module Project's outputs to your Setup Project. When the end user executes the Setup application, the License.txt file will be installed in the same folder as the Setup application's main executable. In addition to the Programs Menus added by the Setup application, the Merge Modules shortcut to the License.txt file will be added. The power of the Merge Module Project type comes when you create your next Setup Project and you add this same Merge Module without having to recreate the Merge Module's functionality.

An alternative to using the Setup and Deployment project template types is the ClickOnce Deployment. ClickOnce Deployment is a new technology introduced with .NET to overcome some of the shortcomings of the Setup and Deployment process.

■ Working with ClickOnce Deployment

THE BOTTOM LINE

Integrated into every WPF, Windows Forms, and Windows Services/Console application is the ability to use the ClickOnce Deployment feature. ClickOnce Deployment is a new technology introduced with .NET to overcome some of the limitations of a typical Windows Installer, Setup, and Deployment project.

Introducing ClickOnce Deployment

The ClickOnce Deployment feature is configured from within the project's Properties window. Use the Signing, Security, and Publish expanders to configure the application's ClickOnce Deployment.

A ClickOnce Deployment is the ability to publish the application to a single location where users can execute the application without having to execute the Windows Installer application. The ClickOnce Deployment feature is controlled by a manifest file that enables the ClickOnce Deployment to know what needs to be executed and when the application has changed. The manifest is configured using the Project Properties feature in Visual Studio. Table 7-6 summarizes the Project Properties expanders used to configure ClickOnce Deployment.

Table 7-6

Project Properties Expanders
and ClickOnce Deployment
Configurations

EXPANDER	DESCRIPTION
Publish	The main area of configuration for ClickOnce deployment. There are three major sections to the Publish expander: the Publish Location, the Install Mode and Settings, and the Publish Version. The Publish Location section determines where your ClickOnce Deployment will be saved. You can publish your deployment to a network shared folder, a CD, or to the internet. The Install Mode and Setting section is where most of the ClickOnce Deployment is configured. You will configure the Application Files, Prerequisites, Updates, and Options. The Publish Version section is where you establish the version number for the application. This is important because ClickOnce Deployment uses the version number to determine when to perform an update. In addition to the ClickOnce Deployment sections, the Publish expander also includes the Publish Wizard and Publish Now buttons that use the configuration information to provide and perform the ClickOnce Deployment operation.
Signing	This is where you can sign your ClickOnce Deployment. The Signing expander has two sections, but only the Sign the ClickOnce manifests section is used in the ClickOnce Deployment feature. The Sign the Assembly section is used for signing the application. Signing is a process that ensures that when a user tries to download your file, the file he/she receives is the file you set up to download. Signing prevents spoofing or phishing security risks. You are not required to sign your ClickOnce Deployment, but if you don't, the user will receive a warning message during install. The warning message will state that the application being installed is not signed, and thus could be a fake and pose a security risk. The warning message will allow the user to continue with the install.
Security	This is where you configure the operating security settings. When users are installing your ClickOnce Deployment, they may have downloaded the install from a network share or from the internet. Typically, files downloaded from these types of places are considered to be untrustworthy or unsafe and require an increased level of operating system permissions or privileges to operate. The Security Expander configures your ClickOnce Deployment to have increased permissions and/or be trusted by the operating system.

Once the necessary ClickOnce Deployment options are configured and deployed, you will be able to make updates to the application and then republish the application again and again. The power of the ClickOnce Deployment can then be used to ensure that the users get proper updates and the application is maintained consistently.

Working with ClickOnce Deployment

> The Publish Expander in the Project Properties contains the majority of the ClickOnce Deployment configuration options.

Configuring your ClickOnce Deployment is accomplished by customizing the project settings on the Signing, Security, and Publish Project Properties Expanders. Table 7-7 summarizes the configurable settings for the Signing Expander.

Table 7-7

Signing Expander ClickOnce Deployment Configurations

CONFIGURATION	DESCRIPTION
Sign the ClickOnce manifest checkbox	An optional configuration—you can publish your ClickOnce Deployment without signing the manifest file. If you do not sign the manifest file, users will be warned that the installation presents a security risk, thus making sure they want to proceed. In some of today's more professional or managed networks, an installation could be blocked when the install is not signed. Signing the manifest file requires the purchase of a security certificate. The security certificate is a file that is generated and maintained by a third-party vendor that ensures that the files signed by a certificate have not been altered or tampered with. If you are developing an internal tool, you will most likely not want to pay for a security certificate because you control all of the resources in the ClickOnce Deployment process. If you are developing a commercial application for the general public, you will want to purchase a certificate to ensure to your customers that the download and application are secure.
Certificate control	Lists the information about the security certificate currently loaded.
Select from Store button	Allows you to select a security certificate from your personal store of certificates. Use this option if you already have the certificate installed on your computer.
Select from File button	Allows you to select a security certificate from the file that you received from the certificate vendor. Use this option if you have installed the certificate. This option is most common.
Create test Certificate button	Generates a temporary security certificate. The test certificate should never be used for external distribution. If the test certificate is used for external distribute, the ClickOnce Deployment is treated as if no certificate was used at all and the user will still receive the warning message.
Timestamp server URL	The web address of the timestamping server you want to use to timestamp your certificate signing. When the user wants to install and the installation process wants to verify the certificate, the timestamp server is used to verify the timestamp of when the application was signed with the certificate.

In addition to the security provided by the signing process, ClickOnce Deployment also provides security for permissions and privileges on the executing host operating system. Table 7-8 summarizes the configurable settings for the Security expander.

Table 7-8

Security Expander ClickOnce Deployment Configurations

CONFIGURATION	DESCRIPTION
Enable ClickOnce Security Settings checkbox	Determines if the ClickOnce Security configurations are enabled at design time. When developing an application for ClickOnce Deployment, you will typically have full control and access on the local machine you are developing. Once you deploy the application, end users may not have the same level of permissions on the deployed machine. This configuration allows you to run the application at various security levels to evaluate how the application will run when security permissions are varied. There are several project types, like the WPF web application, where this setting is configured to be enabled by default.
This is a full trust application	Configures the application to run as a fully trusted application. To be fully trusted means that the application is not restricted from accessing the machine resources like the hard drive. Use this option if you know that your end users will have full permissions on their computers or if the ClickOnce Deployment is in a trusted location, like an intranet site.
This is a partial trust application	Configures the application to run at customer permission levels. By selecting this option, the ClickOnce Security Permissions controls are enabled for configuration. Use this option when you want to evaluate how the application will perform when targeting a type of user who has less than full permissions on his/her machine.
ClickOnce Security Permissions controls	A group of controls that allow the customization of security permissions. There are several zones and permissions for each zone. This option is a more advanced configuration and requires extra planning.

The majority of your ClickOnce Deployment configurations will occur on the Project Properties Publish expander. Table 7-9 summarizes the configurable settings for the Publish expander.

Table 7-9

Publish Expander ClickOnce Deployment Configurations

Section	Configuration	Description
Publish Location	Publishing Folder Location control and browse button	Used to configure where the ClickOnce Deployment will be saved for publishing. The Publishing Folder Location can be a physical location (C:\My Folder), a network share (\\MyServer\My Folder), or an FTP or Web site on the Internet. You must specify a publishing location to use this ClickOnce Deployment feature.
	Installation Folder URL	An optional text control and browse button that configures an alternative location for installing the application. The ClickOnce Deployment feature uses the Publishing Folder Location to check for updates and changes. The Installation Folder URL can be provided as an alternative location for install, but the ClickOnce Deployment feature does not check this folder for updates or changes.
Install Mode and Settings	Application is available online only	Configures the ClickOnce Deployment to allow only the application to be executed from the Publishing Folder Location. Use this option if you do not want the users to install the application directly. You might want to use this option for applications that change frequently and where you want the user to always be using the latest version. You might also use this option for applications that you want to limit to internal intranet use only.
	Application is available offline as well	Configures the ClickOnce Deployment to allow the application to be installed and executed only from the user's machine. Use this option if you want the users to install the application directly. This option is like the typical Setup and Deployment project, but it has the added benefits of the ClickOnce Deployment updates.
	Application Files button	Lists the files included in your ClickOnce Deployment. The list of files is derived from your output folder when the application is built. Thus, if you want to have a file published with the ClickOnce Deployment, you need to ensure that the file is copied to the build output folder.
	Prerequisites button	Configures and lists the features required to use the ClickOnce Deployment and the application. You can choose to create a setup application to install your prerequisites or to unselect the Create setup program. To install a pre-requisite components checkbox, you will not create an install, but rely on the users to ensure that they have all the needed files for execution. If you use the prerequisite setup program, you can publish the setup install to the same folder as the ClickOnce Deployment, from the vendor's Web site for third-party components, or from a specific location.
	Updates button	Configures the ClickOnce Deployment automatic update feature. A ClickOnce Deployment has the ability to check for updates and automatically download and install the updates as needed. The following is a list of all the configurable options on the Application Update dialog: • The application should check for updates. • Check for updates after the application starts. • Check for updates before the application starts. • Check for updates at a specified number of days. • Specify an update minimum required version number. • The location to get the updates from if different from the Publishing Location.

Table 7-9 (*continued*)

SECTION	CONFIGURATION	DESCRIPTION
	Options button	Configures various ClickOnce Deployment attributes. The following is a list of some of the configurable attributes: • Publishing language • Publisher name • Product name • Support URL • Deployment web page • For CD installations, automatically start Setup when CD is inserted • Verifies files uploaded to web server
Publish Version	Major, Minor, Build, Revision numbers	Configure the applications version information. You can change these numbers as needed, but you will want to always have them incrementing higher for each publication. The ClickOnce Deployment feature uses these numbers to determine if a new version of the application needs updating.
	Automatically increment revision with each publish checkbox	Configures the application's version number to always be updated when a publish action occurs. You will want to use this feature whenever possible. Always remembering to increment the version number can be tedious and the application updates will not work properly.
	Publish Wizard	The Publish Wizard button displays the Publish Wizard dialog. The Publish Wizard dialog consists of three steps: • Where do you want to publish the application?: The same configuration information in the Publish Location section. • Will the application be available offline?: The basic configuration information in the Install Mode and Settings section. • Ready to Publish!: The verification of the Publish Wizard actions.
	Publish Now button	Uses the ClickOnce Deployment configuration information and executes the deployment process. Depending on your configuration settings, you can see the deployment web page from the local host web server when the deployment is complete.

 USE CLICKONCE DEPLOYMENT

GET READY. Before you begin these steps, be sure to launch Microsoft Visual Studio and create a new Windows Forms Application named wfaClickOnce.

1. Modify Form1 to have at least one UI control.
2. Select Project→wfaClickOnce Properties to display the Project Properties tab (Figure 7-18).

 To see the wfaClickOnce Properties tab, you can also select the wfaClickOnce project item in the Solution Explorer window, right-click to display the pop-up menu, then select Properties.

Figure 7-18

Project Properties tab

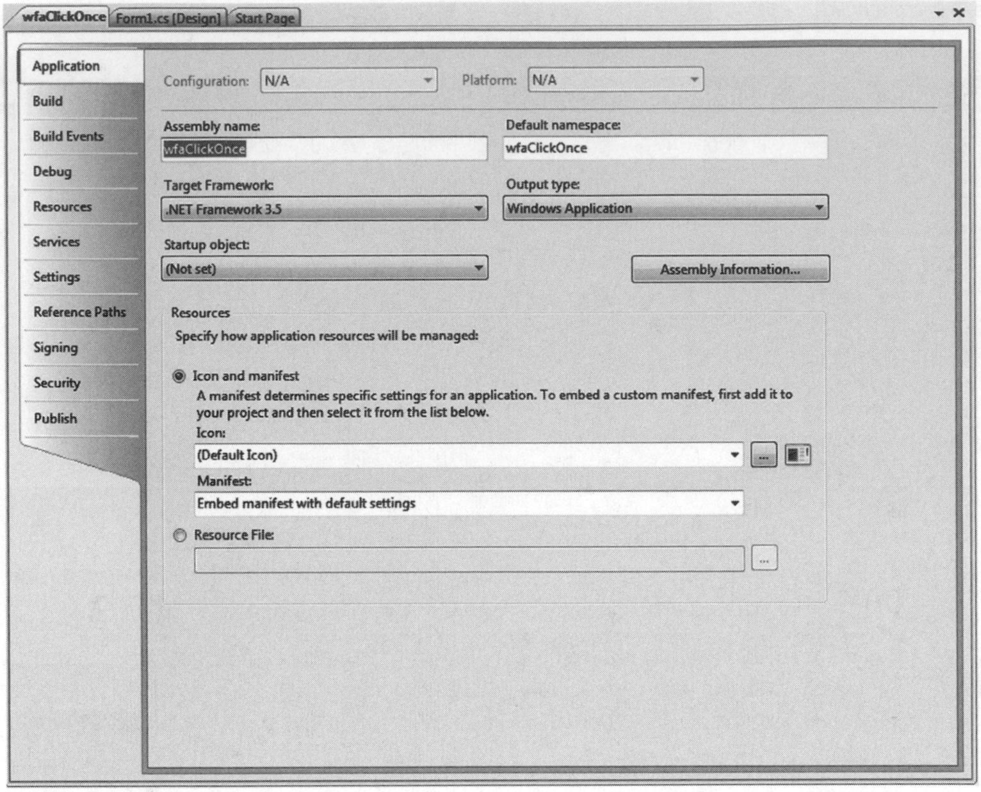

3. Select the Signing expander and verify that the Sign the ClickOnce manifests is unchecked (Figure 7-19).

Figure 7-19

Project Properties tab Signing expander

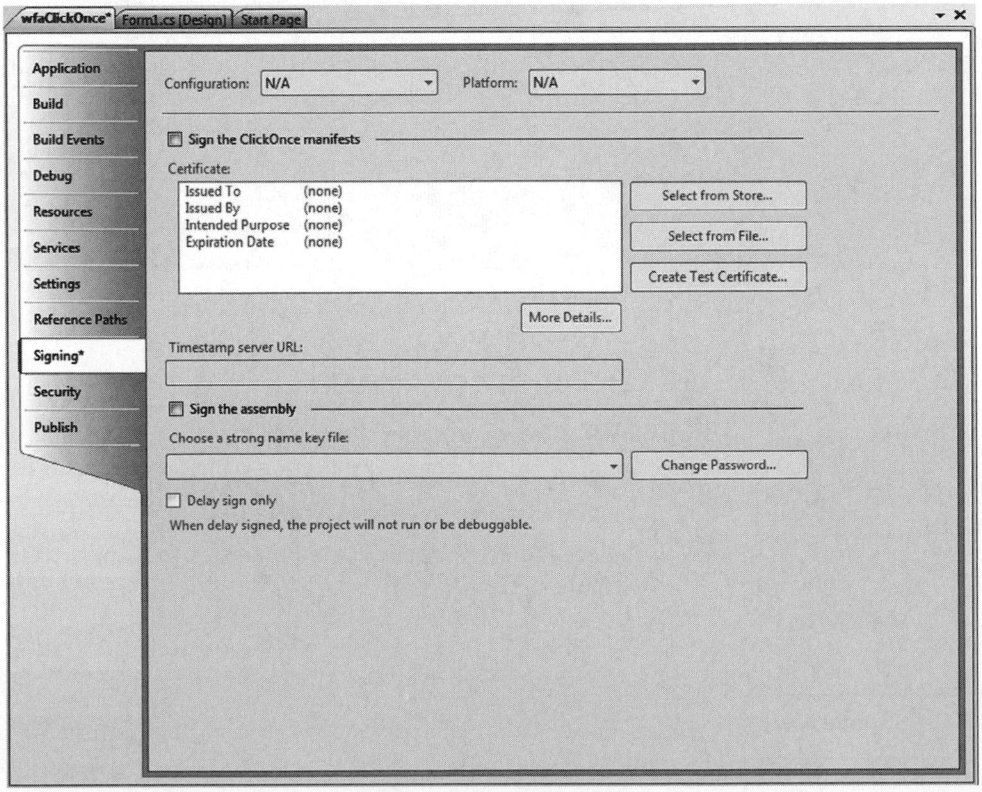

4. Select the Security expander, click the Enable ClickOnce Security Settings and verify that This is a full trust application is selected (Figure 7-20).

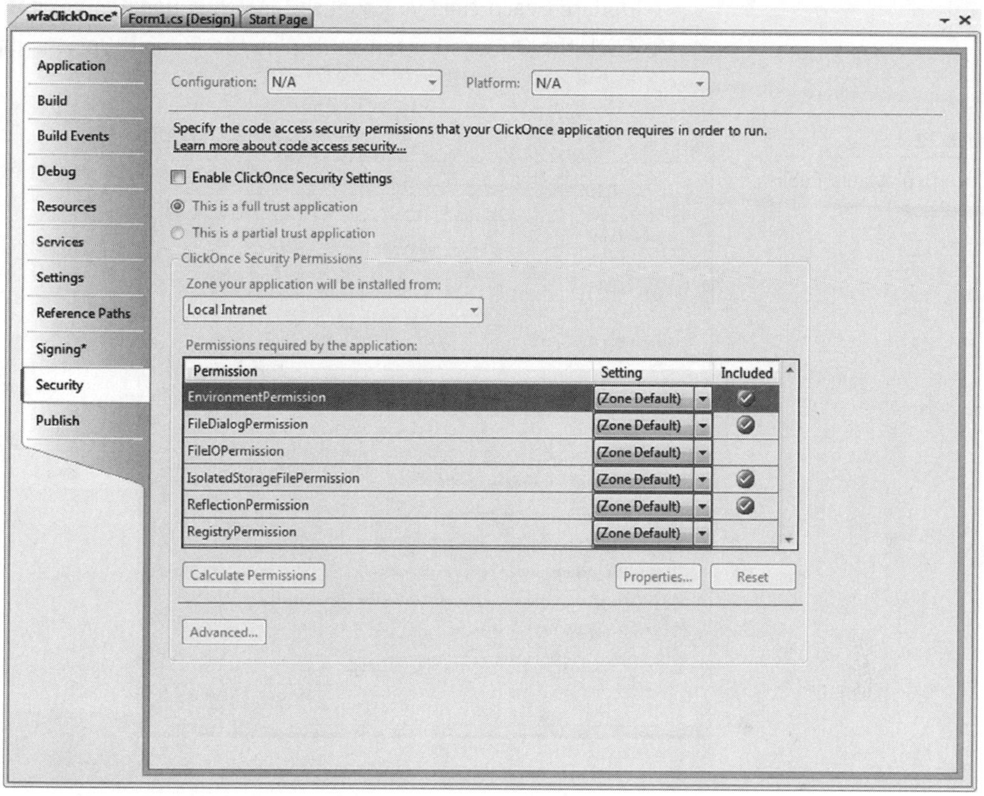

Figure 7-20

Project Properties tab Security expander

5. Select the Publish expander (Figure 7-21).

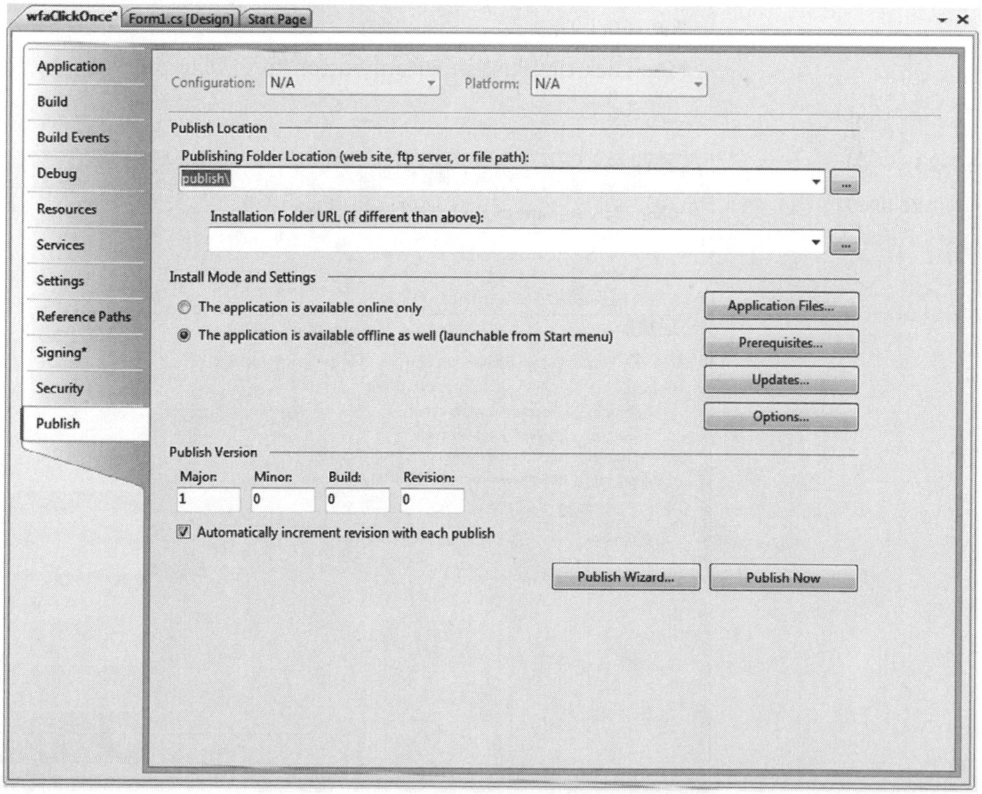

Figure 7-21

Project Properties tab Publish expander

6. Click the The Application is available online only option.

7. Verify that the Updates button is now disabled. Online applications are automatically updated each time you publish, and thus updates are not needed.

8. Click the Options button to display the Publish Options dialog (Figure 7-22).

Figure 7-22

ClickOnce Deployment Publish Options dialog

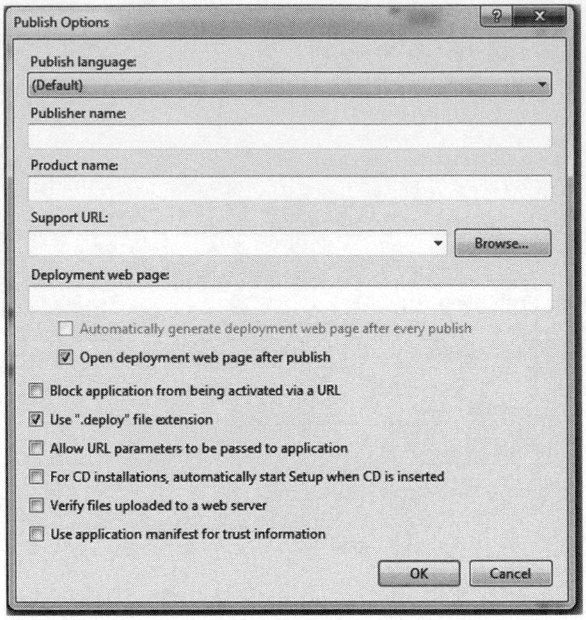

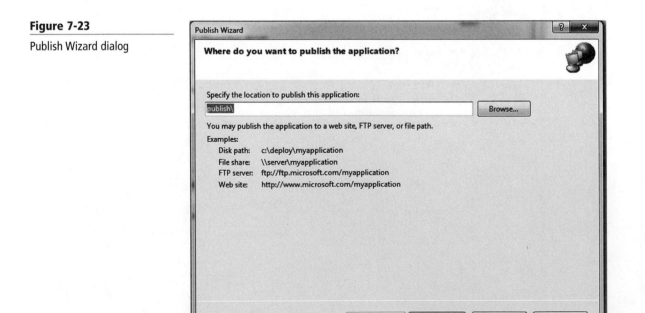

9. In the Publisher Name, key your name.

10. In the Product Name, key **My ClickOnce Deployment Application**.

11. Click OK.

12. Click the Publish Wizard button to display the Publish Wizard dialog (Figure 7-23).

Figure 7-23

Publish Wizard dialog

13. Click Next to display the Will this application be offline? step.
14. Click Next to display the Ready to Publish! step.
15. Click Finish to publish.
16. Verify that the My ClickOnce Deployment Application web page was opened in your default browser.
17. Click Run on the My ClickOnce Deployment Application web page.
18. Click Run on the Security Warning dialog for the setup.exe application.
19. Click Run on the unknown publisher Security Warning dialog.

TAKE NOTE * The second Security Warning dialog box is a direct result of you not signing your ClickOnce Deployment manifest. To eliminate this second Security Warning, you should sign your ClickOnce Deployment manifest.

20. Click Run on the Application Run Security Warning dialog.
21. Verify that the application executed and that you see the controls added in step 1.
22. Close Form1.
23. Modify Form1 to have additional UI controls.
24. Select the wfaClickOnce Tab and select the Publish expander.
25. Click the Publish Now button.
26. Verify that the My ClickOnce Deployment Application deployment web page was loaded into your default browser.
27. Verify that the version number for your My ClickOnce Deployment Application has now changed to 1.0.0.1.
28. Click Run to display the File Download—Security Warning dialog.
29. Click Run to display the Unknown Publisher Security Warning dialog.
30. Verify that the application with the new controls is now executed.
31. Close Form1.

CERTIFICATION READY
Do you know how to create Windows setup and deployment projects?
5.2

STOP. Save or discard the solution. It will not be used again for another exercise.

You have just created a ClickOnce Deployment installation for a simple application. You configured the install to run online and not allow installation. You published the application using the Publish Wizard, then changed the application and republished using the Publish Now functionality.

SKILL SUMMARY

IN THIS LESSON YOU LEARNED HOW TO:

- Use the Windows application distribution options and the differences between each.
- Create a Setup Project using the Setup Wizard and Setup Project components.
- Create a ClickOnce Deployment installation and configure the ClickOnce Deployment options.

■ Knowledge Assessment

Fill in the Blank

Complete the following sentences by writing the correct word or words in the blanks provided.

1. A _____ is a Visual Studio Setup and Deployment project type used to create an installation file for 16-bit and COM application components.

2. A _____ is a Visual Studio Setup and Deployment project type with no user interface.

3. The _____ creates a Setup Project using a step-by-step process.

4. A _____ is a Visual Studio Setup and Deployment project type used to create a Windows Installer Setup Application for a web server application.

5. As a new feature to .NET, the _____ feature can deploy an application without the Windows Installer Application.

6. The _____ Setup Project component defines the main application output.

7. To configure a Setup Project's files and menus, you use the _____.

8. A _____ is a Visual Studio Setup and Deployment project type used to create a Windows Installer Desktop Setup application.

9. The main Project Properties expander used to configure a ClickOnce Deployment is _____.

10. To configure a Setup Project's user interface you use the _____.

Multiple Choice

Circle the letter that corresponds to the best answer.

1. Which of the following Setup Project Editors is NOT supported by the Web Setup Project type?
   a. File System Editor
   b. User Interface Editor
   c. Registry Editor
   d. Custom Actions Editor

2. Which section of the ClickOnce Deployment configuration would you use to test the application with your end user's level of permissions?
   a. Signing
   b. Security
   c. Publish
   d. None of the above

3. Which of the following is NOT a Setup and Deployment Project template?
   a. Setup Wizard
   b. CAB Project
   c. Merge Module
   d. ClickOnce Deployment

4. Which ClickOnce Deployment configuration option would you use if you did not have a security certificate, but you were planning to have one at deployment time?
   a. Select from Store
   b. Select from File
   c. Create Test Certificate
   d. None of the above; you must have a security certificate

5. Which of the following is NOT a File System Editor folder option?
   a. System Folder
   b. System (64-bit) Folder
   c. My Documents
   d. Program Files (64-bit) Folder

6. Which of the following Setup Project Editors would you use to add a copyright notice to the installation application before the installation starts?
   a. User Interface Editor
   b. File System Editor
   c. Custom Actions Editor
   d. Launch Conditions Editor

7. Which of the following Install Mode and Settings configurations enables the end user to install the ClickOnce Deployment?
   a. Application is available online only.
   b. Application is available online and offline.
   c. Application is available offline only.
   d. Application is available offline as well.

8. Which of the following is NOT a Registry Editor key option?
   a. HKEY_CLASSES_ROOT
   b. HKEY_ADMIN_USER
   c. User/Machine Hive
   d. HKEY_CURRENT_USER

9. Which of the following Install Mode and Setting configuration items enables the application to retrieve the latest changes each time it starts from your support Web site?
   a. The application should check for updates.
   b. Check for updates before the application starts.
   c. The location to get the update from.
   d. All of the above.

10. Which of the following Setup Project Editors would you use to make sure that the .NET Framework was installed before installing the application?
    a. User Interface Editor
    b. File System Editor
    c. Custom Actions Editor
    d. Launch Conditions Editor

■ Competency Assessment

Scenario 7-1: Easily Accessible

The application created in Scenario 3-1 has been selected as one of the project pieces that needs an installation. This application will be used often by the users, and thus the installation package needs to install a shortcut in the Start Menu (not a subfolder) and on the desktop of the user's machine. Using these requirements, identify which type of installation method is needed and then implement the installation method within the Scenario 3-1 solution.

Scenario 7-2: Moving Target

The application created in Scenario 4-1 has been selected as another one of the project pieces that needs an installation. Your supervisor is currently not sure that the Login window created is exactly what the users want. You have been asked to create an installation that will allow you to make rapid changes and get those changes to the users with minimal effort. Using these requirements, identify which type of installation method is needed and then implement the installation method within the Scenario 4-1 solution.

■ Proficiency Assessment

Scenario 7-3: Application Copyright

After the initial evaluation of the installation created in Scenario 7-1, the legal organization has raised a concern that the application does not have the company's standard copyright document. You have been asked to integrate the company's standard copyright document into the installation application created in Scenario 7-1. Your supervisor anticipates that you will need to add this document to several installations you are currently working on. Create a generic installation package for the company's standard copyright document and have it installed to the user's desktop.

Scenario 7-4: Install with Updates

Most of the changes for the Login screen have been gathered and implemented. Your supervisor is now ready to allow the users to install the Login screen to their machines. You still want the ability to update the application when changes are made, but modify the installation from Scenario 7-2 to allow the users to install the application.

Index